The Book of Love

The Book of Love

The Story of the Kamasutra

Jᴀᴍᴇs McCᴏɴɴᴀᴄʜɪᴇ

Metropolitan Books

HENRY HOLT AND COMPANY • NEW YORK

Metropolitan Books
Henry Holt and Company, LLC
Publishers since 1866
175 Fifth Avenue
New York, New York 10010
www.henryholt.com

Metropolitan Books® and ® are registered trademarks
of Henry Holt and Company, LLC.

Copyright © 2007 by James McConnachie
All rights reserved.
Distributed in Canada by H. B. Fenn and Company Ltd.

Originally published in the United Kingdom in 2007 by Atlantic Books, London.

Library of Congress Cataloging-in-Publication Data

McConnachie, James.
    The book of love : the story of the kamasutra / James McConnachie.—1st U.S. ed.
        p. cm.
Includes bibliographical references and index.
ISBN-13: 978-0-8050-8818-2
ISBN-10: 0-8050-8818-0
1. Vatsyayana. Kamasutra. 2. Love. 3. Sexual intercourse. I. Title.
HQ470.S3M33 2008
306.7—dc22

                                                          2007047172

Henry Holt books are available for special promotions
and premiums. For details contact: Director, Special Markets.

First U.S. Edition 2008
Designed by Lindsay Nash
Printed in the United States of America

1   3   5   7   9   10   8   6   4   2

Contents

Illustrations

1. Prince Visvantara and his wife Madri, Ajanta. Photo: akgimages, London, Jean-Louis Nou. Scan: courtesy of the Bodleian Library, University of Oxford.

2. Krishna and Radha look at their reflection. Freer Gallery of Art, Smithsonian Institution, Washington, D.C. Gift of Mr and Mrs Charles Page, F1991.90.

3. Statues at Laksmana temple, Khajuraho. Photo: Rajan Atrawalkar, Jalgaon, India.

4. Kamakala Yantra superimposed over an erotic sculpture of the Laksmana Temple, Khajuraho, dated 954. Image from *Tantra in Practice,* edited by David Gordon White (Princeton: Princeton University Press, 2000). Composition by Michael Rabe. Courtesy of Michael Rabe and Princeton University Press.

5. *Bihari Satsai* illustration: 'Stay with me, my love'. Courtesy of Ludwig Habighorst.

6. *Bihari Satsai* illustration: 'Clad in a newly-washed garment, the *nayika* is cooking'. On permanent loan to the Museum Rietberg from the collection of Barbara and Eberhard Fischer. Photo: Rainer Wolfsberger.

Preface

My relationship with the *Kamasutra* began a little over ten years ago, when some teasing Nepalese friends presented me with a glossy, hardback copy of the 'book of love'. It was a classic Indian-produced edition, heavily illustrated with garishly explicit miniature paintings, but lacking any explanation of the origins of the actual text. It matched all my expectations of what an Oriental sex manual would be. It was baroque in its delight in variation and ornamentation, pedantic in its obsessive enumerations and slightly alarming in the freedom of its sexual play. Disappointingly, it was not particularly seductive.

On returning to the UK, I discovered that my gift edition in fact comprised just one of the seven 'books' of the original work. I had, of course, the most notorious section, the one on 'how to do it'. Spotting a 'complete and unexpurgated' paperback copy on a friend's bookshelf, I realized that what had seemed a fairly straight-forward sex manual was more like a book of conduct. It was certainly not pornography, but rather a complex and often beguil-ing guide to negotiating the maze of ancient Indian social relationships. There was a philosophical section on the role of pleasure in life, which also incorporated some satisfyingly rich depictions of the lifestyle of the ideal lover. There were sections on the seduction, enjoyment and lifestyles of, variously, 'Virgins',

'Wives', 'Other Men's Wives' and 'Courtesans', which read like the raw material of some Chaucerian tale. There was also a curious coda on aphrodisiacs and bizarre magical-herbal remedies.

I found this new, greater *Kamasutra* no more arousing than the first, but it was definitely more seductive, its descriptions of a shining third-century world many times more fascinating than the tedious lists of ways of embracing or scratching with the fingernails that I'd first encountered. At times, I was astonished to recognize scenes from an India I knew. More often, I was struck by how distant the world it described seemed to be. It certainly had little to do with my experience of South Asian village life, where I was supposed to ensure the door stood wide open if a woman entered my room. (No woman ever did.) It had still less to do with the India in which the Health Minister of the Hindu-fundamentalist Bharatiya Janata Party had responded to the country's mounting Aids crisis by proclaiming that India's native traditions of chastity and fidelity were more effective than the use of condoms. Or the India in which the film censors demanded that Mira Nair cut no less than fourteen scenes from her sensuous film *Kama Sutra — A Tale of Love* before it could be screened in public.

What on earth could have happened between the apparently carefree composition of the *Kamasutra* in the third century and the problematized publication of my gift copy at the end of the twentieth? Had the colonizing West somehow infected an entire culture with sexual conservatism? Or were the seeds of the *Kamasutra*'s own future downfall already present in the book itself? In tracing the extraordinary life of the *Kamasutra* from palm-leaf manuscript to coffee-table book, across the long intervening centuries, I thought I might find answers. Instead I have ended up writing a book that is only partly about India.

This is as much the story of the modern world's discovery of the *Kamasutra* as it is the story of the *Kamasutra* itself. It is the story of a book that offered men a vision of a libertine paradise and women the (almost) equal right to pleasure, a book that gave the West a new aspiration for personal conduct, a new and sensuous dream in place of centuries of uneasy nightmares. And it is the story of two extraordinary Victorian Englishmen who wanted to change the world in precisely this way: the modest, dogged and entirely obscure Indian civil servant, Foster Fitzgerald Arbuthnot, and the swashbuckling, slapdash and utterly controversial explorer, Richard Francis Burton. Without them and their furtive yet heroic efforts to find, translate, print and ultimately popularize the *Kamasutra*, this rare gem would likely have remained hidden in dusty obscurity.

This is, above all, the story of a book, of how something as fragile as an idea and as evanescent as an image of the world can be cradled between hard covers and nursed down the centuries. The *Kamasutra* has had to survive more vicissitudes than most. It was born in response to the threatened extinction of its entire lineage – the family of scientific works on the subject of sexuality had become scattered and enfeebled, its author tells us, and the *Kamasutra* carried the burden of continuing the bloodline. It was overshadowed through most of its life by older, more robust and often hostile siblings, the great Hindu texts on law, politics and salvation, while its artistic-minded children chose to languish in the exquisite but febrile world of erotic poetry, drama and court painting, forgetting their earnest and dedicated roots. It was slowly forgotten in the land of its birth until, in the nineteenth century, it was dragged out of obscurity by imperialist agents, forced into unfamiliar and misrepresentative clothing and transported overseas. It found little welcome on arrival in the West, and was obliged to scurry furtively between London and Paris, just barely surviving by selling itself to the dubious customers of backstreet bookshops under the constant threat of imprisonment. When it was finally given its freedom, in 1963, it found itself briefly fêted and lauded but, as the years went by, it was increasingly elbowed out of the limelight by clownish impersonators.

Today, the *Kamasutra* is the single most famous 'Oriental' book of all. It is better known than its worthy, mystical Hindu cousin, the *Bhagavadgita*, and more celebrated, even, than the legendary *Arabian Nights*, notwithstanding Richard Burton's own prediction that 'a manual of erotology cannot have the interest of the *Nights*'. Despite its fame, what the *Kamasutra* actually says remains a mystery to most people both in the West and, more surprisingly perhaps, in India. Certainly, its contents are not as often repeated in the bosom of the family as the stories of Sinbad the Sailor or Aladdin and his Lamp.

The 'book of love' seems to have two popular reputations, one as an exotic compendium of absurdly acrobatic sexual positions that would probably be embarrassing or even dangerous to attempt — but might just possibly be rewarding. The other is as a repository of Oriental erotic wisdom, the Ur-text of a profoundly spiritual tradition that makes the crudely physical goals of Western sexuality look laughably superficial and puts the repressive, patriarchal heritage of the Christian world to shame. Either way, the *Kamasutra* is known as the *definitive* exposition of the art of lovemaking, the ancient authority to which all later efforts in the genre must refer. It has become a byword for sex itself. Just as there are 'very Bibles' of rules or advice, and 'veritable odysseys' of journeys or sustained searches, any book or film or intimate afternoon that aspires to

truly baroque sexual variety or astonishing levels of experimentation is a virtual *Kamasutra*. Somehow, an ancient Indian treatise on
the erotic now ranks among that rare body of iconic works whose
title alone can stand for the very thing it represents.

Writing this book has turned out to be something of an odyssey
in itself – by which I mean that there have been endless obstacles
in my path. More than 120 years after the *Kamasutra* was first translated into English, sex is still not an entirely respectable area of
study. The pioneering 1883 edition of the *Kamasutra* was not openly
published in the UK or US until 1963, while the first translation of
the *Kamasutra* directly into English by a professional scholar was
completed only as recently as 2002. (It is Wendy Doniger and
Sudhir Kakar's edition for Oxford University Press, and I owe it a
major debt.) Remarkably little serious research has been done on
the *Kamasutra* itself, or even the context in which it was written.
There are only a few obscure and old-fashioned monographs
published in India, some paralysingly worthy tracts written in
late-nineteenth-century German, and a half-handful of highly
specialized articles by contemporary academics. There is, by
contrast, a torrent of woefully inaccurate and sensationalizing
publications on the Indian erotic, most of it repeating the same old
mildly titillating misinformation.

When it comes to the life of Richard F. Burton, the flood of bad
books surges still higher. Most of the scores of biographies repeat
the same old canards about the *Kamasutra* – principally, the notion
that Burton translated it. (Mary Lovell's *A Rage to Live* and Dane
Kennedy's *The Highly Civilized Man* are superb exceptions.) By contrast, Burton's chief collaborator in the venture, Foster Fitzgerald
Arbuthnot, lacks even a decent obituary to his name, while the
Indian *pandits*, or scholars, who did much of the actual translating

work have all but vanished into historical oblivion. This book attempts to rescue the admirable Bhagvanlal Indraji and the still-shadowy Shivaram Parshuram Bhide from that undeserved obscurity.

Even tracing the afterlife of the *Kamasutra* in the twentieth century has not been smooth. Early editions of the 'Burton' text were, almost exclusively, furtively printed by purveyors of clandestine pornography. Places and dates of publication were often forged, and statements about the contents of the book, or the origins of the text used, were evidently designed as pornographic advertising rather than actual, reliable information. Few libraries bought or kept such publications, and even the ones that did, such as the British and Bodleian libraries, still impose restrictions on how and where the books may be read – even if they can be found at all, given the confused state of the catalogues. In the 1970s, the Bodleian, in Oxford, suffered from a zealous librarian who actually instituted a purge of books that might corrupt students' morals. Hundreds were transferred to the restricted 'phi' shelfmark – where many stay, for want of equivalent liberalizing energy. The *Kamasutra* is among them.

Even in the glossy new British Library, I've had to collect books – even innocuously unillustrated ones – from locked cabinets, then take the long walk of shame over to the isolated 'special materials' area in the Rare Books Reading Room, there to make notes under the avuncular eye of the music librarian. One valuable source of eroto-bibliography, an annotated copy of the infamous *Index Librorum Prohibitorum*, even comes with a note insisting: 'Please replace immediately in Strong Room upon return to storage,' and this is seemingly not because of its value but its sexually explosive properties.

Occasionally, I've been confronted with my own lurking sense of embarrassment. I've found myself concocting tactfully discreet misrepresentations of the nature of my work, and I've fended off endless amused speculation on the exact nature and scope of my research. I've sometimes told outright lies. The respected parents of one Brahmin friend must have wondered why I blushed so deeply when I told them I was writing about 'early Hinduism'.

Competing with these puritanical reactions has been my own growing sense of political purpose. The *Kamasutra* may no longer be the world's most detailed or most practical compendium of sexual knowledge. In India it lost that status as long ago as the twelfth century, when it was supplanted by medieval manuals that were narrower but more explicit – that saw fit to mention, for example, the clitoris. As a text, the *Kamasutra* is no more than the glorious ruin of an ancient pleasure palace, a site to be marvelled at but no longer occupied. It is an archaeological dig rather than a blueprint for the construction of a culture. But as a book, as an object carrying with it all the extraordinary after-history of its adventures since its birth, the *Kamasutra* continues to be potently relevant.

Its life in the West has been defined by the foster-parents who have coaxed it out of the quiet of the library or the darkness of the pornographic bookshop and into the noise of the political battlefield. Each parent has seen different qualities in their adopted child, but the broader battlefield has been the same: the endless campaign of liberalism against repression. Burton and Arbuthnot deliberately placed their translation of the *Kamasutra* at the end of a line of publications opposed to paternalism and prudishness. They planted it like a time bomb in the heart of Victorian polite society and finally, in the wake of the overturning of the *Chatterley* ban, the bomb went off. In the 1960s, astonished readers acclaimed it as 'a picture of a great and highly civilized society' and 'an expression of fundamental Indian attitudes' that delivered a 'salutory shock': the world could be sensuous *and* civilized; the moralists had no monopoly on refinement. In the 1970s, the sexologist Alex Comfort wielded the *Kamasutra* in the cause of pacifism and libertarianism, while in the 1990s it was brandished for gay rights by the idiosyncratic Hindu convert, Alain Daniélou. Today, in India, the *Kamasutra* is still held up as a proud example of that country's alternative tradition of sexual morality.

This 'biography' of the *Kamasutra* is, first and foremost, the story of a life. The first chapter begins with a kind of conception, after all, and with the *Kamasutra*'s birth in ancient India. But I also offer it as a modest sortie in the long war against authoritarianism. If there is a moral to this tale, it is that we can attempt to govern our own desires, but we cannot command the desires of others. As Vatsyayana, the original sage-author-compositor of the *Kamasutra*, wrote some eighteen hundred years ago:

> Therefore, when a man has considered
> the region, and the time, and the technique,
> and the textbook teachings, and himself,
> he may – or may not – make use of these practices.
> But because this matter is secret,
> and because the mind and heart are fickle,
> who could know who should do what,
> and when and how?

PRAGMATISTS SAY: 'PEOPLE should not indulge in pleasures, for they are an obstacle to both religion and power, which are more important, and to other good people. They make a man associate with worthless people and undertake bad projects; they make him impure, a man with no future, as well as care-less, lightweight, untrustworthy and unacceptable. And it is said that many men in the thrall of desire were destroyed, even when accompanied by their troops. For instance, when the Bhoja king named Dandakya was aroused by a Brahmin's daughter, desire destroyed him, along with his relatives and his kingdom. And Indra the king of the gods with Ahalya, the superpowerful Kichaka with Draupadi, Ravana with Sita, and many others afterwards were seen to fall into the thrall of desire and were destroyed.' Vatsyayana says: Pleasures are a means of sustaining the body, just like food, and they are rewards for religion and power. But people must be aware of the flaws in pleasures, flaws that are like diseases. For people do not stop preparing the cooking pots because they think, 'There are beggars', nor do they stop planting barley because they think, 'There are deer.'

Kamasutra
Book One: General Observations
Chapter Two: Achieving the Three Aims of Human Life
translated by Wendy Doniger and Sudhir Kakar (2002)

CHAPTER ONE

The Wheel of Sexual Ecstasy

In the beginning, sings the 'Creation Hymn' of the *Rig Veda*, the holiest and most ancient of India's scriptures, 'there was neither non-existence nor existence'. Then, out of nothing and from nowhere, arose *kama*. *Kama* was sexual desire, the urge to create and procreate, the atom-like essence of creation itself. According to the *Brihadaranyaka Upanishad*, the greatest and oldest of India's philosophical texts, the First Being 'found no pleasure at all; so one finds no pleasure when one is alone. He wanted to have a companion. Now he was as large as a man and a woman in close embrace. So he split his body into two, giving rise to husband and wife... He copulated with her and from their union human beings were born.' *Kama*, then, was the first itch that brought the world into being, and humanity with it. Where the Judaeo-Christian tradition begins with 'light', you could say that Hinduism starts with *kama*. In the beginning was sex, and sex was with god, and sex was god.

By the middle of the first millennium BC, long after the Vedas and Upanishads were composed, *kama* had come to signify not just

3

primal desire, but the particular pleasures of love and lovemaking. In poetic epics of the era like the great *Mahabharata, kama* was transformed from divine essence into personified god: *kama* became Kama, an Eros-like figure of youthful beauty praised as the first-born, the god above all other gods, the son of Brahma, the creator. Kama was said to carry a bow made of deliciously sweet sugarcane, strung with a line of languorously humming bees and capable of firing flower-tipped arrows more deadly than any steel arrowhead. As a god and as an idea, *kama* was the expression of the divine creativity in humans, an essential principle of existence to be celebrated, praised, enjoyed and expressed through procreation. But as ever, there was a serpent in paradise. *Kama* was also a threat to the practice of meditation and the pursuit of the divine. It diverted the questing soul from the ultimate spiritual goal of 'release', or liberation from the world of birth and death. Hindu myths are full of tales of jealous gods sending heavenly nymphs to distract holy men whose austere meditations had made them too powerful. And the ascetic could not be too careful: one spilled drop of semen, like Samson's cut hair, was sufficient to burn away all his *tapas,* or stored-up spiritual energy.

Even the greatest ascetic of them all could be tempted. According to an ancient myth recorded in the *Shiva Purana,* after many thousands of years of perfect lovemaking the god Shiva abandoned his wife Parvati in order to pursue solitary meditation in the cool heights of the Himalayas. Frustrated and angered by her husband's neglect of his sexual obligations, Parvati dispatched Kama to disturb Shiva's concentration by piercing him with one of his potent, flower-tipped arrows. Just as the abstract *kama* had awoken the primal being from his slumber of non-being, the god Kama easily roused Shiva from his meditation. Enraged, Shiva turned the heat of his third, 'spiritual eye' on the god of desire, a heat engendered by aeons of yogic austerities, by centuries of sperm retention. Kama was reduced to ashes, becoming *ananga*, 'the bodiless one', a roving, aerial and ethereal spirit with the power to goad even the greatest ascetics towards the pursuit of pleasure.

The myth vividly dramatizes the bow-taut tension in Hinduism between asceticism and sensuality. The uncertain dating of almost all ancient Indian texts, the *Kamasutra* included, makes it very hard to make general statements about eras, but at the time of the *Kamasutra*'s birth, in around the third century of the first millennium, the ascetic principle seems to have had the whip hand. In the *Bhagavadgita*, the 'Hindu Sermon on the Mount' composed perhaps a little before the *Kamasutra*, the god Krishna virtually froths at the mouth as he fulminates against *kama*. 'By this is wisdom overcast,' he shrieks, 'therefore restrain the senses first: strike down this evil thing!' The so-called 'renouncer faiths' of Buddhism and Jainism, which were flourishing in the third century, rejected the tainted physical world even more emphatically. Asvaghosa's 'Life of the Buddha', which may be a hundred years or so older than the *Kamasutra*, warns that 'the one who they call Kama-deva here-on-earth, he who has variegated weapons, flower-tipped arrows, likewise they call him Mara, the ruler of the way of desire, the enemy of liberation'. For Buddhists, Mara was the ultimate tempter and was even known as the lord of death.

Not all thinkers were so confident in their rejection of *kama*. The poet Bhartrihari legendarily lived a life that oscillated no less than seven times between the severe existence of a monk and an abandoned pursuit of sensuality. For this writer, who probably lived within a century or two of the *Kamasutra*'s composition, there was no middle way between the erotic and ascetic principles. 'There are

two paths,' he wrote, 'the sages' religious-devotion which is lovely
because it overflows with the nectarous waters of the knowledge of
truth' and 'the lusty undertaking of touching with one's palm that
hidden part in the firm laps of lovely-limbed women, loving
women with great expanses of breasts and thighs'. 'Tell us decis-
ively which we ought to attend upon,' he asks in his *Shringarashataka*,
'the sloping sides of wilderness mountains? Or the buttocks of
women abounding in passion?'

The *Kamasutra* was firmly on the side of the buttocks. It mounted
the greatest defence of sexual pleasure the world had ever seen – or
would ever see. Its method, avowed in its very name, was to
capture and distil all previous knowledge on the entire subject of
sexual desire. It was a *sutra*, a scholarly treatise designed to compress
knowledge into a series of pithy maxims – a row of pearl-like
aphorisms strung together in a necklace. Literally, its title means
'the condensed version of the teaching on desire', 'aphorisms on
erotic pleasure' or 'the grammar of sex'. Yet none of these English
translations comes close to conveying the iconic status of the original Sanskrit words. 'The book of love' is less precise, but comes
closer to capturing the breadth of the *Kamasutra*'s scope and the
incredible force of its title's cultural impact.

The author of this extraordinary book of love was a man named
Vatsyayana, about whom nothing is known beyond what he says
about himself in his *Kamasutra*. Which is – rather surprisingly, given
that his book is devoted to sex – that he 'made this work in chastity
and in the highest meditation', and did not labour 'for the sake of
passion'. In the contemporary religious context, Vatsyayana could
be forgiven for sounding a little defensive, but this curious statement may even be true. As Vatsyayana himself explains, the goals
of life are different at each stage of manhood. Youth is for pleasure,

while old age is better suited to contemplation. It's tempting, then, to think that Vatsyayana acquired his sexual expertise as a young man, and composed his *Kamasutra* as a grizzled roué looking back on the adventures of his prime.

When or where those adventures, or the recall of them, took place is a mystery. Vatsyayana does not mention any dates in his book of love, nor where it was written or set. A thirteenth-century commentator, Yasodhara, believed that Vatsyayana lived in the great city of Pataliputra, which is a plausible enough theory, as it later became the home of the highly cultivated and eroticized Gupta court. But Pataliputra lay in the north-eastern part of India (it is now the modern city of Patna, beside the Ganges and bordering eastern Nepal) while most of the geographical references in the *Kamasutra* are to the north-west. Vatsyayana does not even mention the city in his survey of regional sexual preferences – though as the *Kamasutra* expert Haran Chandra Chakladar drily pointed out, perhaps 'he did not like to calumniate his own people by expatiating on their sexual abuses'.

When the book of love was born can only be guessed from a few tantalizing – and rather titillating – clues. The *Kamasutra* must come after the death of Queen Malayavati, as Vatsyayana tells us that she was killed by her husband's incautious use of the 'scissors' method of love-slap. (Perhaps fortunately, its secret is now lost.) Her wretched husband, Shatakarni Shatavahana, is thought to have ruled in the first century BC. And it must predate the fifth-century poet Subandhu, who pungently described in his poem *Vasavadatta* how the local Vindhya mountain range 'was filled with elephants and fragrant from the perfume of its jungles, just as the *Kamasutra* was written by Mallanaga and contains the delight and enjoyment of mistresses'. The commentator Yasodhara confirms that Mallanaga was Vatsyayana's given name, and Subandhu is known to have worked in Pataliputra, at the imperial court of Chandragupta II 'Vikramaditya'.

In fact, the *Kamasutra* is probably considerably older than Subandhu's poem, as it conspicuously fails to mention the glorious Guptas, dwelling instead on two earlier dynasties, the Abhiras and Andhras – and in not altogether flattering terms. Vatsyayana tells the farcical story of how a certain King Abhira was killed by a washerman brother while making an adulterous sortie into another man's home. He also observes that the women of the Abhiras 'like embracing, kissing, scratching, biting and sucking, and although they do not like to be wounded they can be won over with slaps'. As for the Andhras, their women are apparently 'delicate by nature but have coarse habits', such as grasping a man inside them 'like a mare, so tightly that he cannot move'. The Abhira dynasty came to power in the third or fourth decade of the third century AD, while the Andhras are thought to have declined soon after. Vatsyayana, then, must have lived around the early or middle part of the third century AD.

In India, this was a time between empires. The adulterous Abhiras were just one of many minor regional dynasties capitalizing on the collapse of the extensive Satavahana empire, and it would be a hundred years before the beginning of the Classical 'golden age' of the imperial Guptas. Third-century India was divided into endless kingdoms, principalities and even republican states, but the absence of a presiding imperial government did not necessarily lead to war and chaos – any more than the lack of a Roman emperor or a Grand Duke prevented Florence, Siena and Pisa from flourishing during the Italian Renaissance. Across the subcontinent, new cities were being founded at the crossroads of trade and pilgrimage routes by road and river. Caravans were exporting pearls, perfumes, precious stones, gold, finely worked ivory and pottery as far afield as China, Central Asia, the African coast and the eastern Mediterranean. Some luxury goods even reached Rome, while coins and foreign materials – as well as ideas – followed the caravans home again.

The new cities were well ordered and well built, with streetplans meticulously oriented around the cardinal points of the compass, and major thoroughfares neatly cobbled in stone. Segregated quarters were occupied by different castes or trades, while a great central marketplace attracted local peasantry from their outlying cow-herding villages – the appropriate venues, the *Kamasutra* advises, for the very lowest kind of lovemaking, technically known as 'sex with a peasant'. The lowest castes were relegated to satellite villages beyond the city's defensive palisade, while the more prosperous city-dwellers built their homes in sturdy brick, with fine porches overlooking the street. On the balconied roofs of these porches, the *Kamasutra* tells us, lovers lingered together after sex, gazing up at the moon and naming the constellations. At the very top of the house, dovecotes were installed in the eaves, while more birds were painted on the roof, symbolizing the love between the householder and his wife.

The religious-minded may have disapproved, but urban society was luxurious and sensual, the driving force of a highly aestheticized culture that would scarcely be matched again in India. At perfumed and bejewelled courts, poets, scholars and scientists were patronized by minor kings and princes. Women were lavishly adorned with ornamental jewellery, their hair sculpted and held in place by beautifully decorated hairpins, their faces made up in elaborate palettes of colours. Picnic-parties frequented carefully cultivated gardens on the city fringes, where guests swam in pools specially designed to keep out the crocodiles, and frolicked with each other under the trees. As the 'Libertine' tells the prostitute-heroine of the mid-first-millennium Sanskrit play, *The Little Clay Cart*:

> Behold the splendour of the park!
> The trees resplendent in their fruit and bloom,
> Protected by the king's keen guard from doom
> And by the creeper vines closely embraced
> Like husbands with their women interlaced.

At temple festivals in the evenings, the wealthy and urbane rubbed shoulders with prostitutes and professional actors, grazing on roasted grains, lotus stems and mangoes, and indulging in water-fights and puppet shows. At the salons of the *ganikas*, the most exquisite courtesans, the sophisticated gathered for conversation liberally sprinkled with nuggets of philosophy, jokes and elegant literary and erotic references.

The citizens of these young and sensual cities were known as *nagarakas*. Literally, the word translates as 'he of the city', but it means much more than that. In the era of the *Kamasutra*, the word 'city' had many of the connotations it has today, of sophistication, urbanity and fast living. *Nagaraka* has accordingly been rendered into English as 'worldly-wise citizen', 'man-about-town', 'city-bred man of fashion', 'elegant townsman', 'gentleman', 'cosmopolite' and 'urbane playboy'. But these words do not capture the heady odour of danger or corruption that clung to the original *nagaraka*. The more religious-minded citizens of third-century India associated cities with moral turpitude. A play by a near-contemporary of

Vatsyayana's, *The Recognition of Shakuntala*, features a group of ascetics making a journey to a major town. As the ascetics enter the palace, one turns to another: 'Look at these city people,' he mutters to his friend, 'these pleasure-lovers. I feel like a man fresh from the bath caught in a filthy beggar's gaze.'

Vatsyayana positively wallowed in the *nagaraka*'s 'filth'. His book was entirely devoted to these young, urban men who, as he put it, 'incline to the ways of the world and regard playing as their one and only concern'. Whether or not the *Kamasutra* was written *by* a pleasure-seeking playboy – or at least by an older man who used to be one – the book's structure suggests that it was written *for* one. The first of its seven books, or sections, 'General Observations', puts *kama* in its philosophical context and describes how our hero should set himself up for a life of pleasure. Like all the books, it is divided into a number of chapters, the most fascinating of which is devoted to the *nagaraka* himself. It is an astonishing portrait of his lifestyle, and so precise in its detail that if Vatsyayana was not a city slicker when he composed his great work, it is hard to believe that he was not at least recalling private memories. (Unless, like an eminent bachelor don at a fashionable Oxbridge college, Vatsyayana was simply surrounded by *nagarakas* and knew their habits inside out. In which case perhaps the *Kamasutra* was not so much a sex manual as a coursebook on sexual culture.)

The sheer intimacy of the chapter on the life of the *nagaraka* makes it extraordinarily, persuasively immediate. It begins at the beginning: when a man has completed his education, Vatsyayana says, he enters the mature, 'householder' stage of life. He is wealthy from work, inheritance or conquest, and comes without apparent ties – he chooses a city in which to settle solely on the basis of 'where there are good people' or 'wherever he has to stay to make a living'. It's easy to imagine the scion of old money lounging about in modern London's Notting Hill, or a Bombay yuppie jetting off to make fast money in an American bank. On arrival in his chosen city, he now starts to live as a *nagaraka* should. He sets up the perfect home, 'in a house near water, with an orchard, separate servant quarters, and two bedrooms'. One bedroom is for sleeping; the other is entirely devoted to sex. Inside, he keeps all the props of his effortlessly cultivated existence: a *vina* lute for strumming, implements for drawing, a book, garlands of flowers, a board for dice and cages of pet birds such as mynahs and parrots that he delights in teaching how to speak. Vatsyayana notes with typical precision, and sensuousness, that his bed is 'low in the middle and very soft, with pillows on both sides and a white top sheet'; his orchard-shaded swing is well padded; his bench of baked clay is covered with flowers; and his lute hangs not from an ordinary peg but from an ivory tusk. The *nagaraka* wallows in truly sybaritic luxury. His home is like an eligible bachelor's apartment in a designer magazine – and Vatsyayana's description is probably just as aspirational.

On getting up in the morning, the *nagaraka* 'relieves himself, cleans his teeth, applies fragrant oils in small quantities, as well as incense, garlands, beeswax and red lac, looks at his face in a mirror, takes some mouthwash and betel, and attends to the things that need to be done'. He chews lemon-tree bark and betel to sweeten his breath, bathes daily, has his limbs rubbed with oil every second day, wears perfume and 'continually cleans the sweat from his armpits'. Nothing so vulgar as body odour could be allowed to spoil this city boy's perfumed perfection. Scent was an important marker of wealth and breeding. The *Lalitavistara*, a Buddhist text roughly contemporary with the *Kamasutra*, describes how the young prince Gautama, the future Buddha, was endlessly anointed with perfumed ointments, waters, oils and the beloved sandalwood paste, while his palace home was unceasingly adorned with fragrant flowers.

During the day, the *nagaraka* passes his time in cock-fights, games, teaching his birds to speak, chatting to his urbane and rather dissolute friends – his 'libertine, pander and clown'. The 'libertine', a kind of itinerant connoisseur of the aesthetic arts, is characterized by the *Kamasutra* as an effete ne'er-do-well. Although he comes from a good family and is educated to a high standard, he 'has no possessions other than his shooting-stick, his soap and his astringent'. Together, the friends attend horseback picnics involving games, theatricals and, in summer, swimming. One can imagine the smooth-mannered, meticulously scrubbed 'libertine' lounging against his shooting-stick while his *nagaraka* friends show off their lithe bodies in the water, teasingly inviting their lovers to join them.

After a siesta, the *nagaraka* and his hangers-on embark on a tour of the 'salons' – courtesans' houses where fashionable people gathered to discuss art, poetry and women, and where they brought their racier lovers to drink, flirt and graze on fine foods. Later in the evening, the *nagaraka* attends a musical soirée, before retiring to his perfumed bedroom to wait for his women friends. Those girlfriends whose clothes have become wet as a result of coming to join him in bad weather, he courteously helps to change. The *nagaraka* and his lover then retire to the frescoed bedchamber, which has been festooned with flowers, and made fragrant with incense and other heady perfumes. As the lovers chat, joke and flirt with each other, the room is filled with the sounds of singing and the movement of dancers. Before making love, the *nagaraka*

displays his wealth and generosity by rewarding the entertainers
with yet more flowers, along with scented oils and betel nut. Only
then are the musicians sent away – and lovemaking begins.

The *nagaraka* should now turn to the *Kamasutra*'s second book:
'Sex'. It teaches him how to actually do it. Tellingly, it is the longest
and most detailed of all seven books. For having sex, as the
Kamasutra describes it, is a sophisticated affair. Famously, the
Kamasutra describes sixty-four *kama-kalas*, or ways to make love.
These 'arts of love', or 'erotic techniques', are not sixty-four sexual
positions, as they are often said – with awe – to be, but simply a
kind of grand total of the categories into which Vatsyayana divides
the different moods and modes of lovemaking. Theorists, Vatsyayana says, divide sex into eight different topics, namely 'embracing,
kissing, scratching, biting, the positions, moaning, the woman
playing the man's part and oral sex'. As each of these modes of sex
is supposed to have eight different particular manifestations, there
are thus sixty-four ways in which a man or woman could be said to
be having sex in its broadest sense. Mastery of these sixty-four
erotic techniques is essential for an accomplished *nagaraka*. If a man
lacks them, Vatsyayana says, 'he is not very well respected in con-
versations in the assembly of learned men.' The *kama-kalas* are not
just tools for successful love making, then; they lie at the heart of
what constitutes an educated man.

Of course, the fact that knowledge of the arts of love will
impress women is in itself no small matter. 'Virgins, other men's
wives and courtesans de luxe look with warm feelings and respect
on the man who is skilled in the sixty-four arts,' says Vatsyayana,
drily – and success with women is another defining characteristic
of the gentleman. The *nagaraka*'s basic education behind him, he
may now turn to the *Kamasutra*'s next four books, which define all

the different types of women that he may want to pursue. 'Virgins' describes how a man gets married, and how he woos his bride in bed, while 'Other Men's Wives' focuses on how those wives may be seduced. Where seduction is not, apparently, necessary, the *Kamasutra* takes a different tack. The books on 'Wives' and 'Courtesans' sketch the relationship of these women to the *nagaraka*, instructing the wife or the prostitute in her obligations, and informing the *nagaraka* about what behaviour he should expect.

Few ancient books have described the social and sexual lives of women in such intimate, exacting detail, and for this alone the *Kamasutra* is a rare and precious work. From the *nagaraka*'s point of view, however, the *Kamasutra*'s descriptions of women are rather like excerpts from a handy field guide to birds in their various plumages. There are even descriptions of regional variations (in sexual tastes), detailed instructions on how different kinds of women may be spotted and won, and warnings about which types of game must be left alone. Wives can be young and virginal, for example, or senior, or junior, or married to a king and living in a harem, or simply 'unlucky in love and oppressed by rivalry with her co-wives'. If virgins and wives aren't enough, the *nagaraka* may seek out the alluring *punarbhu*, an independent and sexually expert widow seeking remarriage or a mistress-like arrangement with an important official. He may also encounter two particularly exotic types of birds: the lady-boy, who offers oral sex for a living, and the more masculine masseur, who may throw in a hand-job or, if so desired, go so far as to 'suck the mango'.

There was no shame in turning to paid sex. Courtesans are lovingly graded according to their desirability, beauty and sophistication, from 'the servant woman who carries water' and 'the promiscuous woman', to 'the dancer, the artist, the openly

ruined woman, the woman who lives on her beauty and the courtesan de luxe'. This last and highest kind of prostitute is the *ganika*,
a woman of significant independence and high status – the *ganikas*
of the fifth-century Licchavi kingdom of Nepal even had their
own political representative body and were considered one of the
glories of the city. The *ganika* acquires her elevated status,
Vatsyayana says, by distinguishing herself in the 'sixty-four arts'.
Confusingly, these are not the sixty-four *kama-kalas* that mark
out the properly trained *nagaraka*, but the sixty-four *silpa-kalas*, a
finishing-school-type programme of feminine accomplishments
ranging from cooking and testing gold and silver, to making
glasses sing by rubbing their wet rims, and teaching parrots and
mynah birds to talk. Massage and hairdressing, meanwhile, more
obviously lend themselves to the young student of *kama*, as do the
arts of putting on make-up – including make-up for the teeth –
and dressing a bed properly. Mastery of all these skills will apparently allow a prostitute to work in the highest circles, while a
nobleman's daughter, if she learns them, will successfully keep
her husband under her thumb, 'even if he has a thousand women
in his harem'.

The *Kamasutra*'s seductively intimate, naturalistic detail can be
dangerous. The *nagaraka*'s erotic cocoon all too easily becomes the
reader's, and the world outside his shining realm of limitless pleasures can all too easily fade from view. In truth, the *Kamasutra* is no
more isolated from its context than the real *nagaraka* can have been
insulated from the everyday demands of religion, work and family.
Vatsyayana was not just composing a manual for the men-about-
town of his day, nor was he simply describing their world. His
Kamasutra was no 'player's handbook', no proto-*Joy of Sex*. It was
something far more ambitious and profound. It was also far more

wedded to Brahmin traditions of the distant past than its colourful descriptions of the *nagaraka*'s dissipated life suggest.

In its very first chapter, the *Kamasutra* declares itself to be the last scion of an ancient lineage that stretches right back to a '*Kamasutra*' composed by Nandi, the servant of the god Shiva. This divine Ur-*Kamasutra* was supposedly 1,000 chapters long and was itself an offshoot of the original book of Brahma's creation. Sacred or not, this text was clearly unwieldy, so a sage by the name of Svetaketu Auddalaki cut it down to a more memorable 500 chapters. Perhaps this was still unmanageable, for another erotic expert called Babhravya, from the western Pancala country, further edited the book down to a mere 150 chapters. Concocting a legendary geneal-ogy for a text was commonplace, as claiming that a text was descended from a god's original composition was as good as to say that it was correct. The *Kamasutra*'s genealogy, however, was not fabricated for the sake of authenticity – or at least not entirely.

The grandfathers of the *Kamasutra* appear in other texts as well, albeit as sexual lawmakers rather than experts in technique. Svetaketu appears in the already ancient mythological epic, the *Mahabharata*, as a legendary seer from the distant past. He is first mentioned when Pandu, the king of the Kurus, explains to his wife Kunti that women used to be free and sexually autonomous. Promiscuity, Pandu says, was 'not regarded as sinful, for that was the sanctioned usage of the times. That very usage is followed to this day by birds and beasts without any jealousy.' Addressing her as 'Kunti of the softly tapering thighs... lotus-eyed Kunti', Pandu tells her how there was once a hermit called Svetaketu, the son of the great seer Uddalaka, who saw his mother being led away by the hand by a Brahmin, as if by force. Svetaketu became angry and laid down a new rule that 'a woman's faithlessness to her husband shall be a sin equal to aborticide, an evil that shall bring on misery'. (Pandu gets his come-uppance when he shoots a deer with an arrow while it is trying to mate. The deer turns out to a disguised sage taking advantage of the relatively relaxed rules on animal sexuality, who curses Pandu, saying that if he attempts to have sex with either of his two wives he will surely die. Heroically, Pandu tries to have sex with his second wife, Madri – and dies.)

Svetaketu again figures as a patriarch of sexual regulation in the philosophical *Brihadaranyaka Upanishad*, which probably dates back to the sixth or seventh centuries BC. Asking his father for an explanation of the meaning and mystery of sex, he is told that sex is a kind of sacrificial offering of man to the gods by means of woman. It even involves the traditional ritual ingredients of *kusha* grass and the mysterious Soma (an ingredient which has been variously identified as the hallucinogenic fly agaric mushroom and the stimulant desert plant *ephedra*). A woman's vulva 'is the sacrificial ground', Svetaketu hears, 'her pubic hair is the sacred grass; her labia majora are the Soma-press; and her labia minora are the fire blazing at the centre.' Svetaketu is also given magical formulae for ensuring the birth of different kinds of sons. To get 'a learned and famous son, a captivating orator assisting at councils, who will master all the Vedas and live out his full lifespan', the man should open the woman's thighs, saying, 'Spread apart, earth and sky.' He then 'slips his penis into her, presses his mouth against hers and strokes her three times in the direction of her hair' – all the while invoking the assistance of various gods.

Whatever the results in terms of progeny, Svetaketu's recipe would hardly seem to guarantee satisfying lovemaking. It is all a long way from Vatsyayana's resolutely practical *Kamasutra*. Babhravya, however, the other grandfather of the erotic tradition, feels less distant. A certain 'Pancala Babhravya' is supposed to have been the author of part of the *Rig Veda* – which would place him only 1,000 years or so before Vatsyayana. As well as condensing the teaching on *kama* into a mere 150 chapters, Babhravya divided it into the seven topics or 'limbs', which survived as the seven books of the *Kamasutra*.

In doing so, he nearly killed off *kama*. According to Vatsyayana, later scholars fatally dismembered Babhravya's work by choosing to specialize in the different topics. A certain Suvarnanabha was apparently an authority on 'Sex'; Ghotakamukha specialized in 'Virgins'; Gonikaputra in 'Other Men's Wives'; while Kucumara focused on aphrodisiacs – this became the *Kamasutra*'s rather perfunctory seventh and final book. Dattaka – who was cursed to live for a time as a woman, thus giving him a privileged, Tiresias-like insight into male and female pleasure – was apparently commissioned by the courtesans of Pataliputra to compose a new text based on Babhravya's sixth 'limb', the one dedicated to prostitution. Like the ancient works of Babhravya and Svetaketu, the seven works of the seven original sexual specialists are now lost. Only a few mere fragments or quotations survive – but enough to be sure that they existed in the distant past.

Even in Vatsyayana's time, the works of the seven sex specialists were apparently in danger of extinction. In his opening chapter, Vatsyayana announced that the teaching on *kama* had become dangerously fragmented and he was mounting an urgent rescue mission. He set out to pick up the threads of an ancient and perhaps moribund tradition in order to bind them together. He wanted the *Kamasutra* to be quoted and referred to by future generations. In the third century, however, books were a rare novelty. (And it's almost certain that none – including the *Kamasutra* – was illustrated.) Manuscripts existed in the form of dried palm leaves inscribed with a stylus whose pinhead-fine scratch marks were afterwards inked in, and there was even paper to be found, made from the skin of birch trees. But most texts were probably learned by rote rather than written down.

There was only one way to ensure that the *Kamasutra* was remembered and that was to make it literally memorable. Vatsyayana accordingly composed in the tightly woven *sutra* form. A celebrated Sanskrit *sutra*, in the classic two-line form, defines the nature of a good *sutra*: 'Brief, unambiguous, essential, universal, / shining and faultless is the *sutra* known to the *sutra*-sages.' In an era when most texts were probably transmitted orally, one that was both short and memorable – not to mention shining and faultless – had obvious advantages. There were drawbacks, however. Vatsyayana was so concerned that his *Kamasutra* should survive that he made it concise to the point of being cryptic. A *sutra* like 'no hand prevention' might mean 'he does not hold back his hand', and 'a mare, cruelly gripping' might mean 'she grasps him, like a mare, so tightly that he cannot move'. This compressed style would cause serious problems for future translators.

By the time he reached concluding verses of the *Kamasutra*, Vatsyayana was clearly exhausted. The work of 'combining earlier texts / and following their methods', he complained, was only done with 'great effort'. It wasn't even entirely successful. Three of the seven books do not sit easily with the other four. The notorious book on 'Sex' stands out by being focused on matters physical rather than social or ethical, while 'Wives' and 'Courtesans' are, exceptionally, written from the woman's point of view. Maybe Vatsyayana's story about Dattaka being commissioned to write the book by the courtesans of Pataliputra was true. The final book, on aphrodisiacs, meanwhile, is blatantly tacked on at the end. Vatsyayana seems to have had little time for it, even casting doubt on the quality of its recipes by warning his readers not to use techniques that look 'doubtful'.

It's impossible to know whether Vatsyayana really was who he said he was: a white-haired scholar, long past sexual temptations, who sat down one day to stitch together the seven limbs of the teaching on *kama*. Like Homer, he may have been a convenient name for unknown compositors, a figure dreamed up to confer a greater degree of unity on a text that was cobbled together from disparate sources. But whether Vatsyayana was real or notional, 'his' task remained the same: it was to restore the body of teaching on *kama* to the dignity of its original wholeness. The idea was not so much to advance or redefine thinking on the subject of *kama*, but to capture the best thinking from existing schools of thought.

The *Kamasutra* was intended to be a contribution to the great scientific project of the era: the composition of authoritative studies of all aspects of human behaviour and understanding. As Vatsyayana describes it, the teaching of Babhravya, Svetaketu and the other venerable authorities formed a *shastra*, or a learned teaching on a particular topic. And at around the time he composed the *Kamasutra*, new *shastras* were constantly being created. Patanjali had composed his *Mahabhasya*, a definitive commentary on the ancient science of grammar, not long before. Bharata contributed his *Natyashastra*, which examined every conceivable aspect of the teaching and performance of dance and theatre. Collectively, these *shastras* could be seen as a vast encyclopedia striving to present the best wisdom available on all subjects – which, in the Brahminical world-view, meant divine wisdom. Creating such an encyclopedia was less a matter of discovering truth than of recovering it, as if

Brahmin scholars were attempting to reconstitute the 100,000 chapters of Brahma's original creation.

It was Vatsyayana's task to ensure that the chapter on *kama* was up to scratch. It was to be the last word on the subject. But what that subject actually was – what *kama* really meant – was deeply controversial. 'Sex' doesn't begin to cover it. The *Kamasutra* begins by defining *kama* 'in general', which, it says, consists 'in engaging the ear, skin, eye, tongue and nose each in its own appropriate sensation, all under the control of the mind and heart driven by the conscious self'. In Vatsyayana's view, it seems, *kama* is nothing less than the conscious experience of pleasure, a state elevated above mere sensuality by awareness and control. As an idea, it isn't so far removed from Wordsworth's aesthetic theories – albeit applied to actual sweating, heaving bodies, rather than clouds and daffodils. (As the next chapter reveals, Vatsyayana's idea owes much to the theories of poetics and literary appreciation developed at around the time he was writing.)

In its 'primary form', however, *kama* is more immediate, more physical. It is 'a direct experience of an object of the senses, which bears fruit and is permeated by the sensual pleasure of erotic arousal that results from the particular sensation of touch'. On this phrase, 'bears fruit', hangs an entire debate of crucial importance for how the *Kamasutra* should be understoood. According to the translators Wendy Doniger and Sudhir Kakar, 'bears fruit' probably refers to the conception of a child. If so, it would fit neatly with the orthodox Brahminical view that sex is 'for' procreation. The Viennese Sanskritist, Chlodwig Werba, has a more radical suggestion, however. *Kama*, as defined by the *Kamasutra*, he translates as being something that comes about 'in consequence of a special contact' which results in the person who experiences it 'being permeated by a well-being of awareness' and successfully reaching her or his goal. *Kama*, then, is an experience that appears to relate on some level to orgasm, not conception, and this kind of orgasm appears to have been seen as a microcosm of the enlightened liberation of the soul. The difference in translation is the result of no mere academic spat; it echoes the single most debated point in the entire realm of sexuality: is sex 'for' procreation or pleasure? If Chlodwig Werba is right, the *Kamasutra* is unequivocally on the side of pleasure.

In Hinduism, *kama* was – and still is – ranked as one of the three fundamental goals of human existence, which together formed the *trivarga*, or triple path. The three goals were *dharma*, *artha* and *kama*. The terms are famously hard to translate. Fortunately, the *Kamasutra* includes the pithiest definition found in any Hindu text. *Dharma*, it says, 'consists in engaging, as the texts decree, in sacrifice and other such actions that are disengaged from material life'. It covers the concepts of 'law', 'justice', 'religion' and 'duty', as well as the seemingly conflicting ideas of 'principle' and 'practice' – one might call *dharma* 'rules and religion'. As for *artha*, it 'consists in acquiring knowledge, land, gold, cattle, grain, household goods and furniture, friends, and so forth, and increasing what has been acquired' – 'wealth and worldly affairs', one might say. It is the *trivarga*, rather than *kama* alone, that Vatsyayana declares to be the subject of his text. He even opens his book by saluting the trio. They are in 'mutual agreement', he says. Together, they define and underpin all knowledge, all virtue and, ultimately, all human life.

In stressing the relevance of the 'three goals', Vatsyayana was staking a claim for the importance of his composition. It would address one of the three fundamental areas of human experience: sex. And if *dharma* covered not simply 'ritual' but the entire realm of the spiritual and moral, and *artha* dealt not just with money but with the entire world of public life and politics, *kama* could mean far more than just 'sex' in the narrow sense. It could fill the space beyond *dharma* and *artha*, concerning itself with all things physical and social. As such, a book on the subject could discuss not just lovemaking but the entire life of the gentleman *nagaraka* in all his private capacities: his betrothal and marriage, his relations with friends, courtesans and lovers – even his taste in bedroom decoration.

Vatsyayana had another reason to emphasize sex as a life-goal: he was covering his own back. Many of his fellow Brahmin scholars would have had little time for the distractions of *kama* – and still less for a text glorifying the philanderings of *nagarakas* under the banner of philosophy. If Babhravya, Dattaka and the rest of the *Kamasutra*'s predecessors were hoary, it was more a result of the dust of neglect than of silvered reverence. By contrast, study of *dharma* and *artha*, the other life-goals of the *trivarga*, was flourishing. Authoritative works on *dharma* and *artha* had already become standards by the time the *Kamasutra* was born.

The *Manavadharmashastra*, or 'Manu's *shastra* on the subject of *dharma*', was not just authoritative but positively authoritarian. In the family of texts that makes up the *shastras*, it was the *Kamasutra*'s clergyman uncle: somewhat older and more severe, and deeply preoccupied with matters of religion and morality. The *Laws of Manu*, as the work later became known in the West, defined norms on subjects ranging from 'guarding the kingdom' and 'the character and behaviour of outcasts' to 'acts that bring about the supreme good'. It also tried to regulate sexual behaviour. Notwithstanding the praise of Friedrich Nietzsche, who fumed that 'all the things upon which Christianity vents its abysmal vulgarity, procreation, for example, woman, marriage, are here treated seriously, with reverence, with love and trust', *Manu*'s attitude to sexuality and the physical can be terrifyingly monkish. It describes the body as 'foul-smelling, tormented, impermanent... filled with urine and excrement, pervaded by old age and sorrow, infested by sickness, and polluted by passion'.

Manu bans sex 'in non-human females, in a man, in a menstruating woman, in something other than a vagina'. Its ideal is that sex should be strictly procreative and monogamous: a man should only approach his wife on specific days within the first half of the menstrual cycle, and then only after a ritual bath and a prayer. Any kind of sex that threatens the social order is forbidden, to the extent that 'if a man speaks to another man's wife at a bathing place, in a wilderness or a forest, or at the confluence of rivers, he incurs the guilt of sexual misconduct'. Worse still are 'acting with special courtesy to her, playing around with her, touching her ornaments or clothes, sitting on a couch with her' – all of which modest flirtations are the very life-stuff of the *nagaraka*. The penalties for adultery are severe: a woman will be eaten by dogs in a public place, a man burned on a red-hot iron bed – though, generously, *Manu* accepts that this ruling on adultery need not apply to the wives of strolling actors. To underline the danger, *Manu* issues the apocalyptic warning that: 'If men persist in seeking intimate contact with other men's wives, the king should brand them with punishments that inspire terror and banish them. For that gives rise among people to the confusion of the castes, by means of which irreligion, that cuts away the roots, works for the destruction of everything.'

Vatsyayana, of course, includes a whole chapter on 'Other Men's Wives'. He advises his male audience that among the 'women who can be had without any effort' are 'a woman who stands at the door; a woman who looks out from her rooftop porch onto the main street... a woman who hates her husband; a woman who is hated; a woman who lacks restraint; a woman who has not children' – and the list goes on and on, ending with 'the wife of a man who is jealous, putrid, too pure, impotent, a procrastinator, unmanly, a hunchback, a dwarf, deformed, a jeweller, a villager, bad-smelling, sick or old'. One somehow feels for the jewellers.

The point of adultery is, according to Vatsyayana, pleasure alone. And sex for the sake of sex is, conveniently, exactly what the *nagaraka* is looking for. As is his wife: Vatsyayana approves the notion that a woman who does not 'experience the pleasures of love' may leave her husband for another man. But Vatsyayana is careful not to extol the virtues of adultery too highly. The verses that end the chapter on 'Other Men's Wives' pronounce, surprisingly, that a man 'should never seduce other men's wives' as this goes against both *dharma* and *artha*, and they claim that the sole object of describing how a man can be a successful seducer – as the preceding book has done in prolific detail – is supposedly to put husbands on their guard.

It's easy to choke on the cool hypocrisy of this self-justification, but it is the result of Vatsyayana's defensiveness about describing forbidden sexual practices, a pose of legitimacy he adopts while the encyclopedic ideal drives him to describe all possible forms of sexual experience. Vatsyayana's approach seems to be that if you know all the rules, you can choose whether or not they apply to you, and where your best advantage lies. These Machiavellian mores were undoubtedly influenced by Kautilya's *Arthashastra*, the standard treatise on the life-goal of *artha*, or 'wealth and worldly affairs'. As a manual of statecraft addressed to an ideal prince, the *Arthashastra* is the devious politician brother to *Manu's* clergyman uncle. It deals with subjects as diverse as the proper conduct of courtiers, the 'capture of the enemy by means of secret contrivances or by means of the army' and 'detection of what is embezzled by government servants out of state revenue'.

Vatsyayana copied the *Arthashastra*'s supremely organized structure, and even mimicked its stance, employing the same ruthlessly pragmatic approach to seduction that the *Arthashastra* uses for, say, capturing a fortress or dealing with a strong enemy. So close are the forms that the *Kamasutra* might almost be a mischievous parody. The *Arthashastra* itself brushes up against the realm of *kama*. It stipulates the prince's 'duty towards the harem', for instance, and the tasks of the 'Superintendent of Prostitutes' — which include seeing that prostitutes are properly trained in the art of lovemaking. Its morals are more equivocal than *Manu*'s, but the *Arthashastra* is hardly permissive. Its first book, 'Concerning Discipline', has a good deal to say on the personal and intimate conduct of the ideal prince. A chapter on the 'restraint of the organs of sense' describes how a worthy ruler has 'his organs of sense under his control' and should (or should be able to) 'keep away from hurting the women and property of others; avoid not only lustfulness, even in dream, but also falsehood, haughtiness, and evil proclivities'.

A prince was not expected to be an ascetic, however, and the *Arthashastra* briefly sways towards the warmth of the *Kamasutra*'s embracing world-view:

Not violating righteousness and economy, he shall enjoy his desires. He shall never be devoid of happiness. He may enjoy in an equal degree the three pursuits of life, charity, wealth, and desire [*dharma*, *artha* and *kama*], which are inter-dependent upon each other. Any one of these three, when enjoyed to an excess, hurts not only the other two, but also itself.

Vatsyayana says much the same thing, although what the *Arthashastra* deems to be excessive is surprisingly tame. If a woman is engaged 'in amorous sports' she is fined three *panas*. The fine goes up to twelve panas 'if she goes out to see another man or for sports'. It is doubled for the same offences committed at night or 'if a man and a woman make signs to each other with a view to sensual enjoyment, or carry on secret conversation for the same purpose'. Such rules could be designed to target the lifestyle described in the *Kamasutra* as these kinds of flirtations are meat and drink to the *nagaraka* and his lovers.

Vatsyayana was up against powerful enemies – or, at least, rivals. Despite *kama*'s theoretical importance as one of the three life-goals, to actually enjoy a lifestyle based entirely on the pursuit of pleasure was deeply problematic. Both the *Laws of Manu* and *Arthashastra* are stiff with warnings of what constitutes sexual misbehaviour. They groan with precisely stipulated penalties for transgression. The *Kamasutra*, in violent contrast, offers moderating or cautionary notes at most, and these are often preceded with the phrase 'Vatsyayana says' – a stylistic tic borrowed from the *Arthashastra* – thus emphasizing that rules may be a matter of opinion.

Vatsyayana gets his retaliation in first by anticipating attacks on the moral worth of *kama*. Pursed-lip 'pragmatists', he reports, would argue that 'people should not indulge in pleasures, for they are an obstacle to both religion and power, which are more important... They make a man associate with worthless people and undertake bad projects; they make him impure, a man with no future, as well as careless, lightweight, untrustworthy and unacceptable.' They make him, in short, a *nagaraka*. But *kama*, for Vatsyayana, is just as important as *dharma* and *artha*. It is simply a matter of appropriate timing. Childhood, he says, is for knowledge, youth for pleasure, and old age for religion and release – horses for courses, one might say. He adds, with gleeful pragmatism, 'Or, because the lifespan is uncertain, a man pursues these aims as the opportunity arises' – stabbing as the occasion serves, perhaps.

Vatsyayana confesses that some authorities believe that people should not even indulge in *writing* about pleasures, let alone enjoying them. 'Scholars say,' he warns, that while it is appropriate to have *shastras* about *dharma* and *artha*, 'since even animals manage sex by themselves, and since it goes on all the time, it should not have to be handled with the help of a text'. Vatsyayana's answer is typically practical. 'Because a man and woman depend upon one another in sex,' he says, 'it requires a method.' The method is, of course, his book. With an earnest manner – and perhaps a glint in his eye – Vatsyayana then modestly suggests that the pleasures of the flesh 'are a means of sustaining the body, and they are rewards for religion and power'. One must simply 'be aware of the flaws in pleasures, flaws that are like diseases. For people do not stop preparing the cooking pots because they think, "There are beggars", nor do they stop planting barley because they think, "There are deer."' Nor, we may infer, should people stop making love – or writing about it – because they think, 'There are scholars.'

This 'liberal' voice would later resonate with Western readers as a precious survival from the ancient world. Such palpably permissive mores are rare indeed in 'religious' texts from the distant past. The voice is most audible and distinct in the *shlokas* or verses that round off most of the *Kamasutra*'s chapters, acting as a kind of running commentary on the *sutras*. If the *sutras* are like grains of rice

– nutritious, pithy, essential and capable of being stored for long periods – the *shlokas* are spoonfuls of sweetness. To borrow from the *Kamasutra*'s own recipe for virility, they are the honey and butter that transform a plain rice dish into a sumptuous pudding – one that, with the addition of 'the juice from a sparrow's egg', allows a man to 'make love with endless women'.

When the *Kamasutra* was composed, the *sutra* form was already archaic. *Shlokas*, by contrast, had a more contemporary flavour and it seems likely that they are the voice of Vatsyayana himself – or at least of the writers or editors whose work is attributed to him. Many readers in the West have found this voice warmly, comfortingly liberal. It tends to commentate on the *sutras* in order to clarify or modify the rules. The final *shlokas*, for instance, warn that the 'unusual techniques employed to increase passion' are in fact 'strongly restricted', and they are described only because a full survey required it. This is not a moralizing restriction, however, so much as a liberating one. As the *shlokas* continue, the extraordinary relativism underlying the statement becomes clear. 'People should realize,' they observe, 'that the contents of the texts apply in general, but each actual practice is for one particular region.' Rules, in the *Kamasutra*, may not be what they seem.

Ultimately, the *Kamasutra* challenges the very idea of rules concerning love. The *shlokas* that conclude the chapter on 'slapping and the accompanying moaning', from the book on 'Sex', end with a celebrated simile that perfectly expresses the idea that passion prevails over regulation and sex surpasses the dry facts of any textbook – even a textbook on sex. Slapping and moaning, Vatsyayana says, are 'no matter for numerical lists / or textbook tables of contents' – which is exactly what characterizes the *sutras*.

For people joined in sexual ecstasy,
passion is what makes things happen…
For just as a horse in full gallop,
blinded by the energy of his own speed,
pays no attention to any post
or hole or ditch on the path,
so two lovers blinded by passion
in the friction of sexual battle,
are caught up in their fierce energy
and pay no attention to danger.

The simile of the horse perfectly captures the power and (sweaty) energy of lovemaking. It represents neither man nor woman but passion itself: vigorous, autonomous and almost, but not quite, out of control, hurting itself recklessly in delight at the energy of its own speed. Sexual excellence may be the product of self-mastery, the cultivated knowledge of the sixty-four arts and sciences, but passion, Vatsyayana says, 'does not look before it leaps'.

But it is in the verses that close the chapter on 'embraces' in which Vatsyayana most emphatically casts off the dusty gown of the scholar. He stands naked before his audience, declaring that:

The territory of the texts extends
only so far as men have dull appetites;
but when the wheel of sexual ecstasy is in full motion,
there is no textbook [shastra] at all, and no order.

Would Vatsyayana's successors throw away the Kamasutra and strap themselves to the wheel?

$\mathcal{A}$s FOR THE end of sex, when their passion has ebbed, the man and woman go out separately to the bathing place, embarrassed, not looking at one another, as if they were not even acquainted with one another. When they return, they sit down in their usual places without embarrassment, and chew some betel, and he himself rubs sandalwood paste or some other scented oil on her body. He embraces her with his left arm and, holding a cup in his hand, persuades her to drink. Or both of them may drink some water or eat some bite-sized snacks or something else, according to their temperament and inclination: fruit juice, grilled foods, sour rice-broth, soups with small pieces of roasted meats, mangoes, dried meat, citrus fruits with sugar, according to the tastes of the region. As he tastes each one he tells her, 'This one is sweet' or 'delicate' or 'soft', and offers it to her. Sometimes they sit on the rooftop porch to enjoy the moonlight, and tell stories that suit their mood. As she lies in his lap, looking at the moon, he points out the rows of constellations to her; they look at the Pleiades, the Pole Star, and the garland of Seven Sages that form the Great Bear. That is the end of sex.

Kamasutra
Book Two: Sex
Chapter Ten: The Start and Finish of Sex
translated by Wendy Doniger and Sudhir Kakar (2002)

CHAPTER TWO

Pleasure in the Passions

For a time it seemed as if Vatsyayana had succeeded too well, as if his students and *nagaraka* followers really were throwing away their textbooks and freely indulging their erotic appetites. No rival *Kamasutras* emerged to challenge Vatsyayana as the authoritative voice of sex. He even seemed to have killed off the works from which he borrowed — certainly, none of his predecessors' books is known today. Once the *Kamasutra* had been composed, who would try to memorize the 150 chapters of Babhravya, after all? And with the *Kamasutra* to hand, who would commission a new, specialized study of courtesans and their arts? Vatsyayana's book of love was so perfect, so closely observed and finely argued that it couldn't be bettered.

The *Kamasutra*'s success halted the advancement of the science of *kama* — for a time at least — but love soon flowered in another, more perfumed arena: that of the arts. The shimmering cultural summer of the third- and fourth-century Gupta dynasty was the golden age of Classical Sanskrit literature, an epoch in which all the urban delights of the *nagaraka* were given their most refined expression. Poets were lauded and musicians celebrated, but greater than all other delights was the theatre. Crowds of aristocratic arts-lovers flocked to watch plays, especially those with erotic themes. Theatres were profoundly sensual places in themselves, the half-light of smoky lamps and the rows of columns supporting their barrel-vaulted roofs providing perfect opportunities for private conversation or flirtation, even in such a public space. The walls were painted with suggestive images of intertwining creepers and depictions of men and women pleasuring each other. Still more enticing was the perfume of the theatre, the alluring scents of sandalwood, incense, beeswax and betel rising from the audience and combining with the quintessentially theatrical smells of stage make-up and burning lamp-oil.

It was no wonder that Vatsyayana attested to lovers' passion for the theatre. Plays of the Classical era, meanwhile, reflected an equally fierce desire for tales of lovers. Where Shakespeare's theatre resounded with the trumpets of battle, the sighs of romantic lovers and the belly-laughs of low comedy, ancient Indian theatres were supposed to reverberate with one sound above all: the low hum of sensuality. Almost every surviving Classical Sanskrit court drama took *kama* as its central theme, and playwrights used sophisticated techniques of mime, dance and dialogue to capture the very essence of eroticism. Theatre had its own textbook to match Vatsyayana's book of love: Bharata's *Natyashastra* was the definitive work on all aspect of dance, theatre and aesthetics. It set out the exact dimensions for the construction of the ideal theatre and explored complex theories of beauty and artistic appreciation, including the grounding theory of all Sanskrit literature: that of *rasas*. The erotic mood sought by poets and dramatists was, the *Natyashastra* explained, one of nine *rasas*, each of which corresponded to a basic human emotion, but which was elevated above it by artistic expression or conscious appreciation. In Sanskrit, *rasa* can mean taste or flavour, and a *rasa* was like a distilled essence of the raw emotions of everyday experience. Each *rasa* could inspire the tone of a gesture, a look, or even an entire piece of theatre. In the *Poetics*, Aristotle had divided poetry into three genres: comedy, tragedy and epic. Sanskrit aestheticians went further: there were *rasas* for joy and laughter, disgust, wrath, serenity, heroism, fear, grief and wonder.

The greatest, the most fashionable and elegant *rasa* of them all was *sringara*, the *rasa* of the rapturously erotic. It was like the romantic love of the Western stage but underpinned by the force that truly drove that love. It was *sringara* that drew the audiences and inspired the greatest plays. And it was *sringara* – and the playwrights and audiences that together conjured it – that kept the *Kamasutra* alive. A *rasa* was created not only by the playwright; to exist at all it had to take shape in the mind of a connoisseur. The appreciation of the pleasures of love, according to Vatsyayana, was supposed to be 'under the control of the mind and heart driven by the conscious self'. Similarly, *sringara* was to be refined from the actual experience of sexual love as 'a dispassionate pleasure in the passions'. Nothing was supposed to be shown that would make the audience blush, but the articulation of *sringara* in the theatre was far from passionless. Theatre stages had to be raised up on plinths and, it is thought, protected by a wooden railing two feet high that could shield the actors from the excesses of theatre-goers. It isn't known whether the miscreants were raised to such a pitch of erotic fervour that they attempted to cross the divide to enter the idealized world of the play, or whether they simply got so drunk that they attempted to grope the actresses – among whom were prostitutes celebrated for their beauty and their mastery of the sixty-four arts.

The *Natyashastra* was the *Kamasutra's* sexy, clever actress sister —
and the two siblings were very close. This wasn't just a matter of
age, although Bharata and Vatsyayana were probably roughly contemporary, give or take the usual century or two of uncertainty
that blurs most ancient Indian dates. It wasn't even a matter of their
shared, shastric obsession with classification in general and the cat-
egorization of bodily postures in particular, though they were very
similar in this regard — the *Kamasutra's* coital positions need no
introduction, while the *Natyashastra* describes no fewer than ten
modes of standing, seven kinds of pirouettes, thirty-two types of
gaits and 108 'transitory postures'. Their close relationship was born
from a shared sense of the profound theatricality of the erotic.

Sex, for the *Kamasutra*, was theatre; while theatre, for the
Natyashastra, was all about sex. The *Kamasutra* sees sex as a public act
played out to an audience. Even the word it uses for the male lover
is the one that the *Natyashastra* employs for the hero of a play: he is
the *nayaka*, or protagonist. In both works, his lover, or leading lady,
is called the *nayika*. The *Natyashastra* classified her in detail according
to her nature and temperament. The *vasakasajja nayika*, for example,
would dress up in joyful preparation for having sex with her
beloved, anxiously checking her jewels and make-up in the mirror,
strewing her bed with flower petals and gazing longingly out of
the window. The *khandita nayika*, by contrast, was furious with her
unfaithful lover; panting with rage and sorrow, she would not hear
his excuses or even let him come near her. Many of these archetypal romantic situations were also described in the *Kamasutra*.
Tellingly, even the *nagaraka's* three main companions, the 'libertine', 'pander' and 'clown', are stock characters in drama.

Vatsyayana, it seems, was interested not only in the science of
kama. He had a manual of theatrical erotics in mind as much as a

real guide to sexual relationships. At times, the *Kamasutra* itself plunges across the barrier dividing the real from the play-world. At the beginning of each of the seven books, the curtain comes up on the *nagaraka* in a different costume and at a different time of life: he appears as the seducer of virgins, the ideal husband, the pursuer of other men's wives, the client of courtesans and, finally, in the last book, as the man in need of recourse to aphrodisiacs in order to maintain his flagging virility. Sex itself is one magnificent, mannered performance in the *Kamasutra*, part of a whole theatrical lifestyle that begins with the sixty-four arts and ends with the appropriate kinds of cries and moans in bed. The man seducing a young virgin – and the young virgin in turn seducing him – are playing out well-defined roles. Only the courtesan is as consummate a performer: she is hired to 'play the part' of a lover and required to act like a wife 'in order to make him love her'. It is no accident that, as the *Kamasutra* observes, many prostitutes were also dancers or artists, while the *Natyashastra* actually describes prostitution as one of the arts of the dancer.

Lovemaking, in the *Kamasutra*, is elaborately gilded with layers of meaning. Love bites are not just bites, they are mutually understood modes of courtship. Scratches with the fingernails are not the signs of raw passion, they are recognized signals: the 'hare's leap' mark of five 'peacock's foot' scratches close together on the nipple is used to praise a woman for her sexual skill, while a man leaving on a journey also leaves behind 'three or four lines on her thighs or on the upper part of her breasts, to make her remember him'. The *Kamasutra*'s vivid 'scenes' of passionate lovemaking are dramatic depictions as much as portraits of real lovers at play. Many embraces are postures as much as positions, and they owe as much to dance as real sexual behaviour. Take, for instance, 'the twining vine', in which, 'as a vine twines around a great dammar tree, so she twines around him and bends his face down to her to kiss him', or 'climbing the tree', in which she rests one of her feet on her lover's foot and the other on his thigh, and acts as if she were climbing his body in order to claim a kiss. When the woman assumes an 'on top' position to make love, she is described as 'playing the man's part'. And when the lovers engage in sex as 'a form of quarrelling', the woman 'pretends to be unable to bear it' when he 'strikes her on her back with his fist when she is seated on his lap'; and all the while she uses, 'according to her imagination, the cries of the dove, cuckoo, green pigeon, parrot, bee, night-ingale, goose, duck and partridge'. It must have been some performance. The woman's imagination might well have been fired by the *Natyashastra*, which teaches the performer how to mimic the movements of birds and animals, if not how to produce such delicious coos and cries.

Real quarrels are marked by equally elaborate play-acting. If a woman's lover speaks the name of a co-wife, 'or accidentally calls the woman by the other woman's name', or actually betrays her, 'then there is a great quarrel' in which the woman is something of a prima donna. She plays her broken-hearted part

> with weeping, anguish, tossing hair, slaps, falling from the bed or chair onto the ground, tearing off garlands and jewellery and sleeping on the floor... She answers his words by getting even angrier, grabbing his hair and pulling his face up, kicking him once, twice, three times, on his arms, head, chest or back. Then she goes to the door and sits down there and bursts into tears.

This is a feistier heroine than the *nayika* of the *Natyashastra*, who 'should harass him with rebukes made up of words spoken in jealous indignation. But no very cruel words should be uttered and no very angry words should be used either.' Nevertheless, the two heroines are definitely cousins.

If poets and dramatists looked to the *Natyashastra* for the theory, they turned to the *Kamasutra* for the practice, for a model of expression. In the first of the many appropriations that would define the afterlife of Vatsyayana's book of love, the *Kamasutra*'s very language was mined by poets and dramatists, its terminology adopted for erotic authenticity. Sudraka's wonderful, fourth-century play, *Mrcchakatika*, or *The Little Clay Cart*, exists in the very same vibrantly erotic realm described by Vatsyayana. The play has as its hero an elegant and noble *nagaraka* called Carudatta who, by virtue of falling in love with a courtesan, seems almost to walk off the pages of the *Kamasutra*. Carudatta's very house — as described by his friend Maitreya, the 'clown' — could be the the ideal bachelor pad described in the *Kamasutra*, with its terraces, soft bed and couch, its gaming board, orchard garden and caged, melodious songbirds. Writing in around the fourth or fifth century, the greatest of all Sanskrit poet-dramatists, Kalidasa, clearly knew his *Kamasutra* backwards. His poem *Raghuvamsa* dwells on the erotic abandonment of the decadent King Agnivarna, who devolves all his power to his ministers in order to pursue a life of ceaseless sensual pleasure, much like the *nagaraka*'s. In his lap he cradles young women or a *vina* lute; he sits on the terrace of his palace under a canopy, enjoying the moonlight with his harem of graceful virgins; and he leaves bite and fingernail marks on the lips and thighs of women 'practised in the arts' — to the cruel extent that it hurts them to play the flute or *vina* for his entertainment.

Of course, the poets and Vatsyayana could just have been drawing on the same stock images and scenarios, from a common pool of erotic motifs and sexual behavioural norms. But the *Kamasutra* was more than just another literary source: it was the authoritative original. The proof of this is found in Kalidasa's greatest play, the *Recognition of Shakuntala*. In one crux moment in the play, the hero king, Dusyanta, meets the lovely Shakuntala for the first time as she waters fragrant mango trees in a hermit's grove. The scene follows the *Kamasutra* like a rulebook. When a young girl is attracted to a man, Vatsyayana says,

> she does not look at him face to face. When he looks at her, she acts embarrassed. She reveals the splendid parts of her body, under some pretext... When questioned about something, she replies by smiling, lowering her head, and mumbling indistinctly, with unclear meaning, very softly. She delights in staying near him for a long time. When she is some distance from him, she speaks to her attendants in an altered tone of voice, hoping that he will look at her. And she does not leave that place.

Shakuntala obeys Vatsyayana to the letter. She asks her attendants to loosen her blouse, which is 'chafing the youthful swelling of her breasts'; she stands speechless when Dusyanta addresses her, looking down at her feet; she scolds her friends and pretends to quit them and the king – although she ends up staying behind. And when the lovers begin to converse, Shakuntala's friends act as go-betweens – exactly as the *Kamasutra* recommends. Meanwhile, a stage direction notes that Shakuntala 'displays all the embarrassment of erotic attraction', without troubling to specify how this embarrassment might look. It did not need to. The *Kamasutra* had said it all.

The *Kamasutra*'s literary legacy persisted for centuries, Vatsyayana's book of love becoming a manual for the literary representation of love as much as a guide to lovemaking itself. By the seventh century, Magha's poem *Sisupalavadha* was not only borrowing the *Kamasutra*'s technical terms for embraces, kisses and fingernail-marks but, when it came to describing the orgasmic gasps of women, choosing simply to refer its readers to the *Kamasutra* for detail. 'Lovely ladies hissed, purred, wailed, said sweet things and words to the effect of "please stop!", and their laughter and jewellery tinkled,' Magha wrote. He continued, 'All these sounds were the stuff of the *Kamasutra*.' It's tempting to think that the *Kamasutra* was becoming a cliché, and Magha was mocking the ladies for their oh-so-conventional style of lovemaking. More likely, he was using the *Kamasutra* as shorthand for sheer erotic perfection.

Amaru's eighth-century *Amarusataka* — an intimate sequence of one hundred love lyrics, each capturing the mood of a particular moment in an archetypal, passionate love affair — was so incredibly vivid that legend had it that the poems were written by an ascetic named Shankara who had entered the body of a dead man in order to indulge in exuberant erotic experiments. The story is a curious echo of Vatsyayana's own claim to celibacy. Shankara has also taken the opportunity, it was said, to study the *Kamasutra* in depth, and many of the poems' scenes, and the language used to conjure them, were drawn directly from the book of love. Vatsyayana's 'kiss that kindles passion', for instance, which a woman places on the mouth of her sleeping lover, and his 'awakening kiss', which may be provoked by a lover pretending to be asleep, become in the

Amarusataka a real scene from a love affair. At the end of a too-long and too-social evening, a woman is finally left alone with the man she desires. But he is already asleep – or so she believes.

> Overpowered by love my mouth I placed
> Right on his.
> Then it struck me. The rogue's skin had arisen,
> he had just feigned closing his eyes.

Despite the unabashed eroticism of Classical-era literature, India's religious culture was still as troubled by sex as it ever had been. By the time Amaru was writing, however, a movement was becoming established that tried to reconcile Hinduism's erotic and ascetic urges. According to the philosophers of the 'Tantric' cults, desire could be used to overcome desire. Hermetic texts known as Tantras explored the formulation of *mantras*, or mystical utterances, and invoked esoteric theories of cosmology, magic and even anatomy, so that the practitioner could tap into the power of the divine. An important Tantric idea, derived from Patanjali's *Yoga-sutras* of around the first century, held that the Supreme Power of the universe is manifest in occult 'veins' in the human body, taking the form of the sleeping Kundalini serpent. The Tantrin, or adept, was supposed to awaken the Kundalini from its dormant state through ritual, magical – and possibly sexual – practices, uniting the male and female seats of power in the body in the experience of *ekarasa*, the universalized sensation of unitary consciousness. One could describe *ekarasa* as a mystical orgasm, but it could hardly be further from the *nagaraka*'s joyful pursuit of ejaculatory pleasure. The *nagaraka* sought pleasure as an end in itself, while the Tantrin sought to harness it for religious use. The *Kamasutra* stressed the importance of *kama* as a valid life-goal, if kept under proper control, while the Tantric philosophers embraced *kama* as something forbidden and chaotically, darkly powerful.

Among the darkest and most powerful Tantric rites of all was the esoteric *kula prakriya*. It was reserved for high-level Tantric initiates only and sought to purify the devotee's consciousness through ritual acts of transgression, including the expression, exchange, offering and consumption of sexual fluids. Sacramental sex may even have been performed between devotees in mimicry of the divine union of the god Shiva and his own female emanation, Shakti. But even within the already esoteric and transgressive cult of Tantrism, such practices were the province of an extremist, 'left-hand' or 'sinister' minority. Their object was liberation from the world, not joyous participation in its pleasures, and those who followed the left-hand path were supposed to carry out their rituals *without* desire.

In theory, then, ascetic-minded Tantrism could hardly be more distant from the worldly, passionate realm of the *Kamasutra*. From around the tenth century, however, *kama* and Tantra came together – and the results were made stunningly manifest on temple walls all over India. Statues of intertwined couples had existed since Vatsyayana's time, but sculptors, newly gripped by Tantric theories, now began to carve feverishly erotic scenes by the thousand to adorn the exterior walls of temples. This wasn't as shocking as it might seem. Indian temples had always had an intrinsically sexual element. They were centred around a *garba-griha*, or womb chamber, while the chief object of religious devotion, in the Shaivite tradition at least, was the stone *lingam*, a massive, sculptural representation of the ever-erect phallus of the god Shiva, often set in a sculpted base representing the female *yoni*. It is easy to overstate the eroticism of such objects. Gothic cathedrals can also be read as representations of the body, after all, but this does not mean that medieval Christians worshipped the erotic.

Thanks in no small degree to Tantrism, Indian sculptors went further than their Western counterparts. The apogee of erotic temple art was the giant, tenth-century temple complex of Khajuraho, in central India. Erotic sculptures form a mere tenth of the total, but it is a prominent and bewitching fraction. Twisting, broad-hipped and high-breasted nymphs display their generously contoured and bejewelled bodies on exquisitely worked exterior wall panels. These fleshy *apsaras* run riot across the surface of the stone, putting on make-up, washing their hair, playing games, dancing, and endlessly knotting and unknotting their girdles – an activity dwelled on with similar obsession in the *Kamasutra* and the erotic poetry of the golden age. Beside the heavenly nymphs are serried ranks of griffins, guardian deities and, most notoriously, extravagantly interlocked *maithunas*, or lovemaking couples.

Today, Khajuraho is popularly known as the 'Kamasutra temple', but its coupling statues do not in truth 'illustrate' Vatsyayana's positions. They are the child of a strange union of Tantrism and fertility motifs, with a heavy dose of magic. Fertility and conception are of course screamingly absent from the resolutely secular *Kamasutra* – as is Tantrism. It's easy to imagine the hedonistic *nagaraka* shuddering at the very thought of fathering a child, and he certainly never seems to enter a temple – other than to enjoy a moonlit festival where he might pick up women. The famous love-making groups do not reflect the joyous precision of Vatsyayana's embraces but, instead, concealed symbolical-magical diagrams, or *yantras*, which were placed in particular positions on the temple walls in order to magically propitiate evil spirits. At Khajuraho, a sculpture of a washerwoman clinging to the neck of a bearded ascetic may not simply show two people having sex, it may express the Tantric notion that the 'washerwoman', who represents the idea of the subtle energy of Kundalini, residing in the spine, has risen as far as the *chakra*, or subtle centre of life energy, at the level of the neck.

The erotic temple sculptures at Khajuraho primarily symbolize the 'right-hand' Tantric practice of using sex as a metaphor for joyful union with the divine. They celebrate mystical release, not actual ejaculation. But there is a powerful connection with the *Kamasutra*, nevertheless. Behind Khajuraho's Tantric significance lies the fact that, like other 'erotic' temples, it was built by a wealthy and powerful dynasty to advertise its status. Controlled virility was a sure sign of a great ruler, and erotic sculptures were a splendid way to demonstrate that quintessentially regal sexual excellence. The highest expression of control was *alamkara*, or ornamentation, an aesthetic ideal that stood for artistic sophistication, for the ability to improve upon the raw materials of nature. Vatsyayana and the temple sculptors alike delighted in imaginative variation on the theme of sensual pleasure, a delight driven by the urge to tame the erotic by transforming it into art. It is this shared aesthetic vision that throbs through the centuries, ultimately connecting text and temple.

As India entered its 'medieval' epoch, in the early centuries of the second millennium, eroticism was again adopted by religion. This time, the links to the *Kamasutra* were less subtle. The burgeoning *bhakti* cult emphasized the emotional love of the worshipper for god, a love that often flirted with the outright erotic – and, sometimes whole-heartedly, rampantly embraced it. The roots of *bhakti* are at least as old as Tantrism, but the cult established itself in the eighth and ninth centuries around the thrillingly erotic story of the god Krishna and his *rasa lila* or 'love dance' with an entire gang of sexy milkmaids. The tale was most exquisitely told in a ninth-century poem, the rapturous *Rasa-Pancadhyayi*. As the milkmaids dance, it describes how one of them embraces Krishna. She becomes 'elated with bodily ripplings of bliss' and kisses his arm with tenderness. Another, 'decorated with shimmering earrings that swayed to the dance', lays her cheek against Krishna's and accepts a betel nut from his mouth. Another gently brings Krishna's hand to her breasts. Together, they whip themselves, and Krishna, into a sexual-ecstatic fever.

Somehow, this dirty dancing had to be squared with the well-established theory that the milkmaids' love for Krishna was pure and sexless. The only way to do it was to resurrect the old theory from the *Natyashastra*, namely that real emotions could be translated into their idealized, artistic form, as *rasas*. Under the guiding hand of religious devotion, it was said, the passions of *kama* could be similarly transformed and purified into a higher love, which was sweet and sexless. It was divine in essence, even if it was deeply human in its expression. This sleight of theological hand meant poets could get away with as much literary sex as they wanted. Jayadeva's famous twelfth-century poem on Krishna's love dance, the sublime *Gitagovinda*, dared to be even more palpably erotic than the *Rasa-Pancadhyayi*. Its hero was a god, and its ideal was divine love, but it was nothing less than a luxuriantly poetic expression of the very same eroticism sketched in by the *Kamasutra* — so much so that the standard commentary on the poem, by the Mewari King Kumbha, actually quotes from the *Kamasutra* in order to explain the many allusions in the text.

Jayadeva's masterstroke was to elevate one of the milkmaids, Radha, as Krishna's principal lover, thus putting a very human love affair at the heart of the relatively ethereal dance. As the archetypal erotic heroine, Radha is the descendant of the idealized lover of the *Kamasutra*. As she waits in a lonely forest hut for her lover to arrive, in the Sixth Song, her eyelids tremble just as the *Natyashastra* says they should, and when Krishna finally arrives, her eyes 'close languidly' and her body is 'moist with sweat', in the proper manner. Radha then confesses that she 'cooed with the soft sound of the cuckoo; he mastered the procedures of the science of love; my tresses were strewn with loose flowers; the mass of my firm breast was scratched by his nails'. The 'science of love' is, of course, nothing less than Vatsyayana's book. 'O friend!' Radha sighs. 'Make him make love to me.' And Krishna does – masterfully. Radha recalls how 'The jewelled anklets rang out on my feet; he made love to me in various ways; my unfastened girdle jingled; he gave me kisses and pulled my hair. O friend!' she sighs, again. 'Make him make love to me.'

Whether it was the dreamy effect of the love dance, the stirring inspiration of erotic temple sculpture, or the subtle, almost alchemical inflence of Tantrism, as India entered the second millennium *kama* once again became the fashion at India's princely courts. Despite eroticism's literary – and religious – success, study of the original science of *kama* had lapsed. Now, for the first time in centuries, new manuals of eroticism were commissioned by aristocratic patrons. A Nepalese Buddhist monk called Padmasri was one of the earliest writers to take up the erotic baton, in around the tenth or eleventh century. Just as Vatsyayana had turned to ancient predecessors, Padmasri turned to the by now ancient *Kamasutra* – along with a handful of other works, most of which have since been lost. The fact that he considered the *Kamasutra* to be *the* authoritative text, despite the profound social changes that had taken place in the eight hundred or so years since the *nagaraka*'s heyday, is a sign of Vatsyayana's success.

Padmasri's approach to the master text set the standard for the many erotic manuals that followed his pioneering work. His *Nagarasarvasva*, or *Complete Book of the Nagaraka*, barely acknowledged the wider social and philosophical context of the original – perhaps because it was so blatantly out of date – and focused instead on the explicitly sexual content, which it expanded to encompass recent theological and scientific developments. The *Nagarasarvasva* recommends a quite astonishing number of different ways of kissing, for example, and gives endless recipes for cosmetics. Even more up to date was Padmasri's new emphasis on psychology. The 'stallion' man was no longer, as Vatsyayana had it, simply a man with a large penis; according to Padmasri, he was also cunning, smart, bold and sexually voluptuous. The 'doe' woman, meanwhile, was not just a woman with a small vagina; she was jealous, passionate, soft-spoken and skilled in lovemaking.

Padmasri also added a heavy dose of magic, probably under the influence of Tantrism, which had found particularly fertile soil in the lush mountains of Nepal. Magic, of course, was already present in the *Kamasutra*'s aphrodisiac recipes. Luck in love, for instance, required 'beauty, good qualities, the right age, and generosity', but, in the absence of these advantages, holding a gold-plated peacock's or hyena's eye in the right hand would do the trick, as would coating the penis with a powder of milkwort, milk-hedge, red arsenic, sulphur and honey – or even spreading the same mixture, with the judicious addition of dried monkey shit, on the desired woman. But where Vatsyayana's magic was of the country-lore kind, relying on sympathetic magic and traditional medicines, Padmasri's relied on highly developed Tantric-yogic theories.

The *Ratirahasya*, or *Love Secrets*, of Kokkoka took Padmasri's tendencies to another level. It was written 'to satisfy the curiosity of the Most Excellent Vainyadatta concerning the art of love', probably in the late twelfth century. Just like Padmasri, Kokkoka looked back to the *Kamasutra* as the fountain of erotic wisdom while making several innovations and borrowing selectively from alternative scientific traditions. After his invocation to the god Kama – 'Friend of the World, Storehouse of Joys, the Fair, the Divine, the God presiding over Joy in Existence' – Kokkoka granted that while 'the repute and credit of Vatsyayana are worldwide', it had to be admitted that 'other authorities have made plain matters which he left obscure'.

Kokkoka pointed out that where the *Kamasutra* listed three types of men and women, divided according to the size of their genitals, other authorities named four: the lotus-woman, conch-woman, 'varied' or 'marvellous' woman, and the unlovely elephant cow-woman. Like Padmasri, Kokkoka associated each with particular qualities. The elephant-woman, for instance, did not move daintily. Her feet were stout, her toes curling, her neck short and plump and her hair – horrors – red-brown. Her character was no more appealing: 'she is apt to be spiteful,' Kokkoka observed, 'is rather corpulent, and her whole body, and more especially her yoni, has the odour of elephant "tears".' Compare the lotus-woman, who is 'delicate like a lotus bud, her genital odour is of the lotus in flower, and her whole body divinely fragrant. She has eyes like a scared gazelle's, a little red in the corners, and choice breasts that put to shame a pair of beautiful quince-fruits; she has a little nose like a til-flower.' There is a deliciously pornographic flavour to this passage, a sensual savour that is absent from Vatsyayana's clinical dissection of the topic. But Kokkoka was not indulging in salacious description. His task, as he saw it, was to cross-reference the *Kamasutra* with other ancient sources on *kama*, and to tie it to developments in related Sanskrit sciences. In describing the elephant cow- and lotus-woman, Kokkoka was drawing on the Sanskrit science of physiognomy, which was used, along with astrology, to predict a woman's suitability as a bride and as a sexual partner. Each of the four types of women, Kokkoka argued, wants to have sex on different days of the lunar cycle, while 'to obtain the best results' each should be enjoyed at different times of the night. Kokkoka even offered a detailed calendar of lovemaking. On the fourth day, for example, 'Lovers reckon to hold a woman tighter still, pull the two breasts hard together, bite the lower lip, mark the left thigh with the nails, make the "click" several times in the armpits and polish the body of Lady Lotus-eyes with the water that comes from the spring of her own love-juice.' The secret of the 'click' in the armpits is, sadly, lost.

Kokkoka saw himself as writing a new, improved book of love. It was not so much that the techniques of lovemaking had changed or needed to be updated (though Kokkoka was aware of the clitoris while Vatsyayana, apparently, was not). The great task for medieval writers like Kokkoka was not to develop the *shastras*, still less to test them empirically, but to bind them together in one vast and more truly, wholly encyclopedic system. *Shastras* began to encompass everything from Vedic grammar and the *trivarga* to — and this is a mere selection — medicine, weapons-training, music, perfumery, alchemy, penmanship, artithmetic, elephant-training and the noble art of the cutpurse. To this list could be added all or any of the 'sixty-four arts' or *silpa-kalas* of the *Kamasutra*, from needlework and gardening to magic, cock-fighting and, of course, lovemaking. Crucially, texts on even these areas of apparently practical knowledge tended not to describe contemporary reality but an ideal based on venerable – and sometimes ancient – sources. In the world of the *shastra*, truth was seen not as progressive but regressive. The problem, as Vatsyayana himself had pointed out, was that the further in time one moved from the original 100,000 chapters in the mind of Brahma, the more fragmented and unsatisfactory knowledge became.

Kokkoka's *Ratirahasya* and Padmasri's *Nagarasarvasva* were the first major texts to return to the topic of erotic love in a thousand years. They epitomized what would become the *Kamasutra*'s sad legacy: the transformation of the masterwork of erotic culture into a mere rubric for sexual virtuosity. The gulf between the subtlety and sophistication of Vatsyayana and the decadent scholasticism of his successors is nowhere more glaring than in the work of Yasodhara, who wrote a detailed commentary on the *Kamasutra* in the thirteenth century. According to his own account, Yasodhara wrote his *Jayamangala* 'because he was terrified of suffering a lover's separation from sophisticated women'. His other motivation may have been less personal, and less pressing, but it was even more important. A thousand years after the *Kamasutra*'s composition, the medieval scholars attempting to pick up the threads of the *kama shastra* tradition were struggling to make sense of Vatsyayana's words.

The problem was Vatsyayana's use of the *sutra* form. If an ideal *sutra* is 'brief, unambiguous, essential, universal', as the Sanskrit motto put it, Vatsyayana's actual *sutras* had proved rather too brief, too essential and not altogether unambiguous. By the thirteenth century it was felt that the bare bones of the book of love needed some fleshing out. Yasodhara's was the first commentary on the

Kamasutra — at least, if there were other, earlier, works, they have been lost. Despite Yasodhara's relative proximity to Vatsyayana's time, he misunderstood or misrepresented the original again and again. Most significant was the difference he perceived between *kama* in general — that is, pleasure — and *kama* in particular — that is, sex. For Yasodhara, sex itself had become the ultimate focus. Pleasure might be experienced through touch in, say, the hand or foot, but the highest pleasure was 'the reciprocal discovery by man and woman of the natural differences of the lower part of their bodies, which are the vulva and the penis'. Not only was this pleasure higher than non-sexual pleasure, for Yasodhara, but actually different in kind. Genital sexual pleasure produced a *result*, specifically the 'emission of semen' and the accompanying 'bliss' of orgasm. Other pleasures were mere sensations.

Yasodhara's narrow emphasis on sex sometimes led his interpretations bizarrely astray. Where the *Kamasutra* listed woodworking among the sixty-four arts of the cultivated person, Yasodhara felt the need to gloss the art as specifically very useful for the creation of dildos. When it came to the enumeration of the kinds of sex, Yasodhara really lost sight of the bigger picture. Vatsyayana mused that 'since there are nine texts according to each of the criteria of size, endurance and temperament, when they are combined it is not possible to enumerate all the forms of sex'. It is not as if multiplication was unknown to third-century India. The point was rhetorical. *Kama*, for Vatsyayana, was greater than the *shastra*: sex was beyond the study of sex. For Yasodhara, the reverse was true. He pointed out with staggering pedantry that with nine forms in each of the three categories for men and women alike, 'if they mate in all possible combinations, the total comes to 729.' The scholarly weed of classification was now choking the flower of eroticism.

Even as Yasodhara wrote his commentary, Muslim warlords were seizing control of northern India. For a time, the Sanskrit sciences, *kama* included, were insulated from foreign influences by their own innate conservatism, and there was little sign at first that the Islamic courts were much interested in the beliefs or practices of their defeated subjects. Gradually, however, Muslim princes began to extend the same patronage to scholars as would have been offered by their predecessors, the Hindu *rajas*. Islamic and Sanskrit culture could hardly be described as cross-fertilizing, but they were beginning to flirt. Among the Hindu sciences embraced with the greatest enthusiasm was erotics.

One of the sweetest and earliest fruits of this flirtation was the *Ananga Ranga*, whose euphonious title means 'Stage [or theatre] of the Bodiless One', referring to the ancient myth of how the god Kama was scorched to a cinder by Shiva's third eye. The book was written at around the beginning of the sixteenth century, making it one of the last great Sanskrit works of erotology – and one of the earliest to be composed for a Muslim ruler. Its author, Kalyana-malla, begins by invoking the Hindu god Kama, 'thee the sportive; thee, the wanton one, who dwellest in the hearts of all created beings'. He continues, almost in the same breath, by eulogizing his Muslim patron, Lada Khan, the son of King Ahmad, 'the ornament of the Lodi House'. The Lodi family was a Muslim dynasty, reaching its proud zenith as the last ruling house of the Delhi sultanate before it was conquered by Babur, the first Mughal emperor, in 1526. Lada Khan was clearly interested enough in Sanskrit culture to commission this work, yet there is no sense that the fascination was mutual; the Muslim call to prayer does not so much as echo inside the calm, sequestered world of the *Ananga Ranga*.

Sanskrit literature's tendency to look backwards – rather than

forwards, or even outwards – was clearly as strong as ever.
Kalyanamalla claims to have consulted 'many wise and holy men'
before composing his manual, and the wisest and holiest was
evidently Vatsyayana. He is quoted twice by name (a chance that
would save the *Kamasutra* from probable extinction in the nineteenth century, as the next chapter reveals) and is referred to
respectfully as a *rishi*, or divinely inspired sage – once for
recommending a powdered concoction that will render a man or
woman 'submissive and obedient to the fascinator', and once for
his teaching that adultery may be allowed only in certain life-
threatening circumstances. These are, according to Kalyanamalla,
'when he passes restless nights without the refreshment of sleep...
when his looks become haggard and his body emaciated... when
he feels himself growing shameless and departing from all sense of
decency and decorum...when the state of mental intoxication
verges upon madness...when fainting fits come on' and, ultimately, 'when he finds himself at the door of death'.

As with all India's medieval sex manuals, the *Ananga Ranga*
incorporated new material alongside the old. It identified four
types of vagina. The vagina 'which is soft inside as the filaments of
the lotus-flower' was, understandably, the best. Then there was the
one 'whose surface is studded with tender flesh-knots and similar
rises' and the one 'which abounds in rolls, wrinkles, and corruga-
tions'. At the bottom of the list was the vagina 'which is rough as
the cow's tongue'. Kalyanamalla was not only concerned with the
aesthetics of anatomy. The four kinds of vagina were a further
refinement of the traditional four classes of women, and the fruit
of an entire system of thought that also identified four periods of
life, three kinds of humours, eight previous states of existence,
eight signs of indifference, fifteen causes of woman's unhappiness

and twelve periods of greatest desire for sex – including 'through-out the spring season, during thunder, lightning and rain'.

Both spring and storms, tellingly, are archetypal poetic situa-tions for the *nayika* or heroine of erotic literature, and she, rather than any real lover, was Kalyanamalla's true obsession. The *Ananga Ranga* ended with a full rundown of the eight kinds of heroine accepted by Bharata's *Natyashastra* – the ultimate source – and poetic convention. 'The woman who goes to meet her lover' Kalyanamalla described as 'she who, agitated with passion, extremely bold, her ornaments on, stealing out in the night, would go to the house of her lover for love-sport – her, the wise men call the *abhisarika*'. 'The betrayed heroine' was 'she whose husband – his body bearing love-imprints inflicted by the co-wife, his eyes red and bedimmed with sleep – approaches her in the morning, speak-ing coaxingly out of fear – her Bharata calls the *khandita*'. It was these women, the *nayikas* of the poets rather than Vatsyayana's flesh-and-blood lovers, who would be the chief inspiration for the next major development in Indian erotics: the creation of sensual, jewel-like miniature paintings and illuminated manuscripts.

After the *Ananga Ranga*, sex manuals continued to be composed, but they were ever more debased and derivative. The *Kamasutra* itself reared its head in public from time to time, but with ever-decreasing vigour. A certain King Virabhadradeva composed a metrical version of the *Kamasutra* in 1577, while a commentary on the text, the *Praudhapriya*, was written in Varanasi as late as 1788. But despite these occasional stirrings, the *shastra* of *kama* underwent a slow, inexorable detumescence, and awareness of the *Kamasutra* collapsed alongside it. As Hindu court culture gradually crumbled under the pressure of the ever-expanding Muslim presence in India, Sanskrit scholarship diminished and erotic poetry finally became moribund. Brahmin scholars, meanwhile, regarded the erotic with mounting disapproval. Vatsyayana's book of love steadily withdrew into the dusty darkness of religious libraries, to be hoarded among millions of decaying manuscripts.

Even as the *Kamasutra* itself was slowly forgotten, *kama* grew ever more visible — largely thanks to the new influence of Persian painting. It is impossible to trace the thread of any continuity with Hindu art, as almost no painting survives beyond a few fifth-century cave murals in Ajanta. (The alluring scenes of courtly pleasures depicted there may actually be the closest thing there is to an illustration of the *Kamasutra* but the relationship is strained — not just by a couple of centuries but by the fact that the cave-artists of Ajanta were Buddhist.) It is clear at least that erotic art in India long pre-dated the arrival of Islamic culture. The *Kamasutra* itself recommended painting as one of the sixty-four arts — along with 'cutting leaves into shapes' and 'making diadems and headbands'. It even specified that the *nagaraka* should have a drawing board and pencils in his ideal home. The *Natyashastra* described how theatre walls were decorated with male and female figures, patterns of intertwining creepers and depictions of heroic deeds.

Sadly, it is impossible to imagine what the artwork sketched by the *nagaraka* would have looked like, or to reconjure the paintings that adorned the theatres of the Gupta era. If the gulf between the serenity of ancient Rome's statuary and its earthy and often libidinous paintings is anything to go by, even the sensuous sculptures of nymphs and lovemaking couples that adorn Hindu temples may bear little relation to the tradition in painting that preceded them. Still less can we conjure the 'illustrations' that accompanied the *Kamasutra* in pre-Muslim times. There probably never were any. In fact, no Indian illustrated manuscripts whatsoever survive from before the twelfth century, and illuminated texts in any number date back only to the fifteenth and sixteenth centuries. Given the fragility of palm-leaf manuscripts, which were not supplanted by paper until the late fourteenth century, not to mention India's hot, damp climate and thriving insect and rodent life, together with the scholarly habit of replacing rather than hoarding old manuscripts, it is just possible that all older illuminated texts have simply been lost – including those of a putative, illustrated *Kamasutra*. But it is unlikely.

Indian erotic art as it survives today is the beautiful child of the strange marriage between Sanskrit erotic literature and Persian miniature painting. Persian techniques were first introduced into India in the late fifteenth century, and painters were quick to seize on erotic themes, notably Krishna's celebrated love-dance. When the Mughal Emperor Akbar came to power, in 1556, over a thousand local artists trained under famed Persian masters and set about illustrating Hindu books that had been newly translated into Persian. But the greatest achievements in erotic illustration took place not at the great Mughal court, but at the courts of their subject Hindu princes, the Rajputs of north-western India.

Rajput ateliers developed an entire erotic genre, from as early as the fifteenth century. The most popular subjects by far were the *nayaka* and *nayika*, the erotic hero and heroine, who were sometimes specifically identified as blue-black Krishna and his cow-girl lover, Radha. Drawing on their endless flirtations, philanderings and disappointments, Rajput court painters created albums of paintings known as *ragamalas*, or garlands of *ragas* – the *raga* being a kind of inspiring mood (or sometimes a melodic pattern) that was associated with a specific time of day, a season and, in erotic painting, a crux moment in a love affair. The focus was on the psychology of the lovers, and from any given *ragamala* series only a few paintings might be explicitly sexual in content. Nevertheless, the cultivated lover would have used the albums for ambient erotic inspiration. Like the plays of Kalidasa and the poetry of the Classical age, they were intended to stimulate a heightened mood of sensual awareness. They were in a sense, pornography, albeit of a very elevated kind.

Sexual intercourse was, of course, depicted in Indian painting, especially from the eighteenth century onwards. Anyone who has looked over one of the myriad twentieth-century coffee-table versions of the *Kamasutra* will have seen lurid and often improbable scenes, perhaps involving five or six women, a swing, a number of embroidered cushions and impressively yogic levels of flexibility. The roots of this highly explicit representation of sex extended back to the medieval *kama shastra* texts, and ultimately to the *Kamasutra*, but these paintings were no more illustrative of the book of love than had been the temple carvings at Khajuraho and Konarak. Erotic scenes often simply advertised the masculinity, prowess and status of the sitter. Eighteenth-century Indian princes might have themselves painted as consummate lovers, just as – in rather different poses and costumes – they would have themselves portrayed as great hunters or statesmen. Where European noblemen tended to portray their mastery of *artha*, or worldly success, the Indian aristocrat, as ever, was also concerned with *kama*.

The inspiration for erotic portraiture was not so much the *Kamasutra*, then, but the same masculine pride that led English aristocrats to pose with their dogs, horses or daughters in endless paintings by Reynolds or Gainsborough. And at the very same time that erotic portraiture was becoming the fashion in India, Joshua Reynolds was painting portraits of early British adventurers on the subcontinent. These venturesome soldiers, merchants and missionaries may not have taken off their own clothes, but they were more than happy to report back on the exotic and erotic curiosities that had caught the roving colonial eye. If it wasn't talk of sensual sculptures, it was descriptions of alluring 'bayadères' and 'nautch girls' – the *devadasis* or temple-dancer prostitutes who were the distant and diminished descendants of the *Kamasutra*'s exquisitely refined courtesans.

These dancer-prostitutes were one of the few visible survivals of the almost moribund practices of the *shastra* of *kama*. Erotic art was another. In the 1830s, George Eden, one of the first governor-generals of India, visited the court of the Maharaja of Sirmur at his capital of Nahan, in the hills of the Punjab – which had been one of the heartlands of erotic painting. After the ladies left the room, the Maharaja proudly showed off his gallery of lubricious pictures. Many, it seems, had been painted by courtiers themselves; if so, then teaching of the sixty-four arts – which traditionally included painting – was clearly still preserved 1,500 years after the heyday of the *nagaraka*, in aristocratic circles at least. Meanwhile, in the east of India, in Orissa, popular 'posture books' showing a gamut of sexual positions were created by the hundred. Some were picked up by fascinated British travellers and collectors, but they gave little hint of their origins, as the postures rarely acknowledged any *kama shastra* text, and the artistry was usually poor.

Such arts were the last, half-rotten fruits of the tradition that had spawned them. Vatsyayana's book of love, by contrast, was by now all but buried in the past, and discovering it would require painstaking digging. Among the first to put foot to spade was Sir William Jones, a diligent Sanskrit scholar and the first Westerner to roam widely in the great literary treasure-house of Sanskrit

literature. He stumbled across a key relic of India's erotic civilization almost by accident. It was Jayadeva's *Gitagovinda*, and it was so
good that Jones could not help but translate it. He was reluctant,
however, to expose to the world the existence of the most explicitly
erotic material. He observed drily that 'it is remarkable to what a
degree [India's] works of imagination are pervaded by the idea of
sexuality', and to combat this vicious tendency he expurgated the
magnificent conclusion from his 1792 translation. The glorious
lovemaking that concludes Radha and Krishna's tormented affair
was thereby lost, for a time at least.

As India's breathtaking literary heritage was slowly uncovered,
however, it was inevitable that the erotic tradition would eventually be exposed along with it, despite the efforts of the Joneses. But
it would take two unusual Victorian gentlemen, combining the
rare talents of being both Indologists and iconoclasts, to lay bare
the knowledge of that tradition and bring it home triumphantly to
the West. Astonishingly, these two enthusiastic British amateurs
would ultimately be responsible for India's own rediscovery of its
greatest erotic classic.

$\mathcal{W}$HEN THE GIRL accepts the embrace, the man should put a tambula or screw of betel nut and betel leaves in her mouth, and if she will not take it, he should induce her to do so by conciliatory words, entreaties, oaths, and kneeling at her feet… When she is asked by the man whether she wishes for him, and whether she likes him, she should remain silent for a long time, and when at last importuned to reply, should give him a favourable answer by a nod of her head. If the man is previously acquainted with the girl he should converse with her by means of a female friend, who may be favourable to him, and in the confidence of both, and carry on the conversation on both sides. On such an occasion the girl should smile with her head bent down, and if the female friend say more on her part than she was desired to do, she should chide her and dispute with her. The female friend should say in jest even what she is not desired to say by the girl, and add, 'she says so', on which the girl should say indistinctly and prettily, 'O no! I did not say so', and she should then smile and throw an occasional glance towards the man.

The Kama Sutra of Vatsyayana
Part III: About the Acquisition of a Wife
Chapter II: Of Creating Confidence in the Girl
translated by 'A.F.F and B.F.R' (1883)

CHAPTER THREE

The Hindoo Art of Love

In October 1842, a young Indian Army ensign, Richard Francis Burton, arrived in Bombay. He was a pugnacious man of twenty-one with a record of failing to fit in. At Oxford, he had appalled his tutors, quite deliberately, by speaking Latin with a full-blooded Mediterranean accent and had even had the temerity to seek private tuition in Arabic – he was flatly turned down. Burton had shocked fellow students by sporting a luxuriant moustache on arrival at his college and by challenging a rival to fight a duel – a notion so quaint as to be embarrassing. After less than two years, his irrepressible gambling and roistering, and his ostentatious independence of mind, became too much for the college authorities and he was expelled. In the hope that the army might instil some discipline and provide an outlet for his bellicosity, Burton's father bought him a commission in the Bombay Native Infantry for the princely sum of £500. The ongoing campaigns in Afghanistan, it was felt, would provide a speedy road to fame and fortune, or at least to promotion.

Unfortunately, by the time Burton's ship had docked at Bombay, after a four-month voyage, the fighting was over. It was the first blow in what would become a lifetime's pattern of frustration and disappointment, and the first to push him towards other outlets for his aggression and ambition. Burton was sent, instead, to the regimental headquarters in Baroda, where he began, almost obsessively, to learn Indian languages. With the help of his *munshi*, an old Parsee teacher called Dosabhai Sohrabji, and a series of *bubus*, or local servants-cum-mistresses, he passed the army's examination in Hindustani (or Hindi) within a year. Burton later told the story of a certain unnamed Bombay army officer who had shocked his Indian subordinates by 'having learned Hindostani from women' and consequently speaking of himself in the feminine, a linguistic error that 'hugely scandalized the sepoys'. Burton's *bubus*, however, were more than worth the occasional linguistic slip. He later wrote that a local mistress was 'all but indispensable to the student', as she taught him 'not only Hindostani grammar, but the syntaxes of native Life'. It was a prescient comment. Burton would later become the driving force in uncovering India's original grammar of social and sexual life: the *Kamasutra*.

Lacking opportunities to distinguish himself militarily — various mischances and mistimings would ensure that he never fought in a single campaign — Burton devoted himself to the study of Indian languages and, less officially, to the study of Indian sex. He quickly added Gujarati, Marathi, Sindhi and Persian to his Hindustani, and began to revise and improve the basic Arabic he had taught himself at Oxford. In 1844, his unusual linguistic talents were put to use for the Survey Office in the province of Sindh, in modern-day Pakistan. Burton was probably engaged in low-key intelligence work. At least, from this date he began to mix with local people in disguise. In the character of a half-Iranian, half-Arab merchant called 'Mirza Abdullah the Bushiri', Burton began trading from rented shops in Karachi, furnishing them, in his own words, 'with clammy dates, viscid molasses, tobacco, ginger, rancid oil and strong-smelling sweetmeats'. His private interest may have been largely anthropological, but Mirza Abdullah's eavesdropping on the gossip of the bazaar found its way into reports that were passed to Captain William McMurdo, the head of the Intelligence Section under Charles Napier, the conqueror of Sindh.

After a year or two with the Sindh Survey Office, Burton received a special commission to investigate the male brothels of Karachi. 'Being then the only British officer who could speak Sindhi,' he later wrote, 'Mirza Abdullah the Bushiri passed many an evening in the townlet, visited all the porneia and obtained the fullest details which were duly despatched to Government House.' These fullest details, according to Burton, included descriptions of how boy prostitutes were worth twice as much as eunuchs, on the grounds that 'the scrotum of the unmutilated boy could be used as a kind of bridle for directing the movements of the animal'. This kind of exacting, intimate and shocking detail was an early taste of what would become vintage Burton. Inevitably, it profoundly offended his superiors. After Napier left Sindh, the infamous report found its way to Bombay, where someone whom Burton would later only name as 'one of Sir Charles Napier's successors' proposed Burton's dismissal from the service in an 'excess of outraged modesty'. The prudish officer can only have been General Auchmuty or his subordinate, Colonel Corsellis. According to a rare surviving notebook of Burton's, he had already fallen out with Corsellis over an epitaph jokingly improvised one night in the Officers' Mess: 'Here lies the body of Colonel Corsellis,' Burton extemporized. 'The rest of the fellow, I fancy, in hell is.' The offended colonel reported Burton for insubordination.

Whether or not Corsellis privately blackballed Burton for his unseemly interest in boys' scrotal bridles is something of a mystery. Burton's career undoubtedly began to founder. It is possible, however, there was more to it than the notorious Karachi report. Burton's foremost bibliographer, James Casada, spent years trying to trace the report and found nothing. Instead, he uncovered only a consistently positive service record, 'regularly interlaced with commendations and containing no hint of scandals'. Casada concluded that Burton 'retrospectively romanticized and likely fictionalized his parting of ways with the Indian Army'. Equally plausible is the conclusion that such a dangerously obscene report would have been quickly destroyed. There is, however, another possibility: that the man they called 'Ruffian Dick' concocted the whole 'Karachi report' as an elaborate cover for his own, private investigations of India's homosexual brothels. Any potentially damaging rumours about such activities could thus be explained away as a malicious echo of these unacknowledged services to the Crown.

W.G. Archer, the Keeper of the Indian Section at the Victoria and Albert Museum in the 1960s and the first authoritative writer on the *Kamasutra*, mused that he was tempted to regard Burton 'as a character whose unseemly adventures had already given him a vicious aura, to see him as a mystery man, a kind of T.E. Lawrence but with something of the sinister smear of a Roger Casement'. Archer's evidence for Burton's homosexuality was speculative:

> Burton's preference for Arab society, his obsessional studies
> of pederasty, the very thoroughness of his Karachi report, his
> friendship with Swinburne, his long absences from society,
> even his mania for fencing and weapons (itself at times a

symptom of the crypto-homosexual), suggest that behind his
investigation of sex in all its forms lay a need to placate, defend
or justify a latent homosexuality.

This statement is loaded with all the psychological whimsy the
early 1960s could muster. Burton's 'mania for fencing', of course,
hardly proves that he was was gay any more than does James
Casada's observation that Burton had a 'tendency towards emotional involvement with men'.

Burton may well have had homosexual inclinations, or indeed
relationships, but if scandal was behind his career problems, it was
as likely to be as a result of his sexual relations with Indian women.
He was quite open about his relationship with his *bubu*. In the 1840s,
this was not yet socially unacceptable, as it would become under
the Raj, but married officers' wives were already known to strongly
disapprove of such relationships. More damaging to his reputation
was the story circulating among the subalterns that Burton had
buried his love-child beside his bungalow, although the corpse was
in fact that of his deeply mourned fighting cock. More damaging
to Burton's self-esteem was an unfortunate consequence of the fact
that his *bubu* was teaching him not only about 'the syntaxes of
native Life', but giving him a crash course in the grammar of sex
itself. Burton later wrote that he had failed to satisfy his *bubu* as he
lacked the 'retaining art', whose essence, he stated, was 'to avoid
over-tension of the muscles and to preoccupy the brain'.
Defensively, Burton argued that the vegetarian diet of India and
lack of stimulants made the women cold, so that they 'cannot be
satisfied... with less than twenty minutes'. Unlike his monolingual
fellow officers, Burton was able to actually understand what his
bubu said and he may have been almost unique in realizing the

inadequacy of his 'Western' technique. Given the bullish curiosity of the man, it is hardly surprising therefore that sexual performance was a subject to which Burton would return.

Burton's sexual experiences in India were not limited to his *bubus*. He claimed that British officers' wives in Sindh, for all their moralizing, were virtually free of sexual restraint. The officers, meanwhile, had sex with Indian women as often as they wanted – with both married women and prostitutes. In 'Past Loves', an unpublished poem written in India in around 1847–8, Burton claimed, 'I cannot tell the Christian names / Of all my past and present flames.' The reason he gives has less to do with literary reticence – never a virtue of Burton's – and more to do with the sheer number of his lovers:

> One came from far Bokháráa walls
> Another from Gandoppa's falls
>   A fourth from Muskat
> Bagdad gave me a dozen at least
> And Aden many a pretty beast
>   Strong as full-grown muskrat
>
> The Nubians and the Abyssinians
> Sent me at least a score of minions
>   Cashmere was not far behind
> But of them all the fair Núr Ján
> The Venus of Belochistan
>   Was most to my mind

There was talk, much written up by his niece, Georgiana Stisted, of a romance with a Persian princess, and Burton himself leaked other

veiled tales of erotic escapades, including a shaggy dog story about
the attempted kidnap of a Goan nun – a classic Burton tale of the
breaking of taboos. Burton's encounter with Núr Ján, a *nautch* girl,
or dancer-cum-prostitute, is better documented. It also appears to
have been a genuine affair of the heart, judging by the few details
he let slip.

Whatever the truth behind his romantic liaisons, Burton's erotic
discoveries in India weren't limited to the personal. His four Indian
travel books are packed with details of the country's sexual culture.
He discussed Sayyid Hasan Ali's bride-book *Lawful Enjoyment of Women*
and reported that Indian doctors considered the Western lack of
knowledge of aphrodisiacs 'the most remarkable phenomenon'.
In particular, he gave detailed, ethnological descriptions of rites
of passage, including those surrounding circumcision, puberty
and marriage. In his first great book, *Goa and the Blue Mountains*,
he dwelled on the *devadasis*, or temple-dancer prostitutes, and
described how:

> The Numboory family is governed by several regulations pecu-
> liar to it: only the eldest of any number of brothers takes a
> woman of his own cast to wife.... This life of celibacy became
> so irksome to the Brahmans that they induced the Nair cast to
> permit unrestrained intercourse between their females and
> themselves, it being well understood that the priesthood was
> conferring an especial honour upon their disciples.

Burton was, in fact, a pioneer anthropologist, and his two travel
books on the Sindh region are still regarded as classics of the genre.
More uniquely, he was the first writer to pull back the bedsheets to
uncover Indian sexual behaviour and beliefs. He examined the

ancient roots of India's erotic tradition and digressed in unprecedented detail on *shivalingams*, the phallic stones worshipped across
India as a symbol and manifestation of the god Shiva. As to their
meaning, Burton was as yet circumspect: 'You look towards me for
some explanation of these upright stones, daubed with red,' he
wrote, adding: 'I must place the seal of silence upon my lips, much
as I regret to do so.' He would not remain silent for long.

In January 1847, following a dose of cholera, Burton convinced
the surgeon general in Bombay to grant him two years' leave.
Leaving behind the plains, he made his way south to balmy Goa
and the cool, forested highlands of the Nilgiri Hills, a journey
through backwoods India that filled his travel notebooks, eventually providing the voluminous raw material for *Goa and the Blue
Mountains*. During periods of rest, Burton set about an English
translation of the colourful folk fables of Pilpay. It was probably his
first encounter with a Sanskrit text, though it was made through
many veils; lacking serious knowledge of Sanskrit, he was forced to
work from a Hindi version of a Persian rendering of the original.
Pilpay was also Burton's first attempt at the literary translation of a
'dubious' Oriental text — an occupation that would lead to his lifetime's crowning work. The moralizing element of the tales had led
Pilpay to describe the very scurrilous behaviour of which he supposedly disapproved, thus providing Burton with an early chance
to skirmish across the boundaries of acceptability.

Burton's furlough allowed him to tour the private libraries of
scholars and local princelings, where he could indulge his passion
for book-collecting. This was something of a fashionable hobby for
more intellectually minded British residents in India, as it was
exactly in this period that Western scholars were beginning to discover the full, vast extent of Sanskrit literature. As early as the

sixteenth century, European travellers had reported, with great surprise, the existence of Hindu sacred books, but it was only in the second half of the eighteenth century that it dawned on the British that tens of thousands of works remained entirely unknown, metaphorically hidden by the obscurity of their language or literally hoarded by the Brahmins, who were often reluctant to let foreigners see their sacred texts. The study of Sanskrit was as yet a young discipline; Sir Charles Wilkins' and Sir William Jones' landmark translations of what they called the *Bhagvat-Geeta* and the *Institutes of Menu* were only just over half a century old, while the *kama shastra* tradition remained almost entirely unknown. (Jones had in fact translated Kalidasa's play, *The Recognition of Shakuntala*, but neither he nor the many Romantic poets and dramatists – notably Goethe – who acclaimed the work would have been equipped to recognize the references to the *Kamasutra*.)

Here was an opportunity for Burton to make his mark. The library that most captivated the young ensign was in Bombay, at the East India Company's headquarters, and towards the end of his furlough Burton malingered in the city, making repeated visits, and even commissioning new copies of old texts to be made especially for him. The chief glory of the Court of Directors' library was its unique collection of almost 3,000 Sanskrit manuscripts, which had been donated by H.T. Colebrooke, the great Professor of Hindu Law and Sanskrit at Fort William College in Calcutta. Colebrooke had been the first man to proclaim the Himalayas as the greatest and highest mountain range in the world; he was a pioneer after Burton's own heart. Many of his manuscripts had yet to be examined in any detail, and one in particular remained utterly obscure. It was a modest, 150-page volume, a foot long by just four and a half inches wide. Bound together with a later commentary, following the Indian custom, was the *Kamasutra*. Whether Colebrooke was ever confronted with – or affronted by – Vatsyayana's book of love is unknown, as he never described it or indeed referred to it in any way. No more, for the time at least, did Burton. If, one morning in Bombay, Burton picked up Colebrooke's *Kamasutra*, he did not record his thoughts – although it is hard to be sure as, in 1861, all Burton's notebooks went up with the smoke of a warehouse fire. We know only that among the precious papers reduced to ashes was a collection of Persian and Arabic manuscripts that included works of 'aphrodisiac literature'. Colebrooke would not have regretted missing the chance to be known as the discoverer of India's greatest erotic text. Burton, however, would surely have kicked himself black and blue.

Thanks to either ignorance or reticence, the *Kamasutra* remained unknown in the West, for a time at least. It was only after another visitor to the library copied it out by hand that word of the book's existence leaked into print. It was, fortunately for Burton's later career, the slowest of all possible leaks, coming in the form of an entry in an 1864 catalogue of Sanskrit manuscripts held by the Bodleian Library, a laborious work with the unwieldy title of *Catalogi Codicum Manuscriptorum Biblothecae Bodleianae*. It was created by the German Indologist Theodor Aufrecht, an indefatigable researcher and creator of catalogues – and an unlikely candidate for the title of erotic pioneer. In compiling his catalogue, Aufrecht appended the Colebrooke *Kamasutra* to a second 'unknown' copy, which had been discreetly bequeathed to the Bodleian in 1842 by Horace Hayman Wilson, another lion of Sanskrit scholarship. Wilson had most likely discovered the text while studying manuscripts in Benares, in the 1820s, but he was even less likely than Aufrecht or Colebrooke to publicize such a work, being no enthusiast for 'puerile and tiresome' literature, as he once described India's erotic tradition.

Aufrecht's catalogue may not have shaken the world, but it did include the first ever published description of the *Kamasutra*, calling it: 'The book of Vatsyayana, by whom the art of loving is translated not lightly nor ambiguously but as becomes a learned Indian man – even in the matter of disgusting and filthy things.' Aufrecht couldn't decide, it seems, between denouncing the text for its subject matter and praising its author for managing to handle his material with a modicum of delicacy. He quoted the first three paragraphs of the text, hazarded a guess (incorrectly) as to Vatsyayana's identity, and wrote – in Latin – that he hoped that by his action 'the names of the holy men of yesteryear who toiled in the same study will be rescued from oblivion'. It would take far more than this to rescue the *Kamasutra* from the profound obscurity into which it had sunk. It would, ultimately, take Richard Francis Burton.

Before Burton could deepen his explorations into Indian culture, he was forced to leave India under a cloud. At the close of 1848, soon after his return from Goa and the Nilgiri Hills, he was passed over for the job of translator to General Auchmuty, the commander of the Indian Army in the Mooltan and Punjab campaigns of the Second Sikh War. He was devastated: earlier that year he had added success in the army examination in Punjabi to his qualifications in another half-dozen local languages; his rival, meanwhile, was a lieutenant who knew only Hindustani. Burton boarded ship for home on 13 May 1849. 'Sick, sorry, and almost in tears of rage,' as he later put it, 'I bade adieu to my friends and comrades in India.' Burton also said goodbye to his Indian studies, turning, instead, to the Middle East and Africa. It was not as a fearless army officer in Afghanistan that he would make his name in Victorian society, nor as a learned traveller in Sindh and the Nilgiri Hills, but as the bold penetrator of the world's darkest and most dangerous places.

Burton's first great expedition was, typically, horrendously transgressive. In 1853 he set out alone for the forbidden city of Mecca, a version of his old disguise of 'Mirza Abdullah' providing the necessary passport of Muslim identity. At enormous personal risk, he even scribbled notes while actually inside the most sacred space in Islam, the tent surrounding the Qa'aba. The resulting book, the extraordinary *Personal Narrative of a Pilgrimate to Al-Madinah and Mecca*, was a massive success. It enabled him, four years later, to embark on another journey towards the sacred and the forbidden. While in Arabia, Burton had spoken to traders who reported the existence of snow-capped mountains and giant seas in the heart of Africa. Burton knew his Ptolemy, and the legend that the Nile flowed out of a series of great lakes, and he decided to mount an expedition. In the company of the younger and less experienced John Hanning Speke, Burton set out for the African interior from Zanzibar in June 1857. Twenty-one months later, the two men returned, broken by illness and fever. But the source of the Nile had been found, and Burton had filled yet more notebooks with descriptions of 'native' sexual behaviour.

Amazingly, considering their incredible success and the élan with which they were achieved, Burton's pilgrimage to Mecca and his 'great safari' produced as much poison as they did celebrity. This poison, ultimately, would play a crucial role in creating the feelings of disappointment, frustration and alienation that eventually provoked his publication of the *Kamasutra*. Mecca, first, had damaging repercussions for Burton's later career as a British Consul. As a result of his blasphemy in visiting the holy city, countries with Islamic rulers would never be entirely comfortable with Burton. His relatively sophisticated understanding of Arab culture and politics, not to mention his mastery of the Arab language, presented another problem. Men like Mohammed Rashid Pasha, the Turkish Wali governing Syria when Burton was Consul in Damascus, from 1869 to 1871, would always greatly prefer to work with a bluff, blind, John Bull type, who could be trusted to understand little of what he saw and to report less, rather than with the man they called the 'White Nigger'. The Foreign Office were sceptical about Burton's usefulness for much the same reasons. Henry Elliot, British Ambassador at Constantinople, denounced Burton in the strongest terms as a man 'whose character was so well known in the East as to make it a certainty that trouble would come of it... The fact of the matter is that Eastern Travellers are for the most part exactly the people least fitted to fill the responsible positions of Consuls in Turkey.' Careful observers like the Arabist, anti-imperialist and poet Wilfred Scawen Blunt might have realized that most of the celebrated traveller's 'recitals' were performed *pour épater les bourgeois* but the conservatives at the Foreign Office would never be persuaded that 'Ruffian Dick' was a safe pair of hands. Not only did his looks suggest a touch of the tarbrush, his language and behaviour added a distinct whiff of sulphur.

London society, meanwhile, positively throbbed with tales of Burton's outrageous conduct. Most notoriously, Burton loved to thrill his audiences with the story of how a boy in his party of pilgrims to Meccca had seen him urinating from a standing position, European-fashion, rather than squatting in the Arab manner. Realizing that he had accidentally unmasked himself, Burton bragged that he had followed the boy out of the tent and stabbed

him to death, to preserve his disguise and thus his life. Bram
Stoker reported that Burton told him the story 'was quite true'.
In Damascus, Lord Redesdale's enquiry on the same subject was
met with the insouciant answer, 'Well, they do say the man died.'
A young curate in Trieste who dared to probe was famously stung
with Burton's retort: 'Sir, I am proud to say that I have committed
every sin in the Decalogue.' The fact that so many celebrated
diarists saw fit to task Burton with the question is probably more
revealing than the rather dry manner in which Burton answered
it. In London clubs and English country houses alike, Burton was
viewed as some kind of half-tame bear: the main point of having
him around was to make him growl. Burton probably told his
'murder' story less to genuinely provoke and more to advertise his
understanding and absorption of *all* the ways of the Arabs: from his
mastery of the *muezzin*'s call to prayer – which Burton was pleased
to perform for delightedly horrified friends – right down to the
correct way to piss in the desert.

Burton's Nile expedition provoked even greater notoriety. The
source of the great river had at last been found; the trouble was
that Burton and Speke profoundly and vehemently disagreed
about where exactly it was. The quarrel followed them home:
Burton felt that Speke betrayed him by publicizing his claims at the
Royal Geographical Society before Burton arrived back in England,
and by organizing a new expedition with himself in command.
Speke was fêted, Burton sidelined and criticized. Speke's geographical and topographical labours were lauded, Burton's historical and
ethnographic work barely discussed. Worse, Burton believed that
his former companion, now his 'angry rival', was spreading poi-
sonous rumours about him, making arch references to his habit of
noting local sexual customs, and perhaps alleging outright that

Burton's sexual continence – or preferences – were suspect. Burton's poet friend Swinburne claimed that there had been a 'beloved and blue object of his Central African affections', whose 'caudal charms and simious seductions were too strong for the narrow laws of Levitical or Mosaic prudery which would confine the jewel of a man to the lotus of a merely human female by the most odious and unnatural of priestly restrictions'. Burton's secret marriage in January 1861 to Isabel Arundell, the idealistic daughter of an aristocratic, English Catholic family – against the wishes of her parents – may have helped to quell such rumours.

Speke was eventually proved right that Lake Victoria – and not Lake Tanganyika – was the principal source of the Nile, if not for the reasons he gave. Burton's contributions to East African geography and anthropology were undoubtedly of greater value, but the actual discovery of the Nile's source was the only feat of exploration that truly resounded in the Western imagination. It was 'the greatest geographical prize since the discovery of America'. Burton may have better surveyed the ground for imperialism, but Speke had pioneered the road for expansion. Burton's own disappointment was compounded by the quarrel with his former friend, which played itself out in newspaper articles and bitter private correspondence. Speke eventually shot himself – supposedly by accident – on the eve of the two explorers' first public debate, in September 1864. Burton wrote to *The Times* that 'the sad event... must seal my mouth concerning many things'. Refraining from speaking out, however, was very far from Burton's habit, and the contentious question of the exact topographic details of the Nile watershed continued to rumble away after Speke's death, in a national debate that divided geographers and the fascinated public alike. Burton continued to press the claims of his Lake Tanganyika theory until as late as 1881, when the discoveries of his successors in Africa – notably Livingstone and Stanley – caused him finally and publicly to admit defeat. 'There is a time to leave the Dark Continent,' he wrote, ruefully, 'and that is when the *idée fixe* begins to develop itself.' In any case, long before 1881, even before Speke's death, a new obsession had drawn Burton into another, in many ways darker continent: the little-explored realm of erotics.

In 1863, when the recriminations surrounding the Speke affair were at their peak, Burton and a friend, Dr James Hunt, founded a 'new religion' – at least, this was how Burton described his 'Anthropological Society of London' in a letter to his friend and sponsor, the Conservative Member of Parliament and literary patron Richard Monckton Milnes. In many respects, the Anthropological Society was Burton's fighting response to the bitter aftermath of the Nile expedition. Burton's club emphasized the fledgling, modern sciences of ethnology and anthropology rather than old-fashioned, brute exploration. Its aims were intellectual rather than heroic. Geography had hitherto concerned itself with mapping the physical world and, thanks to men such as Speke, those maps were increasingly complete. Anthropologists like Burton intended, instead, to map the beliefs and behaviour models that underpinned human society. To create such a map, sexuality would need to be discussed, and openly.

Burton's first paper was a report on the 'peculiar customs' of Dahomey, notably polygamy, phallic worship and the practice of male and female genital mutilation. The Society also earnestly sat through papers on prostitution, fertility rituals and the *nautch* or dancing girls of South India, who were beginning to aquire Europe-wide fame as custodians of an ancient erotico-spiritual tradition whose details were, as yet, little understood. To say that such topics would not have been well received at the Royal Geographical Society is to put it mildly. Burton's paper was an early skirmish in what became a lifelong campaign against sexual ignorance, censorship and hypocrisy, with his knowledge of the 'Orient', Africa included, as his principle weapon. Burton later protested in the 1886 'Terminal Essay', which concluded his translation of the *Arabian Nights*, that:

> Few phenomena are more startling than the vision of a venerable infant, who has lived half his long life in the midst of the wildest anthropological vagaries and monstrosities, and yet who absolutely ignores all that India and Burmah enacts under his very eyes... Against such lack of knowledge my notes are a protest.... In this matter I have done my best, at a time too when the hapless English traveller is expected to write like a young lady for young ladies, and never to notice what underlies the most superficial stratum.

In 1863, however, the 'Terminal Essay' was as yet unwritten — and probably as yet unwritable. In his travel books, Burton was still censoring his own observations in order to salve the prudishness of his readership. 'As a traveller and a writer of travels,' he wrote, 'I have found it impossible to publish those questions of social economy and those physiological observations always interesting to our common humanity, and at times so valuable.' The Anthropological Society would solve the problem; it would be a refuge for 'a liberty of thought and a freedom of speech unknown to any other society in Great Britain'. It consequently attracted a small group of men who, like Burton, were unusually willing to challenge the unspoken censorship of public mores, especially when it came to talking about sex. Burton described how he had originally wanted to exercise the 'liberty of thought' and 'freedom of speech' in print, as well as in private conversation. His motive was

> to supply travellers with an organ which would rescue their observations from the outer darkness of manuscript and print their curious information on social and sexual matters out of place in the popular book... But, hardly had we begun when 'Respectability', that whited sepulchre full of all uncleanness, rose up against her. 'Propriety' cried us down with her brazen, blatant voice and the week-kneed brethren fell away. Yet the organ was much wanted and is wanted still.

Sex was just one front opened by the original Anthropological Society in their campaign against respectability and propriety. Another was religion. The discovery of religious cultures such as India's, which could not be lightly brushed aside as primitive, had opened the doors to a new religious relativism. Scientific empiricism was the driving force behind anthropology, and thanks to its discipline it was becoming increasingly clear to a growing number of scholars and, indeed, dilettante travellers that Christianity's claim to a unique message was untenable. The discoveries in India, in particular, were increasingly being held up as evidence that God, if God existed at all, must take many forms. Foster Fitzgerald Arbuthnot, an old friend of Burton's from his India days, was one of the first to comment on the 'striking' resemblance between Krishna and Christ. And he went further: pointing out that 'Christna', as he called the Hindu god, 'was mould with years ere Jesus was born', he declared that 'the story of Jesus of Nazareth is so identical with that of Christna in name, origin, office, history, incidents, and death as to make it manifest that the latter was copied from the earlier almost entire'.

Many members of the Anthropological Society were atheist, or at least broadly deist, in outlook – most notoriously Charles Bradlaugh, the founder of the National Secular Society, who later became a cause célèbre in the world of publishing 'obscene' books. Burton usually refused to be drawn on his own beliefs, telling the Society: 'My religious opinions are of no importance to anyone but myself... I object to confessions, and I will not confess.' That said, he pushed a distinctly relativist and atheist point of view in his long satirical poem, *Stone Talk*, printed in 1865. The poem, however, was delivered through the mouth of a Brahmin trapped in a paving stone, and it was both anonymously and privately printed. Burton did not remain circumspect for much longer. He was soon pugnaciously declaring to the National Association of Spiritualists: 'Personally, I ignore the existence of soul and spirit, feeling no want of a self within a self, an I within an I.' Instead, he put his faith in the brand-new theory of evolution: 'I cannot but hold to the apes,' he declared. Darwin's *On the Origin of Species by Means of Natural Selection* had been published a few years before, in 1859.

For some, the Anthropological Society was less a forum for atheism than a mask for more primal passions. An inner cabal of Burton's friends and colleagues met at Bartolini's dining rooms in London, to drink, dine, tell outrageous stories and indulge in what Burton called 'orgies' – though not, apparently, of the sexual kind. Women were not usually tolerated. If the orgiasts became too riotous, a chairman would call for order by thumping the floor with a club – no doubt to raucous cheers. Carved with an African figure chewing on a femur, it symbolized the group's wilful embrace of the transgressive. The father-figure of this 'Cannibal Club' was Richard Monckton Milnes, who was elevated to the peerage as Lord Houghton in 1863. Milnes was also one of the first men both to rise above the earth in a hot-air balloon and to descend into the deep ocean in a diving bell, and he was an ardent (and frustrated) suitor of Florence Nightingale. He was perhaps best known, however, for the weekend house parties at his eighteenth-century Yorkshire home of Fryston Hall, where he gathered explorers, writers, Conservative Party luminaries and other gentlemen of fashion and influence.

Burton's wife, Isabel, described Milnes' stately home in an article on 'Celebrities at Home' for the magazine *The World*. At the heart of Fryston, she reported, was its library. Its style reflected contemporary Oriental fashions. It was 'a long, handsome, comfortable room, soft-carpeted, and replete with ottoman and sofa luxury'. The *nagaraka*'s ideal home springs inevitably to mind. Fryston was 'walled with books, as indeed was the whole house, not in formal rows but in separate cases, each with its own subject — Poetry, Magic, French Revolution, Oriental Thought, Theology and Antitheology, Criminal Trials, Fiction, from Manon Lascaut to George Eliot'. The subjects Isabel listed were almost uniformly unconventional, from the books on 'anti-theology' to those on the French Revolution. Less orthodox still was the section on 'criminal trials', which in fact covered a variety of school punishments. An interest in the Orient was hardly unusual, but Milnes' thinking went against the usual grain. In his 1844 collection of poetry, *Palm Leaves*, he complained that 'We have taken our notions of Eastern domesticity much more from the ballet than from reality, and have coloured them with so much ferocity and vice, that what is really commonplace becomes paradoxical.'

There was one set of bookcases that Isabel did not choose to describe. Secretly, and illegally, Milnes had accumulated the finest library of erotica in Europe, a collection so extensive that intimates of his freethinking inner circle admiringly referred to his house as 'Aphrodisiopolis'. (Curiously enough, Fryston Hall began life as a monastery and is now the Monk Fryston honeymoon hotel.) As well as collecting erotica, Milnes gathered around him a small, rebellious coterie of well-to-do gentlemen with shared passions for rare and pornographic books, Oriental travel and sexual experimentation. The wild young poet Algernon Charles Swinburne was one *intimé* of the circle, Richard Burton another. Swinburne described Milnes as '*the* Sadique collector of European fame'. As Milnes wrote, riddlingly, in *Palm Leaves*,

Who can determine the frontier of Pleasure?
Who can distinguish the limits of Pain?...
And life will be dearer and clearer in anguish
Than ever was felt in the throbs of delight.

The chief procurer of erotic books for Milnes' library was a former Captain of the Guards, Frederick Hankey, who had retired to Paris to take advantage of the city's relatively relaxed moral climate. Hankey's methods were ingenious and he made full use of his well-to-do contacts. Some pornographic books found their way to Milnes courtesy of the deep overcoat pockets of the manager of the Opera House, a certain Mr Harris, some were buried among dispatches sent to Lord Palmerston from Constantinople – Hankey knew the Queen's Messenger personally; others were simply popped into the diplomatic bag, addressed to one of Hankey's Foreign Office friends. In April 1862, Hankey was visited by the Goncourt brothers at his apartment on the rue Laffitte. In a notorious passage expurgated from their published diaries – and only revealed in the Monaco edition – the Goncourts described him with horror as '*un fou, un monstre*... one of those men on the edge of the abyss'. 'Henkey', as they called this 'terrible eccentric', was 'about thirty years old, bald, with temples swelling out like an orange... his head – and this is strange – is the head of one of those emaciated and ecstatic young priests who surround the bishops in old pictures'. Hankey showed the horrified brothers books with metal clasps resembling phalluses, skulls and torture instruments, and described how he liked to pierce prostitutes with pins until they bled. He also pointed out a book which, he regretted, still lacked a decent cover. Looking down at his fingernails in an ostentatious fey manner, Hankey said he was 'waiting for the skin of a young girl... But it's disagreeable... the skin has to be taken from a young girl while she is alive... I have my friend Dr Barth, you know... the one who travels in Africa and at the time of the massacres... he has promised to get me a skin like that, from a living source.' Hankey was a man devoted to the fantastical, but in this he was telling the truth. 'Dr Barth' was none other than Richard Burton, who had visited Hankey in Paris, in 1859. It was Milnes who had introduced them. Burton described the West African festival of massacres in his 1864 travelogue, *A Mission to Gelele, King of Dahome*, and he actually wrote to Milnes from Dahomey to say: 'I have been here three days and am generally disappointed. Not a man killed, not a fellow tortured... Poor Hankey must still wait for his *peau de femme*.'

In 1860, Milnes recorded Burton's impressions of Hankey in his commonplace book. Ever the anthropologist, Burton told him, 'there is no accounting for tastes in superstition. Hankey would like to have a Bible bound with bits of skin stripped off live from the cunts of a hundred little girls and yet he could not be persuaded to try the sensation of f—g a Muscovy duck while its head was cut off.' The tone is of hearty and perhaps facetious amusement, of delight in transgression rather than the frisson of sexual arousal. This is not to say that Burton did not share Hankey's sadistic predilections, although in 1889, writing to the pornographic publisher Leonard Smithers about a proposed English edition of *Justine*, Burton noted that 'the French of Dr Sade is monstrous enough and a few pages choke me off. But what bile it would be in brutal Anglo-Saxon.' Perspicaciously, the Goncourt brothers recognized that Hankey was not in fact a madman or monstrous freak, but the product of a particular strain of English society. 'Through him, as through a torn veil, I glimpsed something abominable, a frightening aspect of a blasé moneyed aristocracy, the English aristocracy which brings ferocity to love, and finds satisfaction only through the sufferings of women.'

Milnes himself was the quintessential example of this abominable aristocracy. He composed a pornographic flagellatory poem of his own, which Hankey showed Burton during his stay in Paris and which was eventually printed in 1871 – anonymously, of course – as *The Rodiad*, and circulated among like-minded friends. For Burton, this was an early lesson in how private printing could get around the obscenity laws. A.C. Swinburne, meanwhile, was writing doggerel on beaten schoolboys for the pornographic magazine, *The Pearl*, and composing an entire mock-epic entitled *The Flogging Block*. (Even Swinburne's public poetry was famously sexually charged, causing the critic John Morley to call him 'an unclean imp from the pit' and 'the libidinous laureate of a pack of satyrs'.) Swinburne, too, knew Hankey, describing his collection of erotic books and engravings as 'unrivalled upon earth – unequalled I should imagine, in heaven'.

The members of the Cannibal Club were not just socialite trans-gressives indulging in recreational titillation. Discussing sex openly was a radical political act in itself. Writing to a friend in 1873, Burton confessed, 'we did not tremble at the idea of "acquiring an unhappy notoriety". We wanted to have the truth, the whole truth, as each man sees it. We intended to make room for every form of thought, the orthodox and the heterodox; the subversive and the conserva-tive; the retrograde equally with the progressive.' The Cannibals were scientists, of an amateur sort; they helped clear the way for the professional sexologists and psychologists who would soon follow them, just as the great amateur Victorian archaeologists, anthropologists and art historians paved the way for professionals to follow in their own fields of enquiry. Rejecting what they saw as the hypocrisy of the English Establishment, the members of the club used the Orient – Africa included – as a mirror to reflect back the sexual habits of their own society. The light so produced was found to be harshly revealing. As Milnes wrote, 'I do not hesitate to say that I can find no superiority in the morals and manners of the West, and am led to fear that the evils connected with the relations between the sexes are more productive of suffering and debase-ment in any, so-called, Christian countries than in those that remain attached to the habits of the elder world.'

Like all true Victorian amateurs, the 'Cannibals' were practi-tioners as well as observers; they explored the erotic not just in other societies but in themselves as well. Milnes, Swinburne, Burton and their pack of satyrs were not just interested in talking, reading and writing about flagellation. Swinburne referred to his mentor Milnes as 'Monsieur Rodin', asking him in one letter of

1863: 'I suppose I may use schoolboyish tone in addressing my scholastic lord & teacher?' In another, he mourned the departure of his 'tempter and favourite audience' – 'I may hope to be a good boy again,' Swinburne mused, 'after such a "jolly good swishing" as Rodin alone can dare administer... The Captain was too many for me.' 'The Captain' almost certainly referred to Burton's rank in the Indian Army. Milnes himself wrote approvingly in his commonplace book that 'Burton says he has remarked several men with the vice of Studholme Hodgson... all men delighting in cruelty.' Hodgson was a member of the Cannibal Club and gloried under the soubriquet of 'Colonel Spanker' – at least until promoted to the rank of General. Burton even dedicated one volume of his *Arabian Nights* to him, describing him as 'my preceptor of past times' to whom he resorted 'so often for good council and right direction'.

Burton asked after Hodgson in several letters to Milnes, asking to be remembered, for instance, in a letter of April 1862, to 'the amiable trio, Hodgson, Bellamy and Hankey'. A letter of March 1863, written while belatedly honeymooning in Tenerife, suggests that the flagellatory antics of the Cannibals were not limited to members only. Referring to Milnes' elevation to the peerage, Burton joked:

Are you a peer yet, do you feel peerish, and how is that strange sensation? Anything of Hankey? I suppose Bellamy is still fending off the angry fiend. The poor Stewart! I had not time to *confectionner un orgie chez elle*. I left Hodgson the Gen'l sweating under the pangs of a baulked ambition & should be glad to know that he has ejected the irrelevant matter.

By 1873, Burton was speculating that 'Fred Hankey must nearly have been burnt out'. He continued, 'What has become of Tall Colonel (Hodgson)? Of Stuart alias Potter?' 'Stewart', or 'Stuart alias Potter', was almost certainly a pseudonym of the flagellant madame Sarah Potter, who kept a series of brothels where her ladies could be spanked and even pricked with pins. Hodgson, Bellamy (who would later sign up for the first subscription edition of the *Kamasutra*), Burton, Milnes, Charles Duncan Cameron (the Abyssinian Consul who later disappeared from England under a cloud) and several other members of the Cannibal Club were almost certainly her clients. The conversation of their dinners must have made the air turn blue.

Hardly were the Anthropological Society and the Cannibal Club up and running than Burton was appointed Consul in Santos, Brazil. Milnes had persuaded the Foreign Office to give his protégé a chance. In May 1865, the Society gave its founding member a farewell dinner. As a special dispensation, Burton's wife was allowed to listen from behind a screen, thrilling with her usual anxious pleasure that her husband would say the wrong thing to the wrong person. 'He adored shocking dense people,' she later recalled. 'I have frequently sat at the dinner-table of such people, praying him by signs not to go on, but he was in a very ecstasy of glee; he said it was so funny always to be believed when you were chaffing, and so curious never to be believed when you were telling the truth.'

Brazil, unfortunately, failed to offer Burton the rich anecdotes and anthropological insights that the East had provided. Even while he was living and travelling in South America, his thoughts began to return to India. He began work on translating another set of Hindu folk tales, freely adapting and generously expanding upon a part of the *Vetalapancavimsati*, a collection of stories within a narrative frame rather like the Scheherazade story of the *Arabian Nights*. In Burton's version, eventually published in 1870 under the title of *Vikram and the Vampire*, a king (Vikram) enters into a bargain with a living corpse or *baital* (the vampire), who tells him a series of riddling stories on successive nights. Burton's feelings about *Vikram and the Vampire* were hardly passionate: he advised his publisher merely that the tales were 'not without a quaintish merit'. It was, however, a first step on the road towards his final incarnation as a translator. As he himself later commented, the work was 'the rude beginning of that fictitious history which ripened to the "Arabian Nights" Entertainments'. It was also the first step towards *The Kama Sutra of Vatsyayana*.

In *Vikram and the Vampire*, Burton grappled with what could be rendered explicitly in a printed book and what could not. As the vampire tells the king:

> Whilst they were making their offerings, a bevy of maidens, accompanied by a crowd of female slaves, descended the opposite flight of steps. They stood there for a time, talking and laughing and looking about them to see if any alligators infested the waters. When convinced that the tank was safe, they disrobed themselves in order to bathe. It was truly a splendid spectacle – 'Concerning which the less said the better,' interrupted Raja Vikram in an offended tone.

The interruption is in fact Burton's own. He also appended a foot-note that, typically, showed off his personal acquaintance with Hinduism: 'Light conversation upon the subject of women,' he claimed, 'is a personal offence to serious-minded Hindus.' And yet, as Burton would have very well known, offence was more likely to be taken by his own bourgeois, English readers than by some imaginary Hindu – serious-minded or not.

Five years after Brazil and *Vikram*, Burton was awarded a far more satisfactory posting: to Damascus. Again, Milnes had been at work on his friend's behalf. It was here, in 1869 or perhaps 1870, that a more promising project seized Burton's attention. He heard some intriguing news from Foster Fitzgerald Arbuthnot, his old friend from India. Arbuthnot told Burton that he and a Bombay coll- eague, Edward Rehatsek, had been discussing the urgent need for Oriental texts to be translated into English. An eccentric man of Hungarian origin, Rehatsek worked as a professor of Latin and mathematics at Bombay's Wilson College, but his principal passion was for the study and translation of texts – many of them erotic – from Persian. Arbuthnot wondered whether Burton, with his Arabic skills and his interest in the study of sexuality, would be interested in developing a series of translations of Eastern erotic classics alongside himself and Rehatsek. For his part, Arbuthnot was thinking of translating Kalyanamalla's *Ananga Ranga*.

Burton may have known the manuscript from his time in India. As it was a relatively recent manifestation of the *kama shastra* tradi- tion and one that had been taken up by the Muslim aristocracy, copies could be found in India with relative ease. A version of the *Ananga Ranga* in Marathi – the language of Maharashtra, the region around Bombay – had even been published in 1842, the very year of Burton's arrival in India. Certainly, by the time Burton wrote his 'Terminal Essay', he had already collected copies

in Sanskrit and Maráthi, Guzrati and Hindostani: the latter is an unpaged 8vo of pp. 66, including eight pages of most grotesque illustrations showing the various Asan (the Figuræ

Veneris or positions of copulation), which seem to be the triumphs of contortionists. These pamphlets lithographed in Bombay are broadcast over the land.

The aside about the Bombay lithographs is classic Burton. Only he, with his unique, disguised entrée into Indian society and mastery of local languages, would have been able to investigate such an aspect of 'native' culture. Equally, only the anthropologist Burton would have cared to: other *sahibs*, corralled as they were in their English-language cantonments, would never learn, or want to learn, what went on in the bedrooms of their inferiors.

Foster Fitzgerald Arbuthnot might have seemed a surprising candidate for the editorship of a notorious work of Indian erotology. A career civil servant in the Bombay government who rose to the position of Collector – a job which required him to set the rate of *toka*, or land tax revenue – Arbuthnot was, in the words of Burton's early biographer Thomas Wright, 'a man of the world, but quite untainted by it'. As a young man he had a rounded, almost effeminate cast of face, with finely arched eyebrows and a sensual mouth. He was known for 'the sweetness and serenity' of his manner. And yet, 'like so many of your quiet men, he had a determination – a steady heroism, which made everything give way. Oppose Burton, and you would instantly receive a blow aimed straight from the shoulder; oppose Arbuthnot and you would be pushed quietly and amiably aside – but pushed aside nevertheless.' Arbuthnot and Burton had first met in India, in 1853, when Burton was staying in Bombay while writing up his pilgrimage to Mecca. Like Speke, Arbuthnot was another of the younger men that Burton periodically took under his wing. Unlike Speke, Arbuthnot would prove a faithful friend and was largely content to remain the junior partner in the relationship. Burton even called his disciple 'Bunny', the only friend he honoured with a nickname.

According to Isabel Burton, writing after her husband's death, Arbuthnot was Burton's 'best friend for the past forty years'. They certainly shared a restless curiosity about matters sexual, and perhaps some private predilections too. During Arbuthnot's first furlough in England, from 1859 to 1860, Burton introduced him to Richard Monckton Milnes, and it is likely that Arbuthnot met members of Milnes' transgressive coterie, perhaps even participating in their activities. A letter from Burton to Milnes mentions hearing from 'Boy Bunny' in the same breath as speculating on Fred Hankey's health and asking for news of Hodgson and the flagellant brothel-keeper Sarah Potter-alias-Stewart. Arbuthnot himself seems to have been at least aware of Potter's business: writing to Bellamy in 1884, to arrange a meeting, he mentioned that he was 'very glad to hear that you saved some of Potter's things from destruction. I saw the man they were left to, who informed me that he ought to have destroyed them all.'

In 1872, during a second furlough in England, Arbuthnot brought with him the finished manuscript of the *Ananga Ranga* and showed it to his friend. Burton was not impressed. He told Richard Monckton Milnes that Arbuthnot's draft was 'rather dull' and mused that it was 'curious to see the deadening effect of Indian air, even upon that merriest of boys. He actually talks of early history!' It seemed that Arbuthnot's more earnest scholarship was already rubbing up against Burton's relatively swashbuckling attitude. This was the beginning of the debate that would later swirl around the *Kamasutra*. Was the *Ananga Ranga* an instructive document with much to teach the West and, as such, an important addition to every Oriental library? Arbuthnot certainly seemed to think so as the worryingly unscientific astrological and alchemical material was relegated to an appendix. Or was it an erotic classic, with wider commercial application? Burton was well aware that he could present the book as anthropological. Just as *National Geographic* photographs of bare-breasted women would be thought acceptable by a later generation on the grounds of their 'ethnological' aspect, so the descriptions of early Indian society in the *Ananga Ranga* could provide a scholarly fig-leaf for the 'pornographic' content. And, of course, erotica could make anthropology sell.

Burton selectively polished up Bunny Arbuthnot's over-earnest draft to his own, more salacious satisfaction. He appended his usual thoughtful, esoteric footnotes, and inserted plentiful local colour to boot. An entire additional paragraph focused on one of his own, private sexual obsessions.

The wife will remember that without an especial exertion of will on her part, the husband's pleasure will not be perfect. To this end she must ever strive to close and constrict the Yoni until it holds the Linga, as with a finger, opening and shutting at her pleasure, and finally, acting as the hand of the Gopala-girl, who milks the cow. This can be learned only by long practice, and especially by throwing the will into the part to be affected... While so doing, she will mentally repeat 'Kamadeva! Kamadeva,' in order that a blessing may rest upon the undertaking.... Her husband will then value her above all women, nor would he exchange her for the most beautiful Rani (queen) in the three worlds. So lovely and pleasant to man is she who constricts.

It's hard to imagine the passionately Catholic Isabel invoking the god Kama under her breath while constricting her *yoni*. Not content with making up his own sexual advice, Burton added a typically anthropological footnote that suggests the point was not so much that Isabel employed the 'pompoir' technique, but that she was ignorant of it.

> Amongst some races the constrictor vaginæ muscles are abnormally developed. In Abyssinia, for instance, a woman can so exert them as to cause pain to a man, and, when sitting upon his thighs, she can induce the orgasm without moving any other part of her person. Such an artist is called by the Arabs, 'Kabbazah', literally meaning 'a holder', and it is not surprising that the slave dealers pay large sums for her. All women have more or less the power, but they wholly neglect it; indeed, there are many races in Europe which have never even heard of it. To these the words of wisdom spoken by Kalyana Malla, the poet, should be peculiarly acceptable.

Following his creative edit, Burton told Arbuthnot in 1873 that he was happy for the text to be sent to the printers. By chance, 1873 was a landmark year for Indology. That winter, the archaeological explorer Alexander Cunningham had investigated the remains of a brick-built city in the Punjab, which would later be dated to the third millennium BC. The private printing of a sixteenth-century sex book might not seem to have the same potential impact as the Harappa finds, but both events represented an important step in the West's discovery of Indian civilization. At least, the *Ananga Ranga* represented a kind of rough archaeological survey of the ground – the digger's spades were yet to strike the *Kamasutra*, the greatest and most ancient remnant of the obscure civilization that was India's erotic culture. In a wider sense, the 'discovery' of both Harappa and the *Ananga Ranga* belonged to the same Western project of absorbing from the East all the aspects of culture that it did not already possess. The staggering antiquity of pre-Classical civilization – a culture soon colonized in retrospect as 'Aryan' or 'Indo-European' – was one such contribution. Erotology was another. Indeed, as the West groped its way towards Freud, an elaborated and authoritative science of eroticism was what it urgently lacked.

Arbuthnot, or more probably Burton, changed the title from *Ananga Ranga* to *Kama Shastra, or the Hindoo Art of Love (Ars Amoris Indica)*. The new title's unwieldy length resulted from its functioning as a series of codes, each aimed at a different audience. The 'Kama Shastra' part of the title hinted at Arbuthnot's and Burton's ambitions for their book's impact on the world of Indology. The new title suggested that the *Ananga Ranga* was a key text from the great tradition of erotic science – rather than simply a handy guidebook on how to have better sex. For the layman pornophile, 'Hindoo Art of Love' was explicit enough, while the Latin subtitle, aimed at the Classicists, was suggestively borrowed from Ovid's erotic poem, *Ars Amatoria*. A brief passage of marketing copy further emphasized the connection: 'This work may fairly be pronounced unique from the days of Sotades and Ovid to our time,' it advertised. The word 'Sotadic' – drawn from the name of the Greek author of a few obscene poetic satires in the third-century BC – would become Burton's favourite euphemism for 'homosexual'.

Not content with altering the title, the translators went to some lengths to obscure their own identities and their ambitions for the book. The title-page bore the legend: 'Translated from the Sanskrit and Annotated by A.F.F. and B.F.R. For private use of the Translators only, in connection with a work on the Hindoo religion, and on the manners and customs of the Hindoos.' Making their book seem subordinate to a larger and more scholarly work only betrayed Burton's and Arbuthnot's nervousness. For a time, they even considered translating the entire text into Latin, 'that it might not fall into the hands of the vulgar'. But

> further considerations satisfied us that it contains nothing essentially immoral and much matter deserving of more consideration that it receives at present. The generation which prints and reads literal English translations of the debauched Petronius Arbiter and the witty indecencies of Rabelais, can hardly be prudish enough to complain of the devout and highly moral Kalyana Malla.

This claim, of course, is blatantly rhetorical, a way of making their motives look more altruistic. Publishing the text in English, it was suggested, was not done to shock or pander to the tastes of the vulgar, but because the text itself was essentially *moral* in its aims. This tendentious statement apparently rested on Kalyanamalla's own conclusion, that 'Monotony begets satiety, and satiety distaste for congress' and that from this in turn result 'polygamy, adulteries, abortions, and every manner of vice'. Accordingly, the book showed 'how the husband, by varying the enjoyment of his wife, may live with her as with thirty-two different women, ever varying the enjoyment of her, and rendering satiety impossible'. In truth, this entire passage was probably another of Burton's creative insertions.

'The vulgar', sadly, never had a chance to get their highly moral hands on the *Kama Shastra, or the Hindoo Art of Love*. The printers ran off only four (or according to Burton, six) copies of the proofs before stopping to examine what they were actually printing. There was, predictably, an uproar and, whether through moral outrage or fear of prosecution, the printers absolutely refused to continue. Ironically, the stated desire of the translators to print their text 'for private use only' was fulfilled, and Burton's and Arbuthnot's desire to become pioneer publishers of Indian erotic texts remained unsatisfied.

The life of the 1873 *Kama Shastra* was not, however, entirely snuffed out. Burton and Arbuthnot sent one of their precious copies to Victorian England's most eccentric hobbyist, the chubby and amiable Henry Spencer Ashbee. Alongside his probable authorship of *My Secret Life*, a compendious work of pornography purporting to be the graphic details of 'Walter's' liaisons with over a thousand women, Ashbee was hard at work compiling an earnest, three-volume descriptive catalogue of pornographic books. Like Richard Monckton Milnes, he combined bibliophilia with a general mania for matters sexual and a particular enthusiasm for flagellation. The first, 500-page volume of his weighty bibliography was printed in 1875 by James Henry Gaball of Brixton Hill, one of London's more prolific clandestine printers. It was archly entitled *Index Librorum Prohibitorum*, after the Inquisition's notorious list of banned books, and was apparently authored by one 'Pisanus Fraxi' – a play on the Latin words *fraxinus* (ash) and *apis* (bee).

The book's elaborate frontispiece showed an altar-like bookcase with a single volume being burned by a miniature devil at its centre; the flames reached up towards a pediment decorated with a satyr's head, from whose horns hung an elaborate strap-on dildo; below, a single bookshelf was filled with volumes including the *New Epicurean*, the *Sublime of Flagellation*, Frederick Hankey's *Instruction Libertine* – and the *Kama Shastra*. Inside the *Index*, Ashbee gave a detailed description of the text, so detailed, in fact, that he must have corresponded at some length with at least one of the translators – probably Arbuthnot, although the two men would not actually meet for another eight years. Ashbee was certainly well aware of the authors' identities. As he noted, in his usual earnest manner: 'The talented translators are F.F. Arbuthnot, and R.F. Burton, the celebrated African Traveller; the initials of their names being reversed.' Ashbee also observed, on Arbuthnot's authority, that 'there are many references to the poets and philosophers of older days', and he speculated that 'it is hardly probable that so awful and artificial a system sprang full-grown from a single brain.'

This observation was an early flicker of awareness of what might lie out there in the darkness of the Indian night. Arbuthnot had held up a candle and seen the light falling on ranks of *kama shastra* manuscripts. As one of the last manifestations of the long *kama shastra* tradition, the *Ananga Ranga*, of course, could not have been further from springing full-grown from a single brain. But it did stem ultimately from a single textual source: the *Kamasutra*. In a later volume of his eroto-bibliography, *Catena Librorum Absconditorum* (*String of Books Worthy of Being Silenced* or, punningly, *The Chain of Books of the Hidden Ones*), Ashbee reported what Arbuthnot had told him about the 1873 *Kama Shastra*: 'at pages 46 & 59, references were made to the holy sage VATSYAYANA, and to his opinions. The pundits informed me that the *Kama Sutra of Vatsyayana* was now the standard work on love in Sanscrit literature, and that no Sanscrit library was supposed to be complete without a copy of it. They added that the work was now very rare.'

Arbuthnot later wrote a fuller description himself of exactly 'how it came about that Vatsyayana was first brought to light'. Arbuthnot's curiosity had been piqued, it seems, following discussions with the *pandits*, or Brahman Sanskrit scholars, who were helping him translate the *Ananga Ranga*. He recalled how, while translating,

> reference was frequently found to be made to one Vatsya. The sage Vatsya was of this opinion, or of that opinion. The sage Vatsya said this, and so on. Naturally, questions were asked who the sage was, and the pundits replied that Vatsya was the author of the standard work of love in Sanscrit literature, and no Sanscrit library was complete without his work, and that it was most difficult now to obtain in its entire state.

In fact, Vatsyayana is referred to only twice in the *Ananga Ranga*. The book's sixth chapter, on 'the art by which man or woman is rendered submissive and obedient to the fascinator, who for that purpose uses certain drugs and charms', gives a list of prescriptions. The first is taken from 'the holy sage Vatsyayana Muni', who

> hath declared that whosoever will take the powder of sensitive plant, the root of green lotus-flowers, the Bassia latifolia, and barley-flower; and, after mixing it up with some of his own *Kama-salila* [translated elsewhere as 'love seed' and the 'water of life'], will apply it as a sectarian mark to his forehead, such an one will subdue the world of women, and she who looks upon his brow cannot fail to feel for him the most eager desire.

The seventh chapter, on 'Different Signs in Men and Women', ends by discussing the ethics of adultery or, to quote the text itself, the circumstances in which, 'despite all this ignominy, disgrace and contumely, it is absolutely necessary to have connection with the wife of another'.

> The book of Vatsyayana, the Rishi, teaches us as follows: Suppose that a woman, having reached the lusty vigour of her age, happens to become so inflamed with love for a man, and so heated by passion that she [is] likely to end in death attended with frenzy, if her beloved refuse her sexual commerce. Under these circumstances, the man, after allowing himself to be importuned for a time, should reflect that his refusal will cost her life; he should, therefore, enjoy her on one occasion, but not always.

If Arbuthnot and Burton were to explore further and deeper into the unknown realm of ancient Indian sexuality, their quest was now to find a complete manuscript of this 'book of Vatsyayana'.

A VIRTUOUS WOMAN, WHO has affection for her husband, should act in conformity with his wishes as if he were a divine being, and with his consent should take upon herself the whole care of his family. She should keep the whole house well cleaned, and arrange flowers of various kinds in different parts of it, and make the floor smooth and polished so as to give the whole a neat and becoming appearance. She should surround the house with a garden, and place ready in it all the materials required for the morning, noon and evening sacrifices. Moreover she should herself revere the sanctuary of the Household Gods, for, says Gonardiya, 'nothing so much attracts the heart of a householder to his wife as a careful observance of the things mentioned above'.

…When the wife wants to approach her husband in private her dress should consist of many ornaments, various kinds of flowers, and a cloth decorated with different colours, and some sweet-smelling ointments or unguents. But her every-day dress should be composed of a thin, close-textured cloth, a few ornaments and flowers, and a little scent, not too much.

The Kama Sutra of Vatsyayana
Part IV: About a Wife
Chapter I: On the Manner of Living of a Virtuous Woman
translated by 'A.F.F and B.F.R' (1883)

CHAPTER FOUR

Rending the Veil

The failure of the *Ananga Ranga* printing meant that Richard
Burton's career and public reputation were safe. But like a
comfortably married man haunted by memories of a stolen
embrace, he could not forget his aborted flirtation with clandestine
publishing. In the years that followed, his frustration and sense of
impotence only grew, feeding on a larger sense of slight and personal injury. In October 1872, shortly before the printing of the
Kama Shastra, Burton had accepted the post of British Consul in
Trieste. To his contemporaries in the Foreign Office, it would have
seemed a fine placement. It was free from the feverish African air of
Fernando Pó, an island off the Bight of Benin, where Burton had
festered between 1861 and 1863; and it was free from the sickness of
Santos, in Brazil, where Richard and Isabel had together dodged
mosquitoes and cholera from 1865 to 1868. It was free, too, from the
diplomatic intrigues of Damascus, so inimicable to Burton's irreverent character, which had resulted in his dismissal as Consul, in
1871, after just two years' controversy-dogged service. A messenger
had brought Burton the humiliating news; two days later he 'left
Damascus for ever; started at three o'clock in the dark, with a big

lantern; all my men crying... *Ever again?* Felt soft. Dismissal igno-
minious, at the age of fifty, without a month's notice, or wages, or
character.'

To Burton, Trieste could never compensate for the loss of
Damascus – still less for the loss of India. Cosmopolitan as it was, it
was not the East. Bram Stoker – who was to write the (deeply
erotic) novel *Dracula* a quarter of a century later – commented that
the Consul's job in Trieste was 'looked on as a resting-place for a
man of letters'. As such, it was far beneath the high-profile app-
ointment that Burton believed was owed to him as an acknowledged
expert on the East. It was, in fact, a profound disappointment, as his
wife Isabel acknowledged: 'Commercial work in a small, civilized
European seaport, under-ranked and underpaid,' she snorted,
'cannot be considered compensation for the loss of wild Oriental
diplomatic life.' Self-pityingly Burton compared himself to the poet
Ovid, exiled by the Emperor Augustus to Tomis, on the Black Sea.
'I, too,' Burton wrote, 'am a neglected book gnawed by the moth',
'a stream dammed up with mud', 'a Phalaris, clapped, for nothing
in particular, into the belly of a brazen bull'. Ironically – and Burton
would have been well aware of the irony – Ovid's exile probably
stemmed from the offence caused by his erotic poem, the *Ars
Amatoria*, or *Art of Love*. For Burton, by contrast, exile in Trieste was
to allow him to make up for a lifetime of disappointment. Isabel
had complained 'how his writings have kept him back from place
or power', but now the translation of erotic literature would be his
life's crowning achievement. One of Burton's first and greatest projects was the preparation of an English edition of the *Kamasutra*.

In their first summer in Trieste, in 1873, the journalist Alfred Bate
Richards paid a visit to the the Burtons. Richards was an old friend
and sparring partner – Burton apparently mastered him with the

sword, but was no match for Richards' punch in the boxing ring – and had been one of only eight people to attend the couple's clandestine wedding in 1861. Richards began his account of the Burtons' fourth-floor, seafront apartment by describing the prominent evidence of Isabel's profound Catholicism in her private rooms:

> Thus far the belongings are all of the cross, but no sooner
> are we landed in the little drawing-rooms than signs of the
> crescent appear. These rooms, opening one into another, are
> bright with Oriental hangings, with trays and dishes of gold
> and burnished silver, fantastic goblets, chibouques with great
> amber mouth-pieces, and Eastern treasure made of odorous
> woods.

Damascus may have been lost to Richard Burton but he was clearly doing his best to turn his rooms into at least a simulacrum of Constantinople.

To Alfred Bate Richards' eye, Burton himself, with his 'hands and feet of Oriental smallness', seemed to have undergone some sort of exotic transformation. 'The Eastern and distinctly Arab look of the man,' he wrote, 'is made more pronounced by prominent cheek-bones (across one of which is the scar of a javelin cut), by closely-cropped black hair, just tinged with grey, and a pair of piercing, black, gipsy-looking eyes.' By the time Charles Ashbee, the son of the erotic bibliographer Henry Spencer Ashbee, met Burton – in the late 1880s, after his landmark translation of the *Arabian Nights* – the Oriental metamorphosis was complete.

> He was the Djinn who brought the hatchet and the cord, he
> was Agib losing his eye, the Barber extracting the bone from

the hunch-back's throat, the Fire worshipper that bound
Prince Assad, the Bird catcher who snared King Beder, he was
Aladdin's Drug merchant, the African magician, king of the
Djinns – there was no end to the possible transformations of
that appalling beard of his.

For young Ashbee, Burton's magical ability to auto-transmogrify
was as much the point as his Oriental appearance. Other writers
who met Burton in the 1870s were more impressed by the erotic
power that seemed to emanate from him. Bram Stoker, who met
Burton on the Dublin to Belfast train in August 1878, found him
'dark and forceful, and masterful, and ruthless. I have never seen so
iron a countenance.' Later, he suggestively told his friend, the
actor-manager Sir Henry Irving: 'He is steel! He would go through
you like a sword!' The writer Frank Harris, now best known for his
candid sexual confessional, *My Life and Loves*, met a sixty-year-old
Burton at a party in London. In his *Contemporary Portraits* he claimed
Burton had 'an untamed air about him... the naked, dark eyes –
imperious, aggressive eyes, by no means friendly; the heavy jaws
and prominent hard chin gave him a desperate air'. Burton's fascination for dirty talk – erotic and sadistic – and matters Oriental
also caught Harris's ear. Burton, he said,

> had a curious liking for 'sabre-cuts of Saxon speech' – all such
> words as come hot from life's mint... He would tell stories of
> Indian philosophy or of perverse negro habits of lust and canni-
> balism, or would listen to descriptions of Chinese cruelty and
> Russian self-mutilation till the stars paled out. Catholic in his
> admiration and liking for all greatness, it was the abnormalities
> and not the divinities of men that fascinated him.

The eccentric poet, Wilfred Scawen Blunt, agreed that 'in his talk he affected an extreme brutality'. Blunt observed that Burton's eyes were 'like a wild beast's' but, perceptively, he spotted something constrained, claiming that Burton reminded him of 'a black leopard, caged but unforgiving'.

For Burton the fighting animal, Trieste was his cage; for Burton the resplendently costumed Orientalist, it was his straitjacket. Burton yearned for the East with a lover's passion. Throughout their time in Trieste, Burton and his wife intrigued with an almost manic persistence to be moved to a worthier and more easterly posting, from that of special commissioner in charge of suppressing the continued slave trade in the Red Sea, to the post of British Consul in Morocco. Burton wrote to his old friend and patron, Richard Monckton Milnes, complaining that he knew 'every stick and stone within a radius of 100 miles... And now I'm sick of it. I want to be up and doing.' In February 1873 he asked Milnes, 'Why does not the F.O. make me resident at Cabul and find out what Russia is doing there? I can ride, outwalk my mare here, speak Pushtu (Afghan), Persian, Hindustani and so forth.' He wrote a similar letter to Queen Victoria's secret envoy, Lieutenant-General William Wylde, adding, 'Do put in a word for me and send me rejoicing Eastward Ho!'

In the spring of 1874, it seemed for a while as if there would be little time for any kind of future, Oriental or otherwise. During an Alpine ascent of the Schneeburg, Burton decided to spend the night out in the snow, instead of inside a mountain hut, with his companions. He wore only light clothing. It was a typical gesture – a mixture of bravado and a real determination to maintain his body in its iron condition. Burton evidently wanted to prove to himself that he was still up to it. He was not: within days, he fell seriously ill. An inflammation in the groin centred on what was described as a 'tumour', and bouts of severe fever over a period of a month brought him close to death. On hearing the news, Swinburne protested how great the loss would have been to his country, made all the greater because 'he has been neglected and thrown away with all his marvellous and unequalled powers'. Swinburne saw to the bitter heart of the matter: his friend's life as yet lacked its crowning accomplishment. Burton himself recognized as much. His diary entry for 6 December 1883 recorded his profound dissatisfaction. 'To-day, eleven years ago, I came here,' he wrote; 'what a shame!!!'

While Burton floundered and raged in Trieste, his friend Foster Fitzgerald Arbuthnot was busy in India with his quest: to locate a manuscript of this 'book of Vatsyayana'. The theory outlined in Ashbee's *Catena Librorum Absconditorum*, that 'no Sanscrit library was complete' without a copy, was all very well but Arbuthnot found the reality very different. On closer enquiry, he was told that the work was 'very rare' and 'most difficult now to obtain in its entire state'. The problem, it seemed, was the parlous state of Indian libraries. Under the British Raj — established in 1858, almost ten years after Burton left India — it was not just traditional royal government that was breaking down; the old structures of scholarship were suffering too. Religious learning was relatively safe in autonomous monasteries and religious institutions, but areas of scholarship traditionally under court patronage, notably the erotic sciences, had long been under threat. The royal libraries were mouldering, their collections sold off or even disposed of outright.

The problem was compounded by the fact that, in the early 1870s, the British study of Sanskrit was only starting to recover from decades of official neglect. The golden age of Wilkins, Jones,

Wilson and Colebrooke had been followed by an era marked by clashes between the 'Orientalists', who favoured the promotion of 'native' learning under the patriarchal guiding hand of the British, and the 'Anglicists', who wanted India to adopt English as the language not only of government, but of education too. In 1835, the great essayist and colonial legislator Thomas Babington Macaulay had outlawed education in languages other than English, declaring that 'all the historical information that has been collected to form all the books written in the Sanskrit language is less valuable than what may be found in the most paltry abridgements used at preparatory schools in England'. Setting Macaulay's prejudice aside, he could not have known of the existence of even a tiny fraction of the Sanskrit texts that were to be discovered some forty years later.

The West was on the cusp of a veritable Oriental renaissance in the 1870s, and many British Indologists felt that it was Britain's imperial *duty* to be in the vanguard, Foster Fitzgerald Arbuthnot among them. England, he urged, 'ought to lead the way in keeping the world informed on all subjects connected with Oriental literature'. Arbuthnot was notorious for his use of a four-in-hand, a fast and somewhat dangerous type of carriage whose four horses were managed by one skilful driver alone, and he reached for a familiar metaphor, arguing that, 'Surely the time has not arrived for her to take a back seat on that coach, and to let other nations do a work which she ought to do herself.' If England did not take the lead, Arbuthnot knew that other countries would. Germany, with its ever-growing ranks of linguists and philologists, was a particular threat.

Fortunately for the imperial cause, one of the key German scholars of Sanskrit, Johann Georg Bühler, was working on the side of the British. As he was a professor of Eastern Languages and Ancient History at Bombay's Elphinstone College, and was also an enthusiastic member of the Royal Asiatic Society, the nationality of 'George Buehler' – as his British contemporaries called him – was not necessarily a problem. He had begun collecting Sanskrit manuscripts for his own private collection, but repeatedly found himself outbid – often by a Bombay antiquarian, Bhau Daji. Funding was one problem, Bühler's non-Indian status another. As Bühler put it, 'the orthodox sentiments of the majority of the Brahmans, who considered the traffic with "the face of Sarasvati" to be impious and hated the very thought of giving their sacred lore to the *Mlechchhas* [foreigners], made operations very difficult'. By relying on 'unknown Brahmans who secretly came to my house in Puna, being in great pecuniary distress', however, Bühler managed to build up a collection of some 400-odd manuscripts, some old, others copied. He began to realize that the sorry state of 'native learning' meant that time was running out. He observed: 'unsaleable MSS in Gujarat usually find their way into the hands of the Borah paper-manufacturers and are destroyed.' Similar dangers threatened the preservation of manuscripts in other regions.

In 1868, Bühler was given official permission to investigate the holdings of India's old libraries on behalf of the Education Service, as part of a monumentally overambitious government scheme to catalogue every Sanskrit manuscript in India and abroad. The actual legwork largely devolved on the various branches of the Royal Asiatic Society, which sent out scholars – British and Indian – on extended library tours of the various presidencies and provinces of India, 'to examine the manuscripts reported upon, to seek new manuscripts, to purchase manuscripts procurable at reasonable rates, and to have copies made of such manuscripts as are unique or otherwise desirable, but which the possessors refuse to part with'. This was a new world: under the efficient patronage of the Raj, the casual, gentlemanly investigations of Wilson's, Colebrooke's and even Burton's day were to be a thing of the past.

Letters were sent out all over the country, and local *pandits* and schoolmasters dispatched to persuade Brahmin librarians to relinquish their jealous hold on their sacred texts. One eminent British scholar, Peter Peterson, complained that his eyes were clouded by a 'dense and far-spreading' cloud that obscured the history of Sanskrit literature. To dispel that cloud, he urgently needed more manuscripts. He was clear-sighted enough to recognize, however, that the 'native community' was working, relatively speaking, in bright sunshine. Agents were chosen, therefore, for their ability to wheedle their way into the confidences of Brahmin librarians as much as for their scholarship. Georg Bühler could testify from personal experience to the difficulties of the work for Europeans. As he wrote to the Director of Public Instruction in his report for the winter of 1874–5:

In May I received letters from the Sir Sûbâ, and from my agent stating that the S'rîpûj had come back and had agreed to show me his books. I, accordingly, made on May 16 a second journey to Pathan, which a sand storm and several thunderstorms that surprised me in the open field, made anything but a pleasure trip. On my arrival the S'rîpûj seemed to have changed his mind. He at first tried to put me off by showing me one *kothalî* or bag full of dilapidated paper MSS. On being pressed further, he produced one after another six more such *kothalîs*, which

contained altogether between 6–700 MSS. He then solemnly
assured me that this was all he had – an asseveration which I
refused to accept as true.

Bühler's persistence was eventually rewarded and in the early 1870s
the manuscripts came rolling in by the thousands.

Bühler and his colleagues targeted some 14,000 known texts in
Sanskrit and other languages, but the *Kamasutra* was not to be found
anywhere on their wish-lists. In fact, the entire field of *kama shastra*
was strangely ignored. It was not as if scholars were unaware of the
existence of 'erotological' material. Even early missionaries had
complained about the wickedness of Indian scriptures, although
they were probably referring to the tradition of popular epics, such
as the *Mahabharata*, and the polygamous philanderings of Hindu
gods. In the early nineteenth century, however, the missionary
Jean-Antoine Dubois, author of *Description of the Character, Manners
and Customs of the People of India, and of their Institutions, Religious and Civil*
(1816), actually described texts from the *kama shastra* tradition
proper. He described finding 'abominable books' treating of 'the
most filthy and disgusting forms of debauchery', 'the art of giving
variety to sexual pleasures' and 'the decoction of beverages calcu-
lated to excite the passions'. It sounds remarkably as if the Abbé
Dubois had picked up a copy of the *Ananga Ranga* or *Ratirahasya*, if
not the *Kamasutra* itself.

Georg Bühler may not have targeted *kama shastra* texts, but some
still found their way into the *kothalî* after *kothalî* of manuscripts that
were bought and eventually catalogued for the government. In
1874, the German scholar Hermann Jacobi actually found and
copied a manuscript of the *Kamasutra* while travelling around
Rajputana (modern Rajasthan), on behalf of Bühler. But like H.T.

Colebrooke and Horace Hayman Wilson before him, Herr Jacobi did not see fit to write about his discovery. (His reputation thus protected, Jacobi went on to become the respected Professor of Sanskrit at Bonn, and his magnificent private library – including the forgotten *Kamasutra* – was eventually sold to the British Museum.) Even if Jacobi mentioned his curious find to Bühler, the latter kept quiet about it too. Like most of his colleagues, Bühler was distinctly prudish in the face of the more explicit references to sex in the Hindu erotic tradition. When Bühler translated the *Laws of Manu*, in 1886, he squeamishly rendered the original's prohibition of 'sex in non-human females, in a man, in a menstruating woman, in something other than a vagina', as a ban on 'a bestial crime, or an unnatural crime with a female'.

The field remained open to bolder scholars and enthusiasts. At some point in 1874 or possibly early 1875, Foster Fitzgerald Arbuthnot contacted Bühler in Bombay to ask for his assistance. The *pandits* who had helped him with the *Ananga Ranga* had proved entirely unable to locate a copy of the legendary Ur-text, Vatsyayana's *Kamasutra*. Frustratingly, a manuscript was proving to be quite as rare as they had assured him it was. Did Bühler, perhaps, have any idea where or how such a manuscript might be found? Bühler regretted that he couldn't assist Arbuthnot directly. Perhaps he didn't know of Jacobi's discovery, or didn't want to admit that he had heard of it. But he did know another way to help. Arbuthnot recounted the story to Henry Spencer Ashbee. 'After some inquiry', he recalled,

Dr. Bühler, now Sanscrit professor in Vienna, but then employed in the Educational Department in Bombay, recommended to me the Pundit BHUGWANTLAL INDRAJI. This Pundit had already been frequently employed by Mr. James Fergusson, and Mr. James Burgess, in copying and translating for them writings found on copper plates, on stone boundaries, and in temples in many parts of India.

Arbuthnot arranged to interview Indraji. He did not know it, but this encounter would set the *Kamasutra* on its slow journey towards the West.

Bhagvanlal Indraji was uniquely qualified to help Arbuthnot in his search. Born in Junagadh, north of Bombay, in 1839, he had been brought up in the traditional Brahmin way. He learned Sanskrit from his father, who belonged to a hereditary Gujarati sub-caste producing mostly doctors, astrologers or readers and interpreters of Hindu sacred literature. He acquired a detailed knowledge of Ayurvedic medicine, developing a candour about matters physical that would later serve him well. While his elder brother followed tradition, becoming the head of a Sanskrit school under the authority of the Nawab of Junagadh, Indraji didn't care for what he later called 'the abstruse lore of the *shastras*'. He was attracted, instead, by 'the historical traditions of his native province'. One British resident of Junagadh, a certain Colonel Lang, fondly called him 'the little antiquarian'. As an adult eking out a living in business in Bombay, he found time to work as the pupil and assistant of the antiquarian and archaeologist, Bhau Daji – the very same Daji who repeatedly frustrated Bühler in his quest for manuscripts.

Between 1861 and Daji's death in 1874, Indraji made numerous exhausting journeys across India on his patron's behalf, unflagging in his search for ancient coins, inscriptions and manuscripts. An obituarist recalled his 'indomitable energy' and the qualities that underpinned it.

He pursued knowledge under difficulties purely for its own
sake, without regard to ulterior advantages. And he pursued
it steadily, ardently, and with remarkable success. For the sake
of knowledge, he spent days and nights in lonely jungles, in
caves, and monasteries, at times in the neighbourhood of the
denizens of forests, regardless of heat or cold, hunger or thirst,
comfort or discomfort.

In May 1874, following Bhau Daji's death, Indraji was forced to consider his position. European sponsorship was perhaps the only
viable way to continue his work, but while he had learned a little
English on his travels, his acquaintance among European enthusiasts was small. Georg Bühler recalled that Indraji suddenly paid
him a visit in the spring of 1875, 'while I was temporarily staying in
Bombay for some official business'. Bühler took a liking to him,
despite his guest's initial diffidence, later recalling that 'after his
natural shyness and distrust of Europeans, which, I think, had been
implanted artificially, were overcome, he became a most amiable
companion'.

Bühler, then, had no qualms about recommending Indraji to
Arbuthnot. His background had given him access to the right kinds
of library, his training allowed him to recognize and understand
ancient manuscripts, while his experience of Europeans gave him
insight into the likely importance of a work such as the *Kamasutra*.
When the two men met, Arbuthnot found himself face to face
with a simply dressed man with soft, cow-like eyes, refined features
and a markedly humble, almost diffident manner. There was
something determined about his chin, however, and Indraji's unaf-
fected demeanour did not quite conceal his passion for history or
his enthusiasm for the great work of unveiling India's heritage.

Conversation was awkward at first, shifting between Indraji's halting English and Arbuthnot's Gujarati, but eventually, across the linguistic divide, a thrilling truth emerged. By extraordinary chance, Indraji himself owned a copy of the *Kamasutra*. Some five years previously, he told an astonished Arbuthnot, he had discovered it in a library in Benares and, recognizing its rarity, had ordered it to be specially copied. He could even show the book to Arbuthnot, if he so wished.

The offer of a manuscript no doubt clinched the deal. Unfortunately, as Indraji told a crestfallen Arbuthnot, the text in his possession was incomplete. Most critically, it lacked the crucial *Jayamangala* commentary that would help explain the many obscurities of the original. Arbuthnot did not hesitate. He engaged Indraji's services at once and set him to work on compiling a complete text of the *Kamasutra* in Sanskrit by tracking down any other manuscripts that could be found. Indraji accordingly wrote to the many contacts he had made in libraries across India during his long journeys. It was like an all-points bulletin for Brahmin librarians. *Kamasutra* manuscripts were wanted; good British money would be paid for information leading to capture. Arbuthnot, in turn, wrote to Burton to let him know that the great project was at last under way, and Burton relayed the exciting news to Richard Monckton Milnes, up at Fryston Hall.

Burton's revelatory letter is dated 'Trieste (purgatory)', 2 March 1875. 'Caro Milnes,' he began. 'As the yank said before the big fight with the Bear "God Almighty it's not often I bother you", but now I have really something worth telling you. Boy Bunny has been behaving like a trump and giving up his mind (as I, his Pa, have ever advised) to the study pure and simple of Hindú erotic literature.' Triumphantly, Burton asked his friend to go to his secret, erotological library, find the copy of the *Ananga Ranga* shelved there – the one translated by 'two ruffians' – and open it at page 46. There he would find an allusion to a certain 'Vátsyáyana Muni', a character who, Burton was delighted to report, was mysterious no longer. Thanks to Bunny's researches, it was now at last known that this Vatsyayana was nothing less than

> the father of *ars amoris* in Sanskrit, lived about AD.100 and wrote a book in 7 chapters that treats '*de omni re scribili et femina*'. He also quotes from no less than 7 other authors whose works have wholly perished. One of his chapters treats of courtesans, another of managing one's own wife and a 3rd of managing other mens wives. It is *the* standard book.

A book containing 'everything that is writable about women' was a book Milnes would surely, dearly wish to have in his library. There was the problem of finding a complete copy, however, and then the small matter of getting it translated. Fortunately, Burton had a man in the field, 'Bunny' Arbuthnot, who 'has ordered the book from Benares, where the "Holy Sage" lived and will begin to translate at once'. (No mention was made, of course, of the Indian *pandits* who would do most of the work.) Burton played down his own ambitions for the book, teasing his old friend with the prospect that 'If it is thoroughly moral I hope to add some notes. And why, when old age creeps on, should one not devote oneself to popularising the precepts of the wise?' Milnes was well accustomed to reading between the lines. Burton, he knew, would wait and see quite how *obscene* the book turned out to be before making up his mind whether it was worth adorning with the scholarly veil of his learned footnotes.

If Vatsyayana's book of love turned out to be everything Burton hoped it was, this was the last opportunity to make his mark. On his Mecca pilgrimage, over twenty years earlier, he had overheard Arab traders talking about the African sources of the Nile. He later described his intense elation, the numinous clarity of a moment in which he felt he had found '*the mot de l'enigme*, the way to make the egg stand upright, the rending of the veil of Isis' – though, as it turned out, it was left to another man, John Hanning Speke, to rend the veil and claim the glory. When Arbuthnot told Burton that the *Kamasutra* was found, that '*the* standard book' on sexual wisdom was (once more?) within his grasp, even if not yet in a complete form, he must have felt a similar sensation. If he couldn't be the first man to physically rend the veil of Isis by standing triumphant at the sources of the Nile, perhaps he could at least be the first man to penetrate the 'Isis' of Indian erotic wisdom.

Burton resolved to make a return journey to India before the end of 1875. Surprisingly, given her popular reputation as a Catholic prude, he owed the idea to his wife, Isabel. As a young, unmarried diarist, Isabel had implored the fates to 'let me go with the husband of my choice to battle, nurse him in his tent, follow him under the fire of ten thousand muskets... Why with spirits, brains, and energies, are women to exist upon worsted work and household accounts? It makes me sick and I will not do it.' It was not only Richard Burton who was reluctant to live comfortably in Trieste. Isabel had heard, and read, endless stories of her husband's early days in India and she proposed returning there as a way to rediscover and savour his youth. Whether or not she had also heard stories of a certain Vatsyayana and his book of love is unknown.

Burton had ambivalent feelings about returning to the 'fatal land'. In his absence, the heady days of East India Company rule had given way to the tight-lipped conventions of the British Raj; and in the wake of the Mutiny of 1857, Burton-style fraternization with the natives was more frowned upon than ever. For Burton, the very journey was less a matter of rediscovering his youth than of being confronted with his age – he had become stiff and weak in the aftermath of his illness and may have struggled with impotence. In his *Life of Sir Richard Burton*, Thomas Wright described how as the ship passed through the Middle East the old warhorse repeatedly asked after former comrades and acquaintances:

> On reaching Yambu, Burton enquired whether Sa'ad the robber chief, who had attacked the caravan in the journey to Mecca days, still lived; and was told that the dog long since made his last foray, and was now safe in Jehannum… At Aden Burton enquired after his old Harar companions. Shahrazad was still in Aden, the coquettish Dunyazad in Somaliland, the Kalandar had been murdered by the Isa tribe, and The End of Time had 'died a natural death' – that is to say, somebody had stuck a spear into him (story in *Nights*). Bombay was reached on February 2nd.

On arrival in Bombay, Burton found his oldest and closest friend very much alive. The Burtons stayed with Arbuthnot at his summer bungalow, beside the sea at Bandra, twelve miles from Bombay proper. It was a fine house, the fruit of thirty years' hard work in the government service. Isabel was utterly charmed, both by the residence and by her husband's bachelor friend, who took them out on long drives in his daring four-in-hand carriage. Together, the trio toured the sights of Burton's youth and were entertained at parties by local boys dressed as tigers, who performed 'native dances' that Isabel found 'exceedingly graceful'. Arbuthnot also introduced the Burtons to his local friends, including the eccentric Hungarian scholar Edward Rehatsek. Recently retired from a professorship at Wilson College, Rehatsek had sequestered himself, hermit-like, in a tiny house built of local reeds. Dressed in threadbare clothing and unencumbered by servants, he worked furiously on endless translations and submissions to the journal of the Bombay Royal Asiatic Society. Together the party debated Arbuthnot's scheme to revive the Royal Asiatic Translation Fund, a project designed to rescue texts in Sanskrit and other languages from linguistic obscurity.

The conversation also turned to the erotic. Arbuthnot explained that he was still waiting for a copy of the *Kamasutra* that included the complete *Jayamangala* – a commentary which, his *pandit* Indraji assured him, was absolutely necessary in order for the translation proper to begin. Rehatsek revealed that he too had been doing research into erotology, albeit in his own field of Persian and Arabic texts, and had an intimate knowledge of hitherto unpublished Persian erotological classics. At this point Burton must have set out his big, bold idea. With the help of friends and contacts at home such as Milnes and the men of the Cannibal Club – plus the services of less prudish printers than those who had aborted the *Ananga Ranga* scheme – these extraordinary works of Eastern erotics could be made available to an eager readership in the West. Burton explained that together they could concoct a spurious 'club' that would masquerade as a publishing house. They would call this club... the Kama Shastra Society. And the censors be damned! Isabel recalled that the three men had 'many a laugh' over the idea, describing the society as a 'bogie name' invented 'for the purpose of puzzling people when they wished to bring out any book that was not for the drawing room table'.

Of course, before it could grace any English table, drawing room or otherwise, the *Kamasutra* needed to be translated. And by the time Indraji finally received delivery of a new manuscript containing the *Jayamangala* commentary from Benares – his manuscript still has the copyist's date 'Samvat 1933', which translates as between roughly March 1876 and March 1877 – Burton had returned to Trieste. The work, however, would go on without him. Together with his own, original *Kamasutra* manuscript, and two others that had arrived from Calcutta and Jaipur, Indraji now had four texts to work with. 'The first thing then to be done,' Arbuthnot recalled, 'was to find a man competent to prepare the Sanscrit text, and after that a competent translator.' The man competent to prepare the text was clearly Indraji. A yellowing note in Arbuthnot's smooth hand, pasted into a bound copy of Indraji's revised Sanskrit text, explains how the work was done:

> The accompanying manuscript is corrected by me after comparing 4 different copies of the work. I had the assistance of the Commentary called 'Jayamangla' for correcting the portion from I to V Chapter but I found great difficulty in correcting the remaining portion; because with the exception of the copy thereof which was tolerably correct, all the other copies I had were far too incorrect, however I took that portion as correct in which the majority of the copies had agreed.

An almost identical explanation appeared in Arbuthnot's introduction to the 1883 edition.

The identity of the 'competent translator' is more mysterious —
and problematic. Arbuthnot declared only that, from the cor-
rected Sanskrit manuscript, 'the English translation was made'. No
mention was made of how much of the work was done by
Arbuthnot and how much by Indraji — leaving aside, for the
moment, the whole question of the extent of Burton's eventual
contribution. In the nineteenth century, it was common practice
for European scholars to employ *pandits* to elucidate difficult
passages in a text and to help them prepare translations in draft
form. In turning to Bhagvanlal Indraji, Arbuthnot the senior civil
servant would normally have been conscious not so much of having a co-translator as a specialized but junior assistant. Indraji's lack
of fluent English — attested by numerous contemporaries — would,
under normal circumstances, have further edged him into a
subordinate role.

But translating the *Kamasutra* into English was not at all a
'normal' process. Arbuthnot later recalled that in their original
interview he had found that Indraji understood English 'sufficiently', but he did not, it seems, mean 'sufficiently to translate
from Sanskrit with me'. In 1898, the German Sanskritist Hermann
Oldenberg reported that 'the good Bühler' — by then ensconced in
his professorial chair at Vienna — had told him that the *Kamasutra*
was actually translated *in its entirety* into Gujarati by Indraji, and
that this version was then translated into English by a 'native clerk'
who knew no Sanskrit, and that 'a high official' in the Indian Civil
Service — that is, Arbuthnot — had then 'revised it to make sure the
linguistic expression was correct'. (If Indraji was translating into
Gujarati, he was simply following his usual practice; every single
one of Indraji's many papers on archaeology was written in

Gujarati and only afterwards translated into English by European friends and supporters.) If Oldenberg was right, translating the *Kamasutra* must have been a titillating affair for Arbuthnot, as Vatsyayana's text slowly emerged from behind veil after veil of language: first Sanskrit, then Gujarati, then *pandit*'s English, and lastly Arbuthnot's own, plain – naked, one might call it – prose.

To produce an accurate translation in this laborious way is an extraordinary feat. Yet it seems this really was the way Arbuthnot and the *pandits* worked. Bühler's story was backed up by the great Indian architectural historian, James Burgess, who later employed Indraji and reported that not only had Bühler told him Indraji was doing paid work on the *Kamasutra*, but that Indraji had been actively searching for 'a student who knew English, to translate for him'. This 'student' – surely the same person as Oldenberg's 'native clerk' – was, then, the first man ever to render the *Kamasutra* into English (albeit from Indraji's Gujarati version, not the original Sanskrit). Frustratingly, of all the men who worked on this furtive project, he has most completely receded from view. Arbuthnot revealed his name to Henry Spencer Ashbee, sparingly admitting that 'with the aid then of another Brahman by name SHIVARAM PARSHURAM BHIDE, then studying at the University of Bombay, and well acquainted both with Sanscrit and English... a complete translation... was prepared.' Arbuthnot's only other remark about Bhide was that he was 'now employed in the service of His Highness the Guicowar at Baroda'. This is the only clue to his later career.

Baroda (now Vadodara, in Gujarat) was a semi-autonomous kingdom within the British-run state of Bombay – close enough to the city that Burton had travelled there as a young soldier to watch sports put on by His Highness such as 'a fight between two elephants with cut tusks, or a caged tiger and a buffalo'. In the 1870s, the Guicowar – or Gaikwar, or Gaekwad – was a less blood-thirsty figure. Maharaja Sayaji Rao III had come to the throne as a twelve-year-old child, in 1875 – after his predecessor had been deposed for attempting to poison the British resident – and within four years he had founded a college for the study of traditional Hindu astrology and Sanskrit language and literature. This was a fledgling, but significant, Indian-nationalist response to British Indology. It seems likely that Shivaram Parshuram Bhide worked at this college, putting his student experience of working on the *Kamasutra* to good use, no doubt. Perhaps he too was seized with Indraji's passion for collecting; at any rate, by the end of Sayaji Rao's reign, Baroda had over 13,000 Sanskrit manuscripts.

Unlike Bhide, Bhagvanlal Indraji went on to become a cele-brated figure – if not for his work on the *Kamasutra*. Bühler put him in touch with a number of European archaeologists who needed a 'man in the field' and over a decade of indefatigable travels he became a leading authority on Indian palaeography and early history, settling the troublesome controversy over ancient number symbols, discovering the famous stupa at Supara with J. MacNabb Campbell, and bequeathing to the British Museum a valuable collection of coins and archaeological fragments – including the beautiful 'Lion Capital' from Mathura. 'His amiable frank charac-ter, his keen intelligence, and his extensive learning, made him very dear to me,' Bühler wrote, and his feelings were shared by many European scholars. Indraji's obituarist, Oliver Codrington, recalled in 1888 that he 'had no wish for money nor luxuries... and his one luxury was the enjoyment of any appreciation of his work by scholars in Europe, which was slow in coming to him, but did come at last'. Indraji was indeed elected an honorary member of the Bombay branch of the Royal Asiatic Society in April 1877 and, after being invited to submit a paper to the Oriental Congress held in Leyden, in 1883, was made a Doctor of Letters. However, neither institution would have had an inkling of what was, perhaps, his greatest achievement: transforming a hoary and almost vanished work of Sanskrit literature into the world's best-known work of erotology.

Restoring the *pandits* to their proper place of honour as translators does not mean that Arbuthnot should be knocked right off his podium. Unless a draft translation somehow magically appears from some lost box of papers, it's impossible to know exactly how the work was done. In his brilliant, *Kamasutra*-obsessed novel, *Love in a Dead Language*, Lee Siegel mocks the idea that any such draft will one day turn up. A character finds a (fictional) manuscript in the (real) Burton collection at the Huntington Library which contains what he calls the *pandit*'s 'first stab'. The passage that eventually became 'The lovers may also sit on the terrace of the palace or house, and enjoy the moonlight, and carry on an agreeable conversation. At this time, too, while the woman lies in his lap, with her face towards the moon, the citizen should show her the different planets, the morning star, the polar star, and the seven Rishis, or Great Bear' is rendered, instead, as 'Veranda going for moon orb watching, Sahib and Mensahib are talking, talking, most talkatively. Sab is saying this star and that star are this and that.' Of course, the early drafts can have looked nothing like this, and the extraordinary accuracy of the final translation proves that Arbuthnot did far more than simply rephrase Shivaram Parshuram Bhide's English. He worked closely with both *pandits*. One can only imagine the trilingual cacophony of the translation sessions at his house in Bombay.

Whether or not Richard Burton should share the laurels as translator is more controversial still. Just as Burton's fellow Indian Army officers sensed a shadow of moral corruption following him about, similar suspicions have long been harboured by Burton scholars concerning his abilities as a translator. According to some, his later translation of the *Arabian Nights* lifted whole passages from that of his rival, John Payne. This rumour has tainted Burton's role in the publication of the *Kamasutra* as well — but with much better reason. Most of his biographers gloss over the problem, apparently unwilling to suffer the posthumous loss of one of their hero's most remarkable achievements. But there is little evidence that Burton was much of a Sanskrit scholar, for all his much-vaunted fluency in anything from two dozen to forty languages and dialects — depending how you count them. The Indian Army required its translators to be expert in living vernaculars, not dead scholarly languages (although in mid-nineteenth-century India, Sanskrit's status was something like that of Latin in Enlightenment Europe). Burton did at least dabble in Sanskrit, taking lessons in 1843, soon after passing his examination in Hindustani. On this basis, he would have been able to 'read' a Sanskrit text with the close assistance of a *munshi* or teacher — and very often, this was exactly the practice of British Orientalists. But Burton, we now know, had left India before Indraji started work.

Instead, Burton's contribution was that of a celebrity editor. Arbuthnot must have somehow arranged for the completed translation to be delivered to his friend at Trieste. Perhaps he used Fred Hankey's old tricks of smuggling documents in the diplomatic bag, or conveniently hidden in the overcoats of well-respected friends; perhaps he waited until he himself returned to England. Certainly, Burton set about giving the *Kamasutra* a final polish and adding a few of his famous footnotes. Quite how vigorous that polish was remains unclear. In 1963, the *Kamasutra*'s latter-day editor, W.G. Archer, guessed that 'Left to himself, Arbuthnot could not have given it rhythmical vigour and assured style.' Burton, in other words, sexed it up. It is true that Arbuthnot's later, solo literary efforts are bluntly and sometimes awkwardly written, but the style of the translated *Kamasutra* is not especially assured or vigorous. It is, for the most part, obtrusively plain. In his translators' 'Concluding Remarks', Arbuthnot referred admiringly to Vatsyayana's unadorned style. 'As a collection of facts, told in plain and simple language,' he explained, 'it must be remembered that in those early days there was apparently no idea of embellishing the work, either with a literary style, a flow of language, or a quantity of superfluous padding.'

Burton's own, solo translations revel in the florid, the rococo and above all the superfluous. The Arabist Robert Irwin criticized his *Arabian Nights* for being replete with 'Victorian vulgarisms' and alleged it had a vocabulary that lurched 'between the erudite and plain earthy'. The English *Kamasutra*, by contrast, cleverly finds a third path, allowing it to avoid the two extremes: the words *lingam* and *yoni* are used throughout to refer to the penis and vagina. Surprisingly, while both are indeed Sanskrit words, Vatsyayana's original scarcely uses the terms at all – the *lingam*, for instance, rears its head just three times. The choice was probably less a matter of draping a verbal fig-leaf over words that readers might find obscene; as the next chapter will show, Burton in particular was resolutely opposed to pusillanimous expurgation. It was, instead, a clever solution to the lack of an acceptably neutral register for talking about sex in English. It was neither erudite nor earthy, neither gross nor gynaecological.

It was, however, misleadingly religious. *Lingam* and *yoni* can mean 'penis' and 'vagina' in Sanskrit, but in the Hindu tradition the words had increasingly come to refer to symbols of divinity. By the late-nineteenth century, a Hindu *lingam* was no more a penis than a cross was a Roman instrument of execution; rather it was a stone column representing the ascetic power of the god Shiva. Arbuthnot knew this very well. One of his last forays into print was a curious little book entitled *Sex Mythology, Including an Account of the Masculine Cross.* It attempted to trace the use of phallic symbols in religious myths, and Arbuthnot observed that 'there is in Hindostan an emblem of great sanctity, which is known as the Linga-Yoni'. He even attempted to coin the word 'yonjic' to match 'phallic'.

When the *Kamasutra* was revived in the 1960s, the egregious *lingams* and *yonis* were in no small way responsible for the surprising new reputation the *Kamasutra* acquired as a spiritual text, rather than one that was merely pornographic. We cannot know who was reponsible for the words, but if Burton felt an original text wasn't flavoursome enough, he was more than capable of adding a pinch of exotic spice. A 'black slave' in the *Arabian Nights*, for instance, becomes 'a big slobbering blackamoor with rolling eyes which showed the whites, a truly hideous sight'. Burton occasionally inserted his own stories into the *Nights*, and he confessed that in his 'translation' of the *Vikram and the Vampire* stories, he had 'ventured to remedy the conciseness of their language, and to clothe the skeleton with flesh and blood'.

He certainly burst exuberantly into the *Ananga Ranga*. To the original's description of the lavish lovemaking chamber, he added what must have been the fruit of his experience of nineteenth-century Indian brothels:

Scattered about this apartment place musical instruments, especially the pipe and the lute; with refreshments, as cocoa-nut, betel-leaf and milk, which is so useful for retaining and restoring vigour; bottles of rose water and various essences, fans and *chauris* for cooling the air, and books containing amorous songs, and gladdening the glance with illustrations of love-postures. Splendid *divalgiri*, or wall lights, should gleam around the wall, reflected by a hundred mirrors.

The anachronistic addition of books 'with illustrations of love-postures' gives away the game, as does the wishful, Victorian recommendation that follows, namely that 'both man and woman should contend against any reserve, or false shame, giving themselves up in complete nakedness to unrestrained voluptuousness'. Burton also gave some narrative flow to the *Ananga Ranga*'s rather po-faced enumeration of sexual positions. At one point he makes 'the poet' interrupt his own text in order to address his audience — a king whose attention, one may infer, is flagging. 'O, Rajah,' he has the poet say,

'there are many other forms of congress, such as Harinasana, Sukrasana, Gardhabasana, and so forth; but they are not known to the people, and being useless as well as very difficult of performance, nay, sometimes so full of faults as to be excluded or prohibited, I have, therefore, not related them to you. But if you desire to hear anything more about postures, be pleased to ask, and your servant will attempt to satisfy your curiosity.' 'Right well!' exclaimed the king. 'I much wish to hear you describe the Purushayitabandha.' 'Hear, O Rajah,' resumed the poet, 'whilst I relate all that requires to be known concerning that form of congress.' Purushayitabandha is the reverse of what men usually practise. In this case the man lies upon his back, draws his wife upon him and enjoys her.

This is all vintage Burton; readers of one of the exceedingly rare original texts of the *Ananga Ranga* will search for this passage in vain.

Arbuthnot's 'Concluding Remarks' seem to give his swaggering collaborator a discreet rap over the knuckles: 'The author tells the world what he knows in very concise language,' he wrote, 'without any attempt to produce an interesting story.' Arbuthnot wanted no added 'local colour' in his *Kamasutra*. It would be entirely faithful to the original. Burton found himself confined to the bottom of the page, where he could squeeze in a few of his characteristically juicy footnotes. When Vatsyayana mentions the 'Lokayatikas' or materialist philosophers, Burton muses that 'These were certainly materialists who seemed to think that a bird in the hand was worth two in the bush.' When Vatsyayana observes that 'a courtesan, well dressed and wearing her ornaments, should sit or stand at the door of her house', Burton remarks that 'In England the lower classes of courtesans walk the streets; in India and other places in the East, they sit at the windows, or at the doors of their houses.' The presence of Burton the traveller – and Burton the anthropologist, treating the *Kamasutra* as if it described contemporary Indian society – is all too palpable.

Burton himself thought of the actual translation principally as his friend's work. In January 1883, he wrote to John Payne. 'Has Arbuthnot sent you his Vatsyayana?' he asked. In the autumn of 1888, Burton was corresponding regularly with the bookseller and publisher of erotica, Leonard Smithers, who had subscribed to the

Nights. In one of his letters to Smithers, now held in the Burton Collection at the Huntington Library, Burton attacked the 'bawdy publisher' Edward Avery, the leading (red) light of London's erotic book trade. 'Avery is a most pernicious rogue,' Burton wrote; 'he pirated my friend Arbuthnot's book and our joint work.' The book in question was, of course, the *Kamasutra*. Even if Burton had only an editor's role, it is hard not to ascribe the marvellous valedictory paragraph of the 'Concluding Remarks' to him.

> And though there may be disputes and discussions about
> the immortality of the body or the soul, nobody can deny the
> immortality of genius, which ever remains as a bright and
> guiding star to the struggling humanities of succeeding ages.
> This work, then, which has stood the test of centuries, has
> placed Vatsyayana among the immortals, and on This, and on
> Him no better elegy or eulogy can be written than the follow-
> ing lines: So long as lips shall kiss, and eyes shall see, / So long
> lives This, and This gives life to Thee.

These final words could as well have been written about Burton as about Vatsyayana – one certainly suspects that they were written *by* Burton, perhaps for that very reason. Arbuthnot, Bhide and Indraji may be owed the true credit for translating the *Kamasutra*, but without Burton's drive and determination, it would likely have festered among Arbuthnot's private papers, or at most have been printed in some obscure and learned journal of Asiatic studies. And without the shadow of Burton's notoriety, the *Kamasutra* would never have acquired its current global celebrity. In the next phase of the book's life, its rebirth in the West, Burton would come to the fore.

$\mathcal{B}$UT WHEN THE man makes advances by himself he must achieve intimacy from the very start. He sees her on a natural or contrived occasion. A natural occasion might occur near his own house, and a contrived one near the house of a friend, relative, minister of state, or doctor, at a wedding, sacrifice, festival, disaster, picnic, or other such occasion. When she sees him, he gazes at her constantly, sending signals, smoothing down his hair, snapping his nails, jingling his jewellery, chewing on his lower lip, and making various other pretences. When she is looking he talks with his friends about her under the pretext of discussing other matters; he displays his generosity and fondness for enjoyments. Seated on the lap of a friend, he shifts the position of his arms and legs, yawns, raises one eyebrow, speaks slowly, and listens to the woman's words.

Kamasutra
Book Five: Other Men's Wives
Chapter Two: Ways of Becoming Intimate
translated by Wendy Doniger and Sudhir Kakar (2002)

CHAPTER FIVE

A Doubtful Book in Old Age

Seven years passed between the translation of the *Kamasutra* into English and its final appearance in print. Burton squandered them, scrabbling around for money. He prospected for gold in the Midian and on the Gold Coast of West Africa, finding none, then launched a patent liver remedy under the label of 'Captain Burton's Tonic Bitters', which failed to find an eager market. His literary schemes were marginally more fruitful. He completed an oddly mannered translation of the sixteenth-century Portuguese poet Camoëns, and published *The Kasîdah of Hâjî Abdû El-Yezdi, A Lay of the Higher Law*, a whimsical poetic confection intended to echo Edward FitzGerald's phenomenally popular *Rubáiyát of Omar Khayyám*. The *Kasîdah* was among Burton's better poetic efforts, but it was not a commercial success, selling only one hundred copies before being remaindered. Burton tried to maintain the fiction that he was merely the poem's translator – as an author and as a traveller, he was still most comfortable in disguise. Few were fooled. One memorable quatrain captured Burton's proud autonomy and his growing obsession with posterity:

Do what thy manhood bids thee do,
      from none but self expect applause,
He noblest lives and noblest dies who
      makes and keeps his self-made laws.
All other life is living death, a world
      where none but phantoms dwell,
A breath, a wind, a sound, a voice,
      a tinkling of the camel-bell.

Foster Fitzgerald Arbuthnot, meanwhile, retired from his post as Bombay Collector and returned to England. He married the widow of a distant cousin, Elinor Stirling, in 1879, and settled into a comfortable villa in Shamley Green, a well-to-do village in Surrey. His cosy home-counties life was a world away from Bombay, Edward Rehatsek and the four-in-hand carriage, but it was not entirely conventional. Elinor Arbuthnot later became a supporter of the Fabian Society, while her husband – who was now President of the local Liberal Association – earned himself a certain local notoriety by choosing to be the first to leave church at the end of the Sunday service, thus enraging the infuriated squire, who railed against the flagrant breach of the 'long-admitted if unwritten rule of good manners in this parish'.

Privately, Arbuthnot was infringing 'good manners' in a far more purposeful fashion. In 1881, under the punning pseudonym 'Anaryan' he cobbled together a collection of popular stories from Sanskrit literature under the bland title of *Early Ideas*. The book contained a tantalizingly brief description of the *Kamasutra*. It was a first, cautious flirtation with the idea of having his translation printed, but Arbuthnot as yet lacked confidence. He bowdlerized his own translations, advising readers of *Early Ideas* that the

Kamasutra contained 'a good deal of matter connected with the domestic and private details of married life to which it is unnecessary to allude, and which are more fitted for Sanskrit manuscript than for English print'. Quoting a passage from the *Ananga Ranga*, he described how the Lotus-woman's 'mouth resembles the opening lotus-bud, and her perfume is as a lily which has newly burst'. This was a travesty of his earlier work. In his own 1873 translation, it had not been the Lotus-woman's 'mouth' that resembled the opening lotus bud, but her 'Yoni'; and it was not her 'perfume' that smelled lily-like, but her 'Love-seed'.

Arbuthnot was troubled less by obscene words than by the thought that they might reach the wrong ears. He warned his readers that while 'many books contain some good things', unfortunately they are too often 'mixed up with such a mass of padding that the gems of the work are lost in their surroundings. In compiling the present work much has been omitted that would be, doubtless, interesting perhaps to the few, but not to the many for whose edification the book has been prepared, and published as cheaply as possible.' By removing the 'padding', as Arbuthnot coyly referred to the sexually explicit matter, the text's philosophical gems would remain untarnished. Equally, the masses would be unable to get their grubby hands on the padding instead of the pearls – which, for Arbuthnot, was a prime concern. Arbuthnot seemed to believe that whether a text was pornographic or not depended chiefly on the audience. He implied that another, unexpurgated edition could be created explicitly for specialists and collectors, and sold at such a price as would protect it from misuse. Such a project would be less a case of casting pearls before swine and more a matter of delivering muck to the manor-house.

Early Ideas hinted at Arbuthnot's ambitions for the *Kamasutra*. Describing the book as a 'subtle analysis' of 'the social domestic economy of the Hindoos', which entered into 'great details about marriages, about the wives of other people, and about courtesans', Arbuthnot regretted that he could devote only a few cursory lines to what was actually in it. 'The matter is all there,' he insisted, 'but a Balzac is required to place it in an interesting way before the public.' The 'Balzac', the necessary controversial, masterful literary giant, was Richard Burton.

To mastermind the publication of the *Kamasutra*, a book that most of Burton's contemporaries would have described unhesitatingly as obscene, filthy and vicious, might seem a surprising move for a Victorian grandee in the later years of an eminent, if already controversial, career. To most minds – including that of his wife, Isabel, who complained that he should 'write from his own clear *understanding* and not from defiance and contempt of rules' – Richard Burton should have been basking in the warm afterglow of his years spent making a name for himself in Africa and the East. Only the friends who understood Burton's passionate hatred of anti-sensualism could have fully understood the motives that provoked his shocking, erotic swansong.

Burton's first task was to persuade his friend not to indulge in any more rabbit-like substitutions of 'mouths' for 'yonis', and the like. Burton was not averse to the occasional insertion, but he was vehemently opposed to any form of bowdlerization. Chief among his many enemies was the Society for the Suppression of Vice, the self-appointed moral guardian of the publishing world. It was a powerful organization, having secured convictions – as well as large fines and prison sentences – from all but four of the first 159 prosecutions it sponsored. Burton called it a 'hideous humbug' and obsessively referred to its members and supporters by the scornful collective term 'Mrs Grundy' – a name coined in the eighteenth century to personify priggish conventionality. Writing to his fellow Orientalist, John Payne, in 1882, Burton roared that he knew Mrs Grundy to be 'an arrant whore' and would tell her so. By the following year he was raging that he 'would rather tread on Mrs Grundy's pet corn than not. She may howl on her big bum to her heart's content.'

Burton and Payne were then working on rival translations of the *Arabian Nights*. They corresponded on the topic of expurgation, but Payne could not persuade his rival to adopt his way of thinking. Looking back, Payne later wrote, 'I could never get him to understand my objection to filth for filth's sake, altogether apart from all question of prudery. He himself had a "romantic passion" for it.' Burton threatened to produce a mirror-image 'Black Book' of the *Nights*, 'with all the horror between two pasteboards', but his true passion was not for 'filth' itself – although he did relish it – but for completeness. When it was finally issued, Burton's *Nights* would be triumphantly different from Payne's precisely because it presented the entire text, unexpurgated. Cutting out the lewd passages, Burton claimed, was like presenting the public with 'the grin without the cat'. To be consistent, he fumed, the censor of morals 'must begin by bowdlerizing not only the classics' but also

Boccaccio and Chaucer, Shakespeare and Rabelais... Sterne, Swift and a long list of works which are yearly reprinted and republished without a word of protest. Lastly, why does not this inconsistent puritan purge the Old Testament of its allusions to human ordure and the pudenda; to carnal copulation and impudent whoredom, to adultery and fornication, to

onanism, sodomy, and bestiality? But this he will not do, the
whited sepulchre!

Burton was unabashedly triumphant that his wife's later,
'family' version of the *Arabian Nights* was a commercial failure,
selling only 500 copies. He declared that 'even innocent girlhood
tossed aside the chaste volumes in utter contempt, and would not
condescend to aught save the thing, the whole thing and nothing
but the thing, unexpurgated and uncastrated'. It is typical of Burton
to conceive of his sixteen-volume set as some kind of resplendent
male member, longed for and demanded by virgins. He saw the
expurgation of a book as nothing less than a sexual mutilation, and
hated and feared the thought of his own books suffering in this
way.

Just as circumcision and genital mutilation had fascinated
Burton as an anthropologist, so editorial censorship obsessed him
in the last, literary phase of his career. When he described earlier
English translations of the *Nights*, he called them 'unsexed and
unsouled', almost as if the two concepts amounted to the same
thing. Similarly, when he called earlier editions 'vapid, frigid and
inspid', he implied that something sexless was not only bland but
empty. It is tempting to relate these opinions to Burton's life in
Trieste, where he told the writer Alfred Bate Richards that he and
his fiercely Catholic wife were 'like an elder and younger brother
living en *garçon*'; Isabel agreed that they lived 'like brothers'. In this
light, biographer Frank McLynn's speculation that Burton was also
impotent seems plausible, and the private, painful sources of his
fierce campaign to publish erotic texts whole and 'uncastrated'
may be better understood.

LEFT: This luxurious wall-painting of the prince Visvantara dallying with his wife Madri is as close to an illustration of the *Kamasutra* as it is possible to get. Created in the fifth century, it survives in the Buddhist cave complex at Ajanta.

BELOW: Taken from a manuscript of the *Kavipriya*, a late sixteenth-century poem, this watercolour shows the divine lovers Krishna and Radha. Their self-consciousness is typical of India's erotic tradition. The image (c. 1640) is from the court of the Sisodia dynasty of Mewar, which ruled from the fabled lake city of Udaipur.

Khajuraho is popularly known as the '*Kamasutra* temple', but its fleshy nymphs and sensuous sculptural groups are in fact the child of a strange union between Tantrism and fertility motifs.

Khajuraho's sculptures may conceal symbolical-magical diagrams, or *yantras*. Michael Rabe suggests that this washerwoman clinging to an ascetic may express the Tantric notion that the subtle energy residing in the base of the spine has risen as far as the neck.

Miniature painters of the Mughal era strove to portray the many moods of love. These illustrations of Bihari's sensuous poem, the *Satsai*, were painted in the 1780s, but they draw on the *nayaka* and *nayika*, the idealized lovers first described in the *Kamasutra*. They are in the delicately domestic style of Guler, one of the Rajput mini-courts of the Pahari hill states. The male hero is shown as Krishna, his divine status indicated by his blue skin. The *nayika* is shown cooking – this being, as the *Kamasutra* had stated, one of the 64 arts of the ideal lover.

This miniature may be late seventeenth century, and post-Mughal, but the scene of aristocratic lovemaking on a garden terrace comes straight from the *Kamasutra*. This is the 'private pleasure' of Prince Muhammad Shah; the miniaturist is Rashid, from the Rajput principality of Bikaner.

RIGHT: After the explorer
Richard Francis Burton
washed up in Trieste as
Consul, he became involved
in a risky and illegal scheme:
to publish an English
Kamasutra. It would be the
last and most brilliant of his
many wilful provocations.

BELOW: Richard Monckton
Milnes was a poet, a Tory
peer and the hapless suitor
of Florence Nightingale. He
was also Europe's greatest
collector of erotica and,
as Burton's patron, the
éminence grise behind the
first translation of the
Kamasutra.

This portrait of the modest
pandit, Bhagvanlal Indraji,
hangs in the Durbar Hall of
Mumbai's Asiatic Society. It
commemorates his work as an
archeologist rather than as the
first translator of the *Kamasutra*.

The *Kamasutra*'s Indian translators struggled to find a complete version of the text. Finally, in 1876 or 1877, they tracked down this manuscript in Benares – modern-day Varanasi – and began work.

Even as Richard Burton's health failed, he worked with furious vigour on erotic translations. A few months before his death, his old friend and collaborator, 'Bunny' Arbuthnot, visited him and his wife at their house in Trieste.

The *Kama Sutra* published in 1936 by the Medical Press of New York was the first to be illustrated. The drawings by Mahlon Blaine perfectly expressed the *Kamasutra*'s double reputation: it was a work of ancient erotic literature and a manual that even modern couples might turn to for 'marital' advice.

LEFT: The first English translators used the *Kamasutra* to campaign for women's rights to sexual pleasure; the first French translator, Alain Daniélou, used it to argue for gay rights. His lover, Raymond Burnier, took this photograph of Daniélou at Khajuraho in 1943.

The 1991 launch of India's KamaSutra condom was a turning point in modern Indian sexual politics. Delight in sexuality, the advertising campaign argued, was not a corrupt, Western import. The *Kamasutra*, after all, was the quintessential sexy book.

BELOW: In the twenty-first century, 'Kamasutra' has become a byword for gymnastically advanced lovemaking, and Vatsyayana's book of love has spawned a thousand imitations. The *Kama Sutra of Vatsyayana in Pop-up* is surely the most inventive — even if the bits that pop up are not necessarily those you'd expect.

That the *Kamasutra* should remain unmutilated was particularly important to Burton. The book's reputation had long rested precisely on the notion that it provided an analysis of sexuality that was definitive and complete. A bowdlerized translation would have been a travesty. Even a subtle concealment of the more obscene words, as Arbuthnot had attempted in *Early Ideas*, would be like 'the bathos of the painter who makes a pretty woman terminate in a damned red herring', as Burton quipped in a letter to his patron, Richard Monckton Milnes. Arbuthnot finally came round to Burton's point of view. At least, he admitted that 'some parts of the work may be considered somewhat objectionable, but it was better to give the whole work without any expurgations, and as the work has only been brought out for the benefit of the learned, and of those interested in all kinds of Oriental literatures it was far better to give it in its original entirety than to cut out parts of it.'

By August 1882, the momentous decision to publish had been taken. Burton took up his pen on Arbuthnot's behalf, writing to Payne to ask him not to 'forget my friend, F.F. Arbuthnot, and benefit him by your advice about publishing when he applies to you for it. He has undertaken a peculiar branch of literature – the Hindu Erotic, which promises well.' By December of that year, Arbuthnot and Burton had gone further, reviving the idea first mooted in Bombay – that of creating a 'Kama Shastra Society' as a cover for publishing a string of Oriental erotic classics. The Society would no longer be an amusing fantasy, they resolved, but a genuine enterprise. For Burton, the Kama Shastra Society was yet another disguise, another way to explore sexual culture – and his own identity. For Arbuthnot, it was as good a nom de plume as 'Anaryan' and it had the advantage of conferring a rather learned air on his activities while simultaneously poking fun at the pretensions of genuine Indological societies.

Arbuthnot and Burton resolved to begin with the greatest work of erotology of them all, the *Kamasutra*, and follow it up with the *Ananga Ranga* — simply a reprint of the *Kama Shastra, or the Hindoo Art of Love* of 1873, with its original title restored. Next would come Burton's landmark translation of the *Arabian Nights*, and finally, the Society would print Edward Rehatsek's translations of two Persian erotic classics, the *Beharistan* and *Gulistan*, which had long waited for an English audience.

The catalogue was like a miniature version of the great translation project of the day: *Sacred Books of the East*. This grandiose scheme, begun in 1879, was steadily translating the key texts of Hinduism, Buddhism, Jainism, Islam, Taoism and Confucianism into English. Two Hindu scriptures were being translated by Georg Bühler, while the editorship was in the hands of F. Max Müller, the leading Sanskritist of the day. Müller's project was determinedly Humanist. He wanted to present Western scholarship with a body of religious literature that could bear comparison with Judaeo-Christian and Classical texts, and perhaps underpin a kind of second Renaissance. If the scheme was to succeed, it was crucial for it to project an image of the Orient as philosophically minded. It didn't matter that, as Burton would have argued, there were countless examples of obscenity or vulgarity in the Western canon; the *Sacred Books of the East* had to be able to stand up to comparison with even the most stately and high-minded Western classics and look them unblushingly in the eye. From Müller's point of view, to include the *Kamasutra* or other erotic texts in the list would entirely spoil the intended effect. It would serve, if anything, to reinforce negative Orientalist notions of the East as childish, fantastical and immoral. When Müller's project finally came to an end in 1904, fifty volumes had been published. None came from within the *kama shastra* tradition.

The Kama Shastra Society's scheme was not only an imitation of *Sacred Books of the East*, but a parody and a challenge. Where Müller presented the East as 'passive, meditative and philosophical', the Kama Shastra Society would show it to be vigorous, pragmatic and distinctly sensual. Burton was quite serious about challenging accepted ideas about the East. He had long railed against the common belief that women in the Orient were more oppressed than those in the West. He believed that to describe the *real* East — including the East in which men and women were relatively free to express their sexuality — was nothing less than his imperial duty. As a translator, he said, 'I venture to hold myself in the light of a public benefactor. In fact, I consider my labours as a legacy bequeathed to my countrymen at a most critical time when England the puissantest of Moslem powers is called upon, without adequate knowledge of the Moslem's inner life, to administer Egypt as well as to rule India.' What was true for Muslims was also true for the Empire's Hindu subjects. Burton argued that 'the free treatment of topics usually taboo'd will be a national benefit to an "empire of Opinion" whose very basis and buttresses are a thorough knowledge by the rulers of the ruled.' Just as a *bubu*'s pleasure had to be understood before the young Indian officer could satisfy her, so the imperialist had to understand his colonial dependencies intimately before he could attempt to master them.

For all the serious Indological and imperialist ideas that motivated Arbuthnot and Burton, as a club the Kama Shastra Society was largely spurious. According to Burton, writing in December 1882, the membership consisted of just Arbuthnot and himself, though Arbuthnot later averred that there was a third member. The society's chief purpose was to confer anonymity on Arbuthnot and Burton, thus protecting them from prosecution, not only under the Customs Consolidation Act of 1876, which banned the importation of pornography, but also under the Obscene Publications Act of 1857. The latter was known as 'Lord Campbell's Act' after its sponsor, a man who called pornography 'a poison more deadly than prussic acid and strychnine or arsenic'. It was extraordinarily broad, defining obscenity as 'something offensive to modesty or decency, or expressing or suggesting unchaste or lustful ideas, or being impure, indecent or lewd'. It enabled the police to search suspected premises and destroy all printed matter they considered to be obscene. The danger for Arbuthnot and Burton was that while the Act was designed to attack publishers of outright erotica, it also enabled the authorities to crack down on other, apparently worthier publications.

The most notorious case of this kind had been brought in 1876 against Annie Besant and her co-campaigner, Charles Bradlaugh. Besant was an outspoken secularist, feminist and sexual radical who would later embrace the quasi-Hindu Theosophist movement. Bradlaugh was President of the London Secular Society, publisher of the radical newsheet, the *National Reformer* and, of course, a former intimate of the Cannibal Club. Together, they had printed and distributed Charles Knowlton's short booklet advocating birth control, *The Fruits of Philosophy, or the Private Companion of Young Married People*, one of a number of neo-Malthusian tracts on population and birth control issued throughout the Victorian era. They attracted the particular wrath of the authorities by daring to republish the pamphlet after its previous British publisher had been convicted of obscenity almost ten years earlier.

In Besant and Bradlaugh's case, obscenity was only the excuse for taking them to court. Their real crime was to separate sex and procreation by openly advocating contraception. They were quite deliberately challenging the Establishment, and the Establishment knew it. In the event, the jury exonerated them from having corrupt motives, but the booklet itself was declared obscene, and the pair were sentenced to six months in prison and a £200 fine. Although the sentence was later quashed by the Court of Appeal on a technicality – and the *Fruits of Philosophy* went on to sell some 200,000 copies in under three years – the scandal of the trial enabled Annie Besant's estranged husband to prevent her from seeing their daughter for the next ten years.

In this context, printing the *Kamasutra* openly, under Arbuthnot and Burton's own names, was just too dangerous. They might well publicly emphasize their book's importance for the study of Indology, but underneath this dusty costume was a distinctly fleshy text. It lacked even the earnest undertone of neo-Malthusian publications, whose professed intention was the combatting of poverty through the promotion of birth control. Instead, the *Kamasutra* painted a glowing picture of unrestrained sexual libertarianism. It contained detailed advice on how to arouse a virgin and how to seduce other men's wives. It discussed sexual positions in exacting detail, albeit without actual illustrations. It gave, moreover, precise instructions on the delights of 'sucking the mango fruit' – or, rather, having it sucked. It made *The Fruits of Philosophy* look like bedtime reading for the nursery.

Since the Besant–Bradlaugh trial, however, Arbuthnot and Burton had been given some reason to hope that 'scholarly' publications could avoid prosecution, even if they contained overtly obscene material. John Payne's only partially expurgated translation of the *Arabian Nights* had so far escaped legal attention. Payne himself may well have encourged Burton to proceed, for by January 1883 Arbuthnot and Burton had got as far as finding a printer, and Burton was writing to Payne gleefully informing him that 'He and I and the Printer have started a Hindu Kama Shastra (Ars Amoris) Society. It will make the Brit[ish] Pub[lic] stare.'

The printer's identity has been all too successfully concealed, but it was probably James Henry Gaball, an established producer of soft-core erotica. Gaball had already produced Henry Spencer Ashbee's *Index Librorum Prohibitorum*, and Ashbee may have recommended him to Arbuthnot. Gaball was a man who could be relied upon not to run squealing to the authorities – or to stop the presses after printing just a handful of copies, as had happened with the 1873 *Kama Shastra*. He also had links with the clandestine booksellers and publishers Robson and Kerslake, who were listed as 'the Society's Agents' on a prospectus of Kama Shastra Society publications.

Known to regular clients as 'the Brothers', the Kerslakes had their first bookshop on Holywell Street, a murky (and now-demolished) backstreet in the Aldwych area that was notorious among contemporaries as London's 'erotica row'. It is telling that the Kerslakes' premises had previously belonged to another erotic bookseller whose shop was closed down by a police raid. By the time Arbuthnot and Burton were on the lookout for an amenable printer, however, the brothers had joined forces with Bartholomew Robson and moved upmarket to Coventry Street – an address that would later become famous as the home of Charles Hirsch's *Librairie Parisienne*, which supplied Oscar Wilde with his 'private' reading matter. The new firm of Robson and Kerslake was relatively highbrow. In 1883, it was responsible for the Earl of

Haddington's bawdy collection, *Select Poems on Several Occasions*. The book (also printed by J.H. Gaball) sold for the staggering sum of £3. This, then, was a team disreputable enough to take on the project and just sufficiently elevated so as not to offend Arbuthnot's and Burton's aristocratic sense of propriety.

The Kama Sutra of Vatsyayana, With a Preface and Introduction finally emerged from the shadows of London's clandestine presses in the spring of 1883. Radical change was in the air. In the same year, a group of clean-living, forward-thinking pacifists founded the proto-Fabian Fellowship of the New Life — the young, virgin, and as-yet-unpublished sexologist Havelock Ellis among them. And in late August, the Indonesian volcano Krakatoa erupted with a force so immense that it would alter the earth's climate for years to come. The *Kamasutra*'s impact on the West would ultimately be no less far-ranging or long-lasting. Its irruption was achieved, however, with far less noise or spectacle.

Arbuthnot's and Burton's edition appeared under a heavy cloak of anonymity and discretion, as a private printing offered to a few subscribers. Neither translator, editor nor printer were acknowledged, beyond a reference on the title-page to the mysterious 'Hindoo Kama Shastra Society' and a couple of obscure clues hidden away among the footnotes. One note pointed readers to Burton's 1870 translation, *Vikram and the Vampire*; another referenced Arbuthnot's utterly obscure (and anonymous) *Early Ideas*. Even the *Kamasutra*'s place of publication was deliberately obfuscated: while the title-page of the first chapter declared that the book had been printed in London, the title-pages of the last six chapters all bore the name of Benares. Benares, of course, was the source of Indraji's complete manuscript, but Arbuthnot and Burton had other, more urgent reasons for making the misleading attribution. They were laying a false trail for the prosecuting authorities and, at the same time, hanging out a lure for their bibliophile and erotophile subscribers, who were ever eager to follow on the perfumed track of the rare and recherché.

As a physical object, the 1883 Kamasutra was remarkably discreet. There were no pictures, and the book was printed in seven anonymous-looking sections, which the subscriber was supposed to bind together into a complete set. Each section had its own card cover in a tasteful shade of fawn or bluish-grey and carried a warning message: 'For Private Circulation Only'. In the event of prosecution, Arbuthnot and Burton hoped, this would allow them to argue that their translation was designed to be circulated among 'members' only. Publishing the *Kamasutra* in this furtive way also left Arbuthnot and Burton with a problem. If the book was not going to be sold through ordinary booksellers, how could it be marketed? A few copies could be sold privately through trusted erotic booksellers, such as Robson and Kerslake of Coventry Street, or Bernard Quaritch of Piccadilly – both shops could be relied upon to keep a few copies of 'private' and 'subscription' editions under the counter for regular customers – but a slow dribble of casual, pornographic bookbuyers would never bring the *Kamasutra* the fame its backers knew it deserved.

To spread word of the book's existence, therefore, Arbuthnot and Burton wrote to their many contacts in the two worlds of Sanskrit scholarship and erotic bibliophilia. Gentlemen who knew gentlemen who were interested in that kind of thing would privately pass on the word; the interested party would then be put in touch with the right people, a subscription would be arranged and the book would be posted under separate cover. It was a process that could scarcely count as publication; it was more like the sharing-around of pornography in a playground, passed from hand to hand under wraps among the more daring boys. On the face of it, however, the book was aimed more at scholars than erotophiles. Crisp capitals on the verso of the title page announced that the *Kamasutra* was:

DEDICATED

TO THAT SMALL PORTION OF THE BRITISH PUBLIC

WHICH TAKES ENLIGHTENED INTEREST IN

STUDYING THE MANNERS AND CUSTOMS

OF THE OLDEN EAST

Copies were sent out to reviewers who received it in precisely this light, or at least appeared to do so. The Dutch bibliographer, R.C. d'Ablaing, wrote – without mentioning the book's overtly sexual content – to record his view that 'The Hindus were very profound thinkers, but they were misled in their philosophical reasonings by the scantity of their truly scientific principles.' Fernand Drujon, a noted reviewer (in certain circles) and bibliographer of erotica, wrote to the publishers to thank them for 'this interesting and very surprising work. Indeed, I know nothing stranger, even in Sanskrit literature, which offers us some very singular traditions.'

The interest of many subscribers, though, was less scholarly than sexual. In 1884, Arbuthnot wrote concerning the book to 'My Dear Bellamy' – this was Henry Edward Vaux Bellamy FRGS: publicly, a stalwart of the Royal Anthropological Society; privately, an enthusiast for erotic flagellation. '*The Kama Sutra of Vatsyayana*,' he observed coyly, 'is being printed by some learned Brahmans who are interested in the humanities.' Bellamy must have snorted with laughter at the disguise. As for the Brahmans being 'interested in the humanities', this was particularly suggestive. The book was 'concerned about the happiness of man and the comfort of woman', Arbuthnot wrote. The po-faced allusion might have slipped past the censors, but Bellamy needed no stronger hint. 'Quaritch in Piccadilly has some copies to sell, but as I have some spare copies by me I should be happy to present you with half a dozen of them for your perusal and for circulation.' Bellamy's reaction is not recorded but, given his tastes, it seems likely that he would have headed post-haste for Golden Square – then, as now, the London home of Bernard Quaritch's bookshop.

Joseph Knight, editor of *Notes & Queries*, was positively aquiver with satisfaction. He reported that the book was 'indeed, as you say, a work of great erudition and enormous contribution to our knowledge of Indian thought' and he promised to provide his copy with a handsome jacket. More viscerally, he felt that 'The things that are said in it about women are marvellously fine and the book is more charged with suggestion than any work I have read.' For all the book's scholarly and erotic qualities, Knight found himself frustratingly unable to express his approval in any forum more public than a personal letter. 'What a misfortune it is,' he wrote, 'that one cannot review a work like this without getting into bother.'

'Bother' was a peculiarly English understatement. 'Bother', in an era of rampant prudery – and, more to the point, in the era of the Obscene Publications Act – might mean not only a crippling fine and the catastrophic loss of one's place in society, but the possibility of a jail sentence to boot. Printing or distributing such a book, never mind reviewing it, risked a potentially explosive amount of 'bother'.

Arbuthnot's most useful contact was Henry Spencer Ashbee, the eroto-bibliographer who had listed the 1873 *Kama Shastra* in his *Index*

Librorum Prohibitorum. The two men had corresponded for some time but met only in May 1883. (Ashbee did not get to meet his hero, Burton, until June 1885, when they were introduced at the East India Club; Ashbee recorded in his diary that Burton 'impresses one at once as a very remarkable man, whose erudition is as vast as his knowledge of the world of humanity'.) Arbuthnot sent a number of copies to Ashbee for distribution among his wide network of friends and like-minded contacts. It was an under-the-counter process, involving sealed parcels within parcels and the like. Ashbee also kept back a single copy for his own, private library of erotica – a collection unrivalled in England since Milnes' library at Aphrodisiopolis had been destroyed by fire in 1875.

In sending a courtesy copy to Ashbee, the quasi-official curator of pornographic books, Arbuthnot was acting curiously like a conventional publisher sending an obligatory copy to the British Museum. He was eager for the *Kamasutra* to be taken seriously, for its publication to be recorded in some way – even if the conventional methods of doing so were closed to him. (Ironically, Ashbee's copy did eventually end up in the Museum after his death, bequeathed along with his entire pornographic collection, which afterwards formed the heart of the long-secret 'Private Case'.)

Ashbee published a notice of the *Kamasutra* in the third volume of his eroto-bibliography, *Catena Librorum Absconditorum*. Arbuthnot had been deeply involved with the process, writing with suggestions for how Ashbee might describe the book and listing over a dozen verses or chapter endings that he might consider quoting. Some, Arbuthnot warned, were 'pretty strong', others 'very moral'; already, the dual reputation of the *Kamasutra*, as pornography and as sexual-spiritual guidance, was being established. Ashbee also submitted a cautious review to *The Bibliographer* magazine,

which appeared in May 1884 under the playful pseudonym of a
certain 'E.H. Shesba'. He guardedly described the work as 'a treatise
on social life and the relations between the sexes'. He noted
Vatsyayana's hair-splitting tendencies, arguing that the book's style
bore a certain Jesuitical resemblance to 'the disquisitions of the
Romish casuists... especially in the minuteness and subtlety of its
definitions'. He also guessed, rather acutely, that the *Kamasutra* was
'evidently written for those who have to teach others'.

Ashbee concluded by saying: 'Few more suggestive works... has
it been my good fortune to peruse, nor any that contribute more
directly and clearly to our knowledge of Indian thought. From
almost every page might be extracted something fresh, or startling
to our Western notions.' The *Kamasutra*, he realized, was both pornography and Indology, and a challenge to the West's attitudes
towards sexuality to boot. In this almost casual fashion, he neatly
summed up Arbuthnot's and Burton's three chief motivations for
printing the book – and the three main areas in which the book
would flourish in the next century.

The first edition of *The Kama Sutra of Vatsyayana* quickly sold out.
Within a year, Arbuthnot and Burton announced and discreetly
advertised a second. This time, they were more confident. Their
new book was a handsome object, ready-bound in a soft, sensual,
all-white vellum cover, the front and back covers featuring a
border elegantly tooled in real gold. More gold featured in the
hand-worked lettering on the spine. It announced 'The Kamasutra
of Vatsyayana' at the top, and 'Benares, 1883' at the bottom. The
package was elegant, distinguished and discreet. And at the ambitious price of £2 10s, it was excitingly expensive.

The elevated price was not simply a question of Arbuthnot and
Burton protecting themselves from prosecution by keeping circu-

lation small. It was a matter of targeting their audience. As they saw it, Oriental erotica was all very well in the soft hands of cultivated men – the *nagarakas* of their day – who could enjoy it from the proper perspective. In the horny-handed public sphere, however, such material risked being read as mere pornography. Burton publicly argued for heavy fines to be imposed on pornographic booksellers who exposed 'indecent' images and 'immoral' books in public shop windows, and he wanted the fate of 'cheap and nasty' literature to be merely left 'to the good taste of the publisher and the public'. His view was snobbish but libertarian. Unfortunately, the law was egalitarian and repressive, and observed no distinction between refined Oriental erotica and popular pornography.

The law may well have been right in the case of the *Kamasutra*. It may have had aristocratic origins in ancient India, but in Britain it instantly became pornographic, or at least partly so. Torn between pride and the necessity for anonymity, Arbuthnot and Burton provided an obscure clue to the true, pornographic origins of their project. On the title-page of the second edition the place of printing was given as 'Cosmopoli: MDCCCLXXXIII: for the Kama Shastra Society of London and Benares'. A select few erotic bibliophiles would have smiled at an in-joke. 'Cosmopoli' was a fairly standard pornographers' stand-in for a place of publication. It was also intended as an oblique reference to the master of 'Aphrodisiopolis' and presiding chief of a club known as 'the Cosmopolitan', Richard Monckton Milnes.

According to Arbuthnot, writing safely after Milnes' death, in 1885, Milnes had been the Kama Shastra Society's third member. The extent of his involvement is uncertain. He may have put up some of the initial capital, or simply have provided advice and encouragement. He had already been helping Burton with his career for decades – both in the Foreign Office, thanks to his access to the prime ministerial ear, and in the publishing world, thanks to his literary contacts. 'Cosmopoli' also concealed a second, coded, pornographical reference – to the more deeply clandestine world of Fred Hankey. Hankey was probably the co-author of an anonymously published, Sadean French novel, *Instruction libertine*, which gave 'Sadopolis' as the fictional place of printing – though in fact the book was roughly run off at a distinctly under-the-counter press in Brussels.

The oblique references to Hankey and Milnes – the avid, sexually transgressive pornographers and tutors of Burton's wilder bachelor years – betray that while Arbuthnot and Burton were eager for their book not to sink to the level of public pornography, they were well aware that it would be read for erotic pleasure within the small, private sphere of their own coterie. Compared to explicit erotica such as *My Secret Life* – a compendious pseudo-confessional of the outrageous sexual exploits of 'Walter', which was published in the 1880s and probably written by Henry Spencer Ashbee – the *Kamasutra* was soft soap. But there was still plenty in the book to titillate and arouse, and the exotic, Oriental associations provided an additional sexual charge.

One section, in particular, they knew would kindle the interest of their Sadist friends. Fred Hankey no doubt would have approved of the chapter 'On Pressing, or Marking, or Scratching with the Nails', and perhaps the one 'On Biting, and the Means to be Employed with Regard to Women of Different Countries'. Love marks appear to have been a major fetish in ancient India; at least, Vatsyayana recommended an elaborate array of patterns that could be left on the lover's body. 'The line of jewels', 'the broken cloud' and 'the biting of the boar' far exceeded Western nibblings in ambition and imagination.

The *Kamasutra* even asserted that sexual intercourse itself could be compared to a quarrel, 'on account of the contrarieties of love and its tendency to dispute'. It listed no less than six areas that may be struck with passion, as well as four kinds of striking – with the back of the hand, with the fingers a little contracted, with the fist, and with the open palm – and eight sounds of pain that striking may provoke. At this point, in the chapter treating 'Of the Various Modes of Striking and the Sounds Appropriate to Them', the translators made an egregious error. According to their *Kama Sutra of Vatsyayana*, to the four modes of striking may be added, 'the wedge on the bosom, the scissors on the head, the piercing instrument on the cheeks, and the pincers on the breasts and sides'. 'The wedge', 'the scissors' and 'the pincers' are interpreted today not as real instruments but as illustrative descriptions of hand positions forming part of a highly elaborated theory of lovemaking. It is tempting to believe that the misreading was Arbuthnot's or Burton's own, and that they were misled by their own Sadistic impulses.

In fact, like the more thoughtful Victorian Sadists, Vatsyayana's vision simply encompassed an entire range of possible sexual responses to violence. He described these ways of striking as 'peculiar to the people of the southern countries' and opined that 'the practice of them is painful, barbarous, and base, and quite unworthy of imitation'. With characteristic relativism, he went on to add that 'the various modes of enjoyment are not for all times or for all persons, but they should only be used at the proper time, and in the proper countries and places'. Burton the sexual anthropologist could not have put it better. And Burton knew it. He wanted to use

Vatsyayana to show that the cool, relativist permissiveness that his own sexual studies had led him to espouse had deep and ancient roots. For Burton, publishing the *Kamasutra* was not only a matter of playing out his private desires in public; his literary transgression had a political purpose.

Burton's famed skill with the sword may have deserted him in age, but he was still eager to take on his old enemies – the censors, the prudes and the hypocrites – in print. And the *Kamasutra* was his chosen weapon. He shared with Arbuthnot the sense that the hitherto hidden, erotic side of the Sanskrit literary tradition needed to be exposed. And as an inveterate self-publisher, he longed to expose the hypocrisy of sexual censorship. He wanted to use the *Kamasutra* to prick Victorian society out of its sleep of sexual ignorance, be it pretended or actual.

Arbuthnot was right behind him. In *Early Ideas,* he revealed that he considered the *Kamasutra* to be 'simple and good'. It proved, he claimed, that 'the Hindoos of that age possessed a civilization far in advance of our own at that time, while the exact details of everything to be done by husbands and wives seem to point out that marriage obligations were fully recognized at that period'. 'Marriage obligations' were much on the mind of this former long-term bachelor. Arbuthnot believed that ancient Hindu civilization was not only 'far in advance of our own at that time' but more sophisticated than the English society of his own time. He skimmed over the fact that the *Kamasutra* discussed sex in a wide range of contexts, including with 'other men's wives', and co-opted it for the cause of advocating sexual pleasure within marriage. The 'Preface' to the 1883 *Kamasutra* – which, on the grounds of style alone, was almost certainly written by Arbuthnot, although presumably with Burton's help or at least agreement – ended with a similarly heartfelt plea. It concluded that too many Englishmen were completely ignorant of 'certain matters intimately connected with their private, domestic and social life', and that this ignorance had 'unfortunately wrecked many a man and many a woman'. 'Wrecked' was a strong word, a word that placed sexuality at the core of what constituted a man – or a woman.

Burton was no less passionate about the need for sex education. 'The England of our day,' he wrote in 1888, 'would fain bring up both sexes and keep all ages in profound ignorance of sexual and intersexual relations.' 'The consequences of that imbecility,' he warned, 'are particularly cruel and afflicting' – especially for virgin brides. 'How often do we hear women in Society lamenting that they have absolutely no knowledge of their own physiology; and at what heavy price must this fruit of the knowledge-tree be bought by the young first entering life? Shall we ever understand that ignorance is not innocence?' Burton claimed he had heard of brides in their thirties 'who had not the slightest suspicion concerning what complaisance was expected of them'. He blamed the parents: 'out of *mauvaise honte*, the besetting sin of the respectable classes, neither father nor mother would venture to enlighten the elderly innocents'. One of his favourite after-dinner stories was that of the newly-wed husband who ascended the stairs to his young bride in bed, only to find her chloroformed and unconscious, with a note beside her on the pillow saying, 'Mamma says you're to do what you like.' The darker side of the joke – and Burton's serious point – lies not just in the bride's inability to accept her own sexual nature, but in the sexual horrors that may have been visited on the bride's mother by her inept, careless or brutal husband.

In correspondence with Henry Spencer Ashbee, Arbuthnot enlarged on the same theme. 'It is difficult to get Englishmen to acknowledge that matrimonial happiness may in many cases be attained by a careful study of the passions of a wife, that is to say admitting that a wife be allowed to feel passion,' he wrote.

> Many a life has been wasted and the best feelings of a young woman outraged by the rough exercise of what truly become the husband's 'rights', and all the innate delicate sentiments and illusions of the virgin bride are ruthlessly trampled on when the curtains close round the couch on what is vulgarly called the 'first night'. The master either swoops down on his prey like a vulture or, what is just as bad, sins by ignorance, appearing to the trembling creature either as a cruel brute or a stupid bungling fool.

Arbuthnot's and Burton's depiction of the horrors of sexual ignorance should not be entirely trusted. 'Victorianism', in its more extreme, aggressively anti-sensual forms, was effectively constructed by its opponents – and Burton and Arbuthnot were among the first to define the enemy. The truth about sexual satisfaction, or lack of it, in Victorian marriages is less clear. Recent studies have turned up new evidence suggesting that Victorians were as sexually competent and enthusiastic as people of any other era. The age-old belief that the woman had to have an orgasm in order to conceive was still widespread, after all, and many Victorian doctors actually advised couples who could not conceive to try foreplay. Lecturing to the Royal College of Physicians in 1883, the Scottish gynaecologist J. Matthews Duncan presented his survey of sterile women. Among 190 respondents, 152 felt sexual desire and 134 claimed to have orgasms. Duncan could therefore concur with what he called the 'almost universal opinion': that 'in women, desire and pleasure are in every case present, or are in every case called forth by the proper stimulants'.

Many more surveys and anecdotes, however, confirm Arbuthnot's and Burton's view. James Russell Price, a contemporary Chicago physician who castigated parents for not educating their children 'in matters of sex hygiene', interviewed one hundred women who sought legal separation from their husbands. Sixty-eight of them attested to sexual trauma on their wedding night, one eighteen-year-old bride avowing that she was utterly incapable of forgiving or forgetting how her husband locked the bedroom door on their first night together and raped her.

Elizabeth Blackwell, the first American woman to gain a degree in medicine and the author, in 1884, of *The Human Element in Sex*, blamed 'the prevalent fallacy that sexual passion is the almost exclusive attribute of men'. The fallacy was certainly well represented in the medical establishment. H. Newell Martin's textbook, *The Human Body* (1881), cites a doctor as saying that sex is at best 'a nuisance to the majority of women belonging to the most luxurious classes of society', while William Acton, a doctor of medicine and the author of the influential textbook *The Functions and Disorders of the Reproductive Organs* (1857), notoriously maintained that 'the majority of women, happily for them, are not much troubled with sexual feeling of any kind'.

Acton in general, and this quotation in particular, are sometimes presented as exemplifying 'Victorian' attitudes. In fact, far from being the arch-villain of Victorian sexual repression, as he has often been presented, Acton was partly motivated by concern for the sexual sufferings of 'the modest English female' suddenly introduced, in the aftermath of her marriage, to 'what in most instances is to her, at least, a most painful and distressing climax to her other agitations'. Acton, indeed, agreed with Elizabeth Blackwell, who wrote that 'at the very time when marriage love seems to unite them most closely, when her husband's welcome kisses and caresses seem to bring them into profound union, comes an act which mentally separates them, and which is often either indifferent or repugnant to her'.

The problem was not biology, but cultural expectations. Women were 'not truthfully instructed in relation to the central force of human emotion and action', Blackwell wrote, and they remained woefully ignorant of 'the intense physical pleasure which attends the caresses of love'. Sex education, according to Blackwell, was what women sorely needed. The problem was that there was precious little on the subject to be found in print that wasn't outright pornography, fringe medical literature – such as Blackwell's own book – or bizarrely dated. Men were no less in need of expert help. 'Walter', the prolific seducer and hero of *My Secret Life*, finally discovers the secret of the clitoris in a dog-eared sex manual known as *Aristotle's Masterpiece*, though it had precious little to do with Aristotle, having been written (and regularly rewritten) in the seventeenth and eighteenth centuries. But the *Masterpiece* was not easy to come by in the censorious 1880s, and in any case it was far more interested in conception than in what it described as 'venery'.

While the Victorian home was served by endless household manuals advising on all aspects of domestic economy, few dared venture into the bedroom. Those 'marriage manuals' that did were moralizing and restrictive. Pleasure, as often as not, was the enemy – and men remained firmly on top. Arbuthnot and Burton wanted their *Kamasutra* to fill the gap. In his Preface, Arbuthnot compared the sorry state of the sexual sciences in contemporary England with their detailed treatment by the ancient Hindus. He managed to find just two English texts that 'also enter into great details of private and domestic life'. The true identity of the author of the first, *Every Woman's Book*, was not 'Dr Waters', as the 1826 title-page claimed, but the radical republican agitator, Richard Carlile. His tract was part of a modest wave of pamphlets that campaigned for the physical and social wellbeing of women in the 1830s, influenced partly by Malthus's work on population and partly by the growing medical understanding of the reproductive system. (*Every Woman's Book* later influenced *Moral Physiology*, by the American Congressman and social reformer Robert Dale Owen – a treatise on birth control that prompted Charles Knowlton to write the *Fruits of Philosophy*, which in turn influenced Arbuthnot.)

Carlile's goal was to publicize what he called the 'remedy' or the 'physical check', a device that 'has long been known to a few in this country, and to the aristocracy in particular'. For the sake of pregnancies that were planned, healthy and legitimate – for the sake, ultimately, of society itself – he described the vaginal sponge, 'the glove' (the condom) and the practice of coitus interruptus. Carlile's advocacy of contraception concealed another agenda: that 'sexual commerce, where useful and desired, may be made a pleasure'. He embraced what he called 'the disposition to reproduce', describing sexuality as 'a natural passion, or a passion of the body, which we hold in common with every other animal'.

Carlile's reforming zeal extended to a critique of religion, which he called 'a mental disease that turns love into a fancied sin, and commits dreadful ravages, in excluding due sexual intercourse'. Western sexual culture, with its assumption of superior morality, was the enemy. 'The notions of indecency and immorality, which unreasoning minds attach to all discussion about sexual commerce,' he protested, 'may be combatted by referring to the history of mankind, and by showing that through all the varied customs of different nations upon the subject, whatever was the prevailing custom was always the moral right of the matter.' In the hands of Arbuthnot and Burton, the *Kamasutra* could provide detailed evidence of exactly those 'varied customs'. It could act as a foundation stone for cultural relativism.

The second work Arbuthnot cited was one of the century's most influential and subversive sex books. *The Elements of Social Science, or Physical, Sexual and Natural Religion* was probably originally published in 1854–5, as part of a second wave of tracts on 'the most important, though unfortunately most neglected, subjects': birth control and sexual health, with a side-order of sexual libertarianism. Charles Bradlaugh promoted *The Elements* in his *National Reformer* – to which the author, Dr George Drysdale, was an anonymous contributor. Sales soared after the Besant and Bradlaugh trial, with 7,000 copies issued in 1876 alone, and by the end of the century *The Elements* had sold in the region of 100,000 copies, despite being virtually unobtainable in any conventional bookshop.

Almost single-handedly, the book roused Mrs Grundy to a peak of anxiety and repressive fervour. Drysdale began his earnest, passionate work by declaring that 'there is nothing from which mankind in the present day suffers more, than from the want of reverence of the human body'. He deplored the lack of sex education and appreciation of physical beauty. The 'sensual passions', he wrote, 'are viewed in a most degrading light, and the youth is warned to beware of indulgence in them, and rather to train himself in the vastly nobler enjoyments of the moral and reasoning faculties'. Drysdale professed himself in hope, however, 'that the time is not far distant... when the subjects of the following pages shall be generally understood, and openly discussed'.

Swathes of the book dealt with neo-Malthusian issues of population and the condition of the urban working classes, but there was also sexually explicit material. 'Spermatorrhea' and the 'Evils of abstinence' were dealt with alongside venereal diseases and menstrual dysfunctions.

But for all his frankness, Drysdale was just as anxious as William Acton. Both men were greatly concerned by the potentially deleterious effects on the moral constitution of sexuality in general, and 'solitary indulgence' in particular. It was only Drysdale's conclusion that was radical: 'the true and only remedy for the evils arising from abstinence,' he urged, 'is a moderate indulgence in sexual intercourse.' This noble course of action 'braces and ennobles body and mind', he wrote. *The Elements* was hardly a useful handbook for lovers, however. It could not compete with the *Kamasutra*. It was also intended for a very different market from Arbuthnot's and Burton's book; it was aimed not at the leisured, hedonistic, intellectual classes, but at the low-brow masses. But the book's most serious failure, from Arbuthnot's point of view, was that it was steeped in the puritanism of its nonconformist heritage. Drysdale was advocating only *moderate* indulgence. He actually warned against becoming 'steeped in sexual indulgences, as some of the southern nations are', as the inevitable result of such dissipation was that: 'The mind becomes effeminate, and the nerves lose their tone; the power of thought becomes impaired, cloyed as it were by sweetness.'

This was a fairly standard argument of nineteenth-century imperialism, which liked to compare the active, manly rationalism of the West with the passive, effeminate sensualism of lesser nations; it created the fantasy figure of the dissipated and idle Oriental, feminized by excessive lubricity – and thus ill equipped to run his own country. Arbuthnot and Burton, in contrast, were quite happy to steep themselves in 'southern' (or Eastern) sensualism, and they saw the West's failure to do likewise as hypocrisy based on ignorance – and as a failure, therefore, of the rational mind. In his Preface, Arbuthnot compared the 'materialistic, realistic and practical point of view' of the Hindu tradition with Western practices, in which the vast majority thought sexuality 'to be quite incomprehensible, or... not worthy of their consideration'. If an ancient text from a barbarous country could so far surpass the most scientific-minded Western treatises of the day, then either the East was less stagnant, irrational and backward than had previously been admitted, or the West was less open-minded, rational and forward-thinking.

Arbuthnot cited a third book that was, he claimed, the only work in the English language that was 'somewhat similar to these works of the Hindoos'. T. Bell's *Kalogynomia or the Laws of Female Beauty* was published in London in 1821. It did indeed discuss many of the same topics as the *Kamasutra*, and at times in such a similar manner that it is tempting to think that Bell must somehow have been acquainted with at least one of the *kama shastra* texts. He described how people in the East 'make an almost continuous use of aphrodisiac substances of exciting drugs and of philters'. He also categorized different types of women by their sexual behaviour and the manner of their orgasm – if not by the physical dimensions of their vaginas, as the *Kamasutra* had done. The 'cold' woman, Bell observed, has only 'one evanescent emotion when the paroxysm reaches its crisis'. 'The warmer, but yet experienced woman,' he continued, 'strives to conceal her sensibility and fixes her features; but, some time before the crisis of the passion, that fixity becomes contraction of the features, and their paleness betrays her interior sensation.' As for the 'voluptuous' woman, she is 'at the first warm, blushing, yielding and free from constraint – successive and grad- ually increasing chills soon take the place of the flush; – the features seem to contract as well as to become pale; – the eyelids drop over the eyeballs, which are convulsively drawn upward and inward, while the lips are half opened.' Bell also analysed the phe- nomenon of orgasm, and discussed whether or not it was related to conception – a question long pondered in both West and East. Like many *kama shastra* texts (and like William Acton), Bell wondered whether women or men experienced greater sexual pleasure. He concluded that women, having greater 'sensibility' in general, had better orgasms, but ultimately ducked the issue by saying 'it would require a new Tiresias to determine this point'.

The *Kalogynomia* would have been more useful to the sexual tyro than *Every Woman's Book* or *The Elements of Social Science*. Bell may not have enumerated the postures, but he did describe the sexual act with unprecedented precision, giving a helpful sense of the kind of movements that the man might be expected to perform. 'In this operation… it is not one and the same contact, but a repetition of contacts, which communicates pleasure. Hence in coition, the male and female alternately withdraw and approach in manners which are modified by the sensibility, the disposition, the taste, and the experience of each.' Unfortunately, this was about all Bell wrote on the specific topic of how to actually perform the sex act. It was hardly a detailed breakdown of coital positions, still less an eight-part disquisition on how to give oral sex. As Arbuthnot noted, the *Kalogynomia* had its uses but offered little more than 'ele- mentary principles' when compared to the *Kamasutra*. Writing to Ashbee, Arbuthnot compared the woeful state of European – and, worst of all, English – sex education with 'the philosophy and knowledge of conjugal arts peculiar to the people who dwell under a hotter sun than we do'. Referring to 'the writings of the old Indian sages', he concluded that 'Europeans and modern society generally would be greatly benefited by some such treatises'.

The *Kamasutra*, then, was designed not just to fill a gap in the market but, by virtue of its exoticism, to show how anomalous and culturally determined that gap was. Burton scornfully compared 'the ultra-delicacy, the squeamishness of an age which is by no means purer or more virtuous than its ruder predecessors' with the superiority of what he considered to be Oriental attitudes. He admired the worthy pragmatism of 'Moslems and Easterns in general', who

> intelligently study the art and mystery of satisfying the physical woman... I have noticed among barbarians the system of 'making men', that is, of teaching lads first arrived at puberty the nice conduct of the *instrumentum paratum plantandis avibus*: a branch of the knowledge-tree which our modern education grossly neglects, thereby entailing untold miseries upon individuals, families and generations. The mock virtue, the most immodest modesty of England and of the United States in the nineteenth century, pronounces the subject foul and fulsome: 'Society' sickens at all details; and hence it is said abroad that the English have the finest women in Europe and least know how to use them.

Burton's jocularity — the Latin translates as 'the instrument designed for the ploughing of birds' — belies his outraged sincerity. As well as witnessing the behaviour of the contemporary East, Burton had absorbed the arguments of the *Kamasutra*. These described sexual expertise as nothing less than a social and moral obligation, especially for men. According to Vatsyayana, women should be at least acquainted with the science of *kama*, but it was particularly incumbent upon men to educate and improve themselves in this respect. Knowledge and employment of the 'sixty-four arts' guaranteed the *nagaraka* respect among the learned, made him a leader in society and earned him the love of his wife – as well as the wives of others, not to mention courtesans. As Burton put it, 'where then is the shame of teaching what it is shameful not to have learnt?'

In Vatsyayana's view, it was only by proper study and self-improvement that humanity was elevated above the animals, and this applied to sexuality as much as to any other field of human activity. According to the *Kamasutra*, animals merely rut unrestrained in season, their 'intercourse not being preceded by thought of any kind'. Humanity, by contrast, distinguishes itself by cultivation. Or, as Vatsyayana put it, 'sexual intercourse being a thing dependent on man and woman requires the application of proper means'. The argument that art improved nature was a standard of the Western classical tradition, it was just that the West, at this time, did not apply it to the realm of sexuality.

After the flurry of activity surrounding the printing of the *Kamasutra*, two watchful years passed without any further sign of the Kama Shastra Society – and without prosecution. Emboldened, in 1885 Arbuthnot and Burton issued another Indian erotic classic: the *Ananga Ranga*. This time it bore a more confident title-page declaring it to have been 'Translated from the Sanscrit and annotated by A.F.F. and B.F.R.' The Kama Shastra Society's subscribers must have raised their eyebrows at the audacity. The translators were deliberately challenging and goading the censors. The book's

introduction touted the 'extreme delicacy' with which the sixteenth-century author, Kalyanamalla, had handled his theme,
while also giving a fairly unequivocal idea of the actual contents.
Readers were promised that 'all you who read this book shall know
how delicious an instrument is woman, when artfully played
upon; how capable she is of producing the most exquisite
harmony; of executing the most complicated variations and of
giving the divinest pleasures'.

In the same year, the Kama Shastra Society produced the first
volumes of a monumental translation of the *Arabian Nights*, or *The
Thousand Nights and a Night*. Unlike the *Kamasutra* or the *Ananga Ranga*,
it was not a new and entirely original translation, but it was the first
to present the original stories unexpurgated, complete with what
its publishers called all 'the naïve indecencies'. The book was
another private printing, to be sold to subscribers only, but it was
not considered so outrageous that the translator's name had to be
concealed behind the mask of a fictitious society. His identity was
plainly announced. It was none other than Her Majesty's Consul in
Trieste, the cunningly disguised penetrator of Mecca, the bold
discoverer of the Great Lakes region of Africa, the brilliant swords-
man, controversial diplomat and polyglot Orientalist: Captain Sir
Richard Francis Burton. As the sexologist Alex Comfort later put
it, the djinn was right out of the bottle. If Burton was behind the
Nights, the public would know that he was behind the Kama
Shastra Society – at least, those members of the public who had
ever heard of it would know. Dazzled by Burton's celebrity,
perhaps, no one troubled to enquire into the identity of his original
co-translator, 'A.F.F.'

Touting his *Arabian Nights* to Bernard Quaritch, who had been
one of the first booksellers to stock FitzGerald's *Rubáiyát of Omar*

Khayyám, Burton had wondered, 'What *will* Mrs Grundy say?' He promptly answered his own question: 'I predict read every word of it and call the translator very ugly names.' He was right: *The Arabian Nights* was a massive commercial success, albeit a controversial one. So successful were the ten volumes of the *Nights* that a further six *Supplemental Nights* were issued the following year. They too sold out. At last, Burton's career was crowned with financial reward. He commented bitterly that 'I struggled for 47 years. I distinguished myself in every way I possibly could. I never had a compliment nor a "thank you" nor a single farthing. I translated a doubtful book in my old age and immediately made 16,000 guineas. Now that I know the tastes of England, we need never be without money.'

Despite his earnest protestations that his books were aimed at serious scholars, despite his lofty aims to shame hypocrisy and expose ignorance, Burton had discovered in the most tangible way possible that, as sex became an ever greater preoccupation in Western society, books about sex would sell in ever greater numbers. As the 1880s drew to a close, Burton set about translating erotica with a furious energy. If the Midian and West Africa could not be made to produce gold, perhaps dirty books would do it. It was as if he could sense the approaching end – and sense the direction in which social mores were moving.

Burton believed that Anglo-American society was temporarily aberrant, and that natural good sense would eventually be restored. In 1888, he wrote that the public was 'slowly but surely emancipating itself from the prudish and prurient reticences and the immodest and immoral modesties of the early nineteenth century'. His own work would be judged, in good time, with 'full and ample justice'. In May 1889, he wrote to the publisher Leonard Smithers to say that 'It appears to me that the national purity is going too far and that a reaction will presently set in.' Smithers was a self-consciously bohemian figure who dressed as an undertaker and legendarily had himself photographed buggering his wife in a basement print works on the west side of Shepherd's Bush (an act bizarrely reminiscent of the eighteenth-century *maharajas* having themselves painted having sex with their wives and courtesans). In the coming decade he would become the celebrated 'Publisher to the Decadents' – notably Oscar Wilde, Arthur Symons and Aubrey Beardsley.

In early 1890, Burton began work on a revised translation of *The Perfumed Garden of the Sheik Nefzaoui*, a sex manual sometimes referred to as 'the Arab *Kama Sutra*'. The Kama Shastra Society had already issued a subscription-only English edition back in 1886, but it was little more than a rip-off of a French translation printed in Paris by the highbrow Parisian pornographer Isidore Liseux – with the added bonus of plentiful creative additions from Burton's own hand. Burton, as ever, was quite happy to add material; what he could not bear, as a translator, was to excise it. The French version of *The Perfumed Garden* had lacked a crucial section on homosexuality found in the Arabic original, but Burton finally tracked down a complete manuscript after a long search. In his declining months he strove to rectify his former work, labouring every day from half past five in the morning until dusk. He gave his manuscript the new title of *The Scented Garden* and asked Arbuthnot by letter to take care of the manuscript in the event of his death.

In May, Arbuthnot came to Trieste to visit his old friend. Together they sat out on the verandah, listening to the nightingales, recalling their Indian days and no doubt arguing about their latest translation projects. A photograph shows the two men sitting together with Isabel in the garden. A jovial and mischievous

Bunny, his bowler perched cheekily on his head, looks across at his white-haired, white-bearded and obviously failing friend. Burton described Arbuthnot's stay as 'like a whiff of London in the Pontine marshes of Trieste'. If so, it was the last breath of that cosmopolitan air. As the summer waned, Burton's health declined. By October, according to his early biographer, Thomas Wright, 'His eyes, though still fierce and penetrating, were sunk into hollow cavities. His body was emaciated, his hands were thin to transparency, his voice was sometimes inarticulate.' Together with Isabel, he took to releasing caged birds in the garden. On 29 October, Isabel returned from Sunday Mass to find her husband working on the last page of the twentieth chapter of *The Scented Garden*. By midnight, he was complaining of severe gout pain. His condition quickly deteriorated. Shortly before dawn, frantically gasping for air, he cried out, 'I am dying, I am dead,' and collapsed.

A few weeks later, a grieving Isabel wrote to Arbuthnot and his wife Elinor to thank them for their sympathy. 'I am so thoroughly stunned that I feel nothing outside, but my heart is crucified,' she said. 'I have saved his gold watch-chain as a memorial for *you*.' Arbuthnot might have preferred her to save Burton's work, especially the manuscript of *The Scented Garden*. But this was not possible. In the wake of her husband's death, Isabel had burned the text, claiming she had 'reason to know that *I did what he wanted me to do, what he wished himself*'. The legend of an 'insane orgy' of manuscript burning that accompanied the destruction of *The Scented Garden* is ill-founded, although certainly Isabel cleared out the house in Trieste with a recent widow's manic thoroughness, and she ordered many more papers to be destroyed after her own death – including, it seems, everything that related to the *Kamasutra* or the Kama Shastra Society.

Isabel is often supposed to have been so shocked by discovering what her husband was really up to in his study that she cleansed her house by fire. In fact, she later wrote that while 'Richard wished that his men friends shd think I did not know what he was engaged upon', she knew perfectly well what he was about. She read his draft manuscripts. Coyly, she protested, 'I cannot afford to be particular what words I *see*, nor do they do me any harm.' Even in the first weeks after her husband's death, Isabel was impressively methodical, not maniacal. She took care to make a copy of the first and last lines of every page of *The Scented Garden*. She was clearly well aware of the speed and ruthlessness with which the pornographic book industry worked, and felt she needed to be able to defend her husband's reputation against unscrupulous publishers trying to claim their own, pirated versions as the work of 'Burton'.

Isabel could not, however, stand guard over books that had already been published – although, ironically, if she had chosen to preserve the papers relating to the Kama Shastra Society, Burton's supposed authorship of the 1883 translation of the *Kamasutra* would long since have been exposed as dubious. In her *Life of Burton*, Isabel explained that she was afraid not of the nature of her husband's work but of its possible reception. She feared that his publications 'would by degrees descend amongst the populace out of Holywell Street, the very opposite result to what the upright, manly translator would have desired, and the whole contents might be so misunderstood by the uneducated that the good, noble stories [and the] life of Richard Burton... might be handed down to posterity in a false light'. The funeral pyre of Burton's *The Scented Garden* may have run scandalously counter to his lifelong campaign against hypocrisy and bowdlerization but, judging by what happened to the *Kamasutra* after his death, Isabel was remarkably prescient. The next century in the life of the book would largely belong not to the upright and manly worlds of thrusting explorers and penetrating anthropologists, but to the murky realm of pornographic publishing. The *Kamasutra*'s future would belong to Holywell Street and its descendants — to the *nagarakas* of the modern world. As ever, scholars would have to fight to reclaim the book as their own.

*I*F A MAN is attached to her and has done favours for her in the past, even if he now yields but little fruit, she keeps him around by lying. But if he has nothing left at all and no resources to do anything about it, she gets rid of him by some contrivance, without any consideration, and gets support from another man. She does for him what he does not want, and she does repeatedly what he has criticized. She curls her lip and stamps on the ground with her foot. She talks about things he does not know about. She shows no amazement, but only contempt, for the things he does know about. She punctures his pride. She has affairs with men who are superior to him. She ignores him. She criticizes men who have the same faults. And she stalls when they are alone together. She is upset by the things he does for her when they are making love. She does not offer him her mouth.

Kamasutra
Book Six: Courtesans
Chapter Three: Ways to Get Rid of Him
translated by Wendy Doniger and Sudhir Kakar (2002)

CHAPTER SIX

Overwhelming Obscenity

Without Richard Burton's presiding genius, the *Kamasutra* would be no better known today than Tung-Hsüan's seventh-century *Art of Love*, Ovid's *Ars Amatoria* or any one of a host of other sex manuals or erotic treatises from distant countries or times. It was Burton's list of erotomaniac contacts that ensured the initial success of the Kama Shastra Society's printings. It was Burton's status as a great explorer and Orientalist that lent the *Kamasutra* authenticity as a piece of anthropological archaeology, offering a fig-leaf cover of at least semi-respectability. Ultimately, it was Burton's reputation as a Romantic, counter-culture hero, waving goodbye to – or giving the finger to – Victorian values with one hand, and beckoning in the world of modernity with the other, that ushered the *Kamasutra* towards its fame and ubiquity in the twentieth century.

More immediately, it was Burton's decision to publish 'his' translation of the *Kamasutra* as a limited edition for subscribers only that, perversely, ensured its worldwide fame. The fact that the 1883 *Kamasutra* was a secretive private printing meant that its publishers could not establish copyright; and in any case they would hardly dare bring a prosecution for any infringment of their rights. This lack of legal protection did not escape the attention of the buccaneer pornographers of London and Paris – in some cases, the very same people who had supplied Fred Hankey and Richard Monckton Milnes with their 'private' libraries. As Isabel Burton had feared, the British public was less interested in the 'manners and customs of the olden East', as the 1883 *Kamasutra*'s dedication had phrased it, than in sex.

Exotic, aristocratic sex was particularly fascinating. The vellum-bound second printing was hardly off the presses before the first pirated editions were being sold on Holywell Street. This was the first pulse of the feverish underground life of the *Kamasutra*, a life that would continue for as long as England's obscenity laws lasted. The earliest editions were classy affairs, physically at least, reflecting the perceived tone of the *Kamasutra*. The notorious pornographer Edward Avery carefully copied the Kama Shastra Society's pristine white-vellum bindings for his copycat editions, while in 1885 the Parisian publisher of erotica, Isidore Liseux, produced a French 'édition privée' in a limited run of 220 copies, each of which cost the princely sum of 75 francs. Such high production qualities advertised the fact that this was no mere sex guide; it was a precious and elegant work. This was lovemaking for lords and princes.

Isidore Liseux's original advertisement assured readers that no book was 'more capable of exciting curiosity', that they would 'enter into a civilization full of mysteries, a kind of virgin forest in which they would march from surprise to surprise'. Readers of the *Kamasutra* felt themselves to be explorers of exotic realms. The advertisement also suggested a surprisingly close acquaintance with the story of how this 'virgin forest' was originally discovered.

'This extraordinary work only exists, even in India, in manuscript,' it boasted. 'Hardly more than a few copies are known, and these are carefully hidden from the eyes of the profane in the libraries of Benares, Calcutta and Jaipur.' This was quite true. As Arbuthnot and Burton had discovered in the 1870s, far from being the well-thumbed Bible of a living erotic tradition in India, the *Kamasutra* was in fact extremely difficult to find. Manuscripts were rare, and printed copies of the original Sanskrit simply did not exist. The erotic tradition in India had fallen into a long sleep.

In 1883, however, everything had changed. The printing of the English *Kamasutra* acted as a starting gun to Europe's pornographic publishers, causing them to fall over each other to see who could pirate the book fastest. The noise they made was loud enough to wake up even Sanskrit scholars – some as far away as India itself. The truth is that it was Arbuthnot and Burton – along with Indraji and Bhide, of course – who stimulated India to rediscover the Ur-text of its own, almost-vanished erotic tradition. In 1891, Pandit Durgaprasad, of Jaipur, published an edition of the Sanskrit text in Bombay. It was the first time that Vatsyayana's original *sutras* had ever been printed. Despite the title-page's warning – printed in English – that the book was 'For Private Circulation only', it managed to excite ripples in learned circles. In July, the eminent Sanskritist Peter Peterson actually dared to read aloud a review of the new edition to the Bombay branch of the Royal Asiatic Society. The reactions of the audience were, unfortunately, not recorded.

Peterson had been a personal friend of both Bhagvanlal Indraji and Georg Bühler, and had, he claimed, himself secured a fragment of the *Jayamangala* for the Bombay government collection back in 1883. He was interested not in the *Kamasutra*'s explicit material but in the extraordinary way in which it had evidently influenced Sanskrit drama. Peterson avowed that the book was 'a work which is destined, I believe, to throw a great deal of light on much that is still dark in the ancient history of this country'. He would be proved right. The *Kamasutra* was a kind of key to the treasure-house of Sanskrit erotic literature. Indian eroticism was clearly no decadent medieval sideshow, and Indian *pandits* and Western Indologists alike would have to change the way they thought about India — as, ultimately, would the rest of the world.

Pandit Durgaprasad did not know it, but he had also won a race with Foster Fitzgerald Arbuthnot — thereby, in a small way, reclaiming the *Kamasutra* for India. Even as his Sanskrit edition was about to reach the presses, Arbuthnot was struggling to get his own (or rather, Bhagvanlal Indraji's) Sanskrit text published in Britain. Arbuthnot's slow, quiet — and ultimately ineffectual — approach reveals quite how crucial a role Burton had played in making sure the English translation saw the light of day. Back in March 1884, Arbuthnot had written to the head of Oxford's Bodleian Library, E.W.B. Nicholson, to say that he had given Max Müller, Oxford's stylish and extrovert Professor of Comparative Philology, a copy of his *Kamasutra*, and had asked him 'to be good enough to give it to you with my compliments'. Arbuthnot's next sentence was written in red ink, and underlined for good measure: '*The Sanscrit mSS he will hand over to you for the Bodleian when has done with them.*' Nicholson must have wondered what on earth Müller was doing with the manuscripts. The answer did not arrive until seven years later, in July 1891, when Müller wrote to Nicholson from his rooms in one of the brand-new villas of Norham Gardens, in the academic enclave of north Oxford. He had lent the *Kamasutra* manuscripts to the Sanskritist Maurice Winternitz, he explained, who had been thinking about publishing the Sanskrit text. 'But as the text has now been published in India,' Müller continued, 'he has given up the idea.'

Arbuthnot had missed his chance. His manuscripts – Indraji's revised text of the *Kamasutra* and the original Benares copy – were quietly deposited in the Bodleian, where they have since gathered dust, unrecognized. Even if rich British pornophiles and Bombay *pandits* were ready for the *Kamasutra*, Oxford Sanskritists were not. Arbuthnot threw himself instead into more mainstream projects, reviving his idea of an Oriental Translation Fund and contributing generously to the Royal Asiatic Society from his own pocket for the purpose. Thirteen volumes were published by the time of his death in 1901; not one of them was an erotic work.

The disappearance of Arbuthnot's manuscripts, fortunately, did not mean that the *Kamasutra* vanished from sight. It was given a new impetus by the distinguished German Sanskritist Richard Schmidt, who published his own translation in 1897. As had been the case in 1883, Schmidt was keen for his book not to fall into the hands of the profane. Instead of limiting the print run, as Arbuthnot and Burton had done, Schmidt took the extraordinary decision to translate all the *Kamasutra*'s sexually explicit material into Latin rather than German, thus creating a bilingual text. The result was that only linguists – or of course gentlemen with the benefit of a Classical education – would be able to understand the book's dirty bits. Partly thanks to its lack of obscenity – vulgar obscenity, at any rate – Schmidt's translation became accepted as the academic gold standard. It would never become anything like as well known as the 1883 *Kamasutra*, but the distance that it had marked out for itself from the world of smutty books allowed it to be read in influential circles.

The ripples of the stone cast in 1883 were now spreading outwards. Schmidt's *Kamasutra* was picked up by the Berlin dermatologist and 'father of sexology', Iwan Bloch, who discussed Vatsyayana's work in an essay he wrote on 'Indian Medicine' in 1902. Bloch, in turn, was read by Havelock Ellis, Britain's pioneer sexologist. It's likely that Ellis knew about the 1883 *Kamasutra* early on, perhaps through his membership of the Fellowship of the New Life, a pacifist-leaning, liberal-radical club dedicated to self-improvement. Many members of the Fellowship were fascinated by Indian mysticism, notably Annie Besant, the celebrated Theosophist (and erstwhile publisher of *The Fruits of Philosophy*), and Edward Carpenter, a homosexual activist and close colleague of Ellis's who had travelled in India and was a devoted student of the *Bhagavadgita*. Ellis had also worked with Burton's old flagellant friend A.C. Swinburne on the Mermaid series of unexpurgated Elizabethan dramas, and had collaborated closely with John Addington Symonds on their landmark 1896 study of homosexuality, *Sexual Inversion*. Symonds, in turn, had corresponded at length with Richard Burton, then England's chief authority on the topic of homosexuality, thanks to the essay in his *Arabian Nights*. (*Sexual Inversion* accused Burton of being 'wholly unacquainted with the recent psychological investigations into sexual inversion', thus distancing what Ellis liked to consider his new, modern, psychological approach from Burton's catch-all, literary-ethnological approach.)

It's impossible to be sure how exactly Ellis first heard about the *Kamasutra*, but certainly, by the time he published *Sex in Relation to Society*, in 1910, he knew enough about it to write: 'there has long existed an English translation of this work.' Ellis was fascinated by the *Kamasutra*'s discussion of erotic pain and seductive techniques, and described both at length in his book. He also affirmed that 'The old Hindu erotic writers attributed great importance alike to the man's attentiveness to the woman's erotic needs... He must do all that he can to procure her pleasure, says Vatsyayana.' Ellis pronounced the author of the *Kamasutra* to be 'one of the greatest of authorities' and approved the 'spirit of gravity' found in Indian erotic treatises in general. 'Nowhere else,' he wrote, 'have the anatomical and physiological sexual characters of women been studied with such minute and adoring reverence.'

Through Havelock Ellis, Vatsyayana's book of love would finally be recognized by Western science. It took longer for it to be absorbed into the burgeoning realm of Western sex manuals. The *Kamasutra*, for instance, was probably unknown to Dr Elizabeth Blackwell, another intimate of the Fellowship of the New Life and author of *The Human Element in Sex, Being a Medical Enquiry into the Relation of Sexual Physiology to Christian Morality*. Writing in 1884, Blackwell attacked 'the prevalent fallacy that sexual passion is the almost exclusive attribute of men' and praised 'the beneficent control which the human mind can exercise over the passion'. Both sentiments are central to the *Kamasutra*, but hardly unique to it. Even Marie Stopes's 1918 bestseller, *Married Love*, showed small sign of any acquaintance with the Indian arts. At most it is possible to catch a dim echo of the *Kamasutra* in Stopes's answer to the question: 'Is not instinct enough?' No, she declares, 'instinct is not enough. In every other human activity it has been realized that training, the handing on of tradition are essential.' Or as Vatsyayana put it, 'because a man and a woman depend upon one another in sex, it requires a method'.

When Stopes wrote *Married Love*, the *Kamasutra* had evidently not penetrated the consciousness of Western sex writers. It was still hovering around the shadier edges of society, at best. One problem

was that the earliest campaigners and sex writers tended to come
from nonconformist, liberal or medical backgrounds. All too often,
their works were laudably sensible and, in their efforts to steer clear
of any suggestion of lubriciousness, any sense of pleasure in eroticism was lost. Such authors were likely to take a dim view of a
salacious work of Oriental eroticism. Until the 1960s, few sex
writers, if any, straddled the worlds of politics and pornography as
comfortably as Arbuthnot and Burton.

Politics was one problem; sheer availability was another. In the
1890s, London's harried erotic publishers had decamped from
Holywell Street and resettled in the relatively liberal climate of
Paris. Even Havelock Ellis had been able to lay hands on only a
pirated French translation of the *Kamasutra*, which had been printed
in Paris in 1891 and illegally shipped back across the Channel. Erotic
books, whether Oriental or more homely, were banned under
obscenity and postal censorship laws that were policed with vigour.
In the first part of the twentieth century, the risks for British publishers and booksellers were just too great. It was only in the 1920s,
when a few American publishers began to take an interest in this
Indo-pornographic curiosity, that the *Kamasutra* was pushed
towards a less clandestine market. For the first time, the book of
love would reach an audience wider than a few eccentric experts
and dissipated aristocrats.

At first, the climate of the US was scarcely any more favourable
to erotica than Europe's. In 1923, the pornographic publisher
'Broadway' Samuel Roth was sentenced to ninety days in jail, under
the repressive Comstock Act, for sending a $35 limited edition of
Burton's *The Perfumed Garden* through the US mail. If the prosecution was meant as a warning, however, it failed. The American
'Society of the Friends of India' dared to reprint the 1883 Kamasutra

in 1925, while the Risus Press of New York published a few short extracts in the same year, although both editions were limited to under 1,000 copies. This kind of publishing programme would no doubt give a few lucky buyers tremendous excitement, but it would hardly bring the wisdom of the *Kamasutra* to the masses.

Far more significant was the compilation, the following year, of a tiny, flimsy booklet entitled *A Hindu Book of Love (The Kama Sutra)*. It squeezed excerpts of the 1883 text into the sixty-four-page format of the famous – and sometimes infamous – Little Blue Book series. This was a quasi-philanthropic operation set up by the socialist publisher Emanuel Haldeman-Julius, 'the Henry Ford of literature'. The idea was to mass-produce classic works of literature at bargain prices; workers, the theory went, would order the staple-bound books by mail and thus acquire the rudiments at least of a full Humanist education – including sex education; also on the Little Blue list were *Prostitution in the Modern World* and *Strange Marriage Customs*. Just as in 1883, a printing of the *Kamasutra* in Girard, Kansas, in 1926, was about more than recovering an ancient classic. The editing was done by Leo Markun, a hack writer with radical, anti-censorship leanings who was also responsible for the alarming *Mrs Grundy: A History of Four Centuries of Morals Intended to Illuminate Present Problems in Great Britain and the United States*. Richard Burton would have been proud. *A Hindu Book of Love* duly took its place alongside other Little Blue Books presenting radical, alternative lifestyles such as that of the homosexual, the agnostic and the man who knew *How To Be Happy Though Married*. Perhaps the *Hindu Book of Love* was intended to achieve the same effect, at least among the 70,000 Americans who bought a copy.

In the wake of the March 1930 judgement of the splendidly named Justice Augustus Hand, which reversed the conviction of Mary

Ware Dennett for mailing her pamphlet *The Sex Side of Life*, the atmosphere in the US brightened a little. Justice Hand found that 'an accurate exposition of the relevant facts of the sex side of life in decent language and in a manifestly serious and disinterested spirit cannot ordinarily be regarded as obscene'. In the same year, amendments to the Tariff Act allowed 'classics or books of recognized literary or scientific merit' to be imported from Europe – although some senators fought the amendment with everything they could throw at it. Senator Reed Smoot, of Utah, actually sermonized from behind a pile of 'obscene' books, a private printing of Lawrence's *Lady Chatterley's Lover* and the *Kamasutra* among them. Clearly, even if Vatsyayana's book of love was not reaching mass audiences, it was acquiring a reputation as one of the world's more dangerously sexual works – and also as a classic.

Smoot's theatricals didn't do him any good and, in April 1931, Federal Judge Woolsey lifted the ban on Marie Stopes's classic, *Married Love*. Tolerance, if not acceptance, was growing. But still, the *Kamasutra* failed to find a mainstream publisher. In 1932, Edward Windsor and the aptly named Panurge Press, of New York – a dubious enterprise run by friends of Samuel Roth specializing in mail-order pornography – published an Indo-erotological compilation grandly entitled *Cultural and Anthropological Studies in the Hindu Art of Love*. It incorporated most of the 1883 *Kamasutra*, albeit turned into 'explanatory extracts and summations', along with excerpts from the *Ananga Ranga* and other *kama shastra* works. It looked like an impressive product, aiming to expose the third of what it called the 'three great fundamentals of Hindu civilization: the caste system, child marriage, and the Ars Amoris Indica'. These secrets would be revealed exclusively to the 'private collectors of erotica' who had $5 to spare for one of the 1,500 numbered copies. The book, however, was much less worthy than it seemed. Most of it was ripped off, unacknowledged, from Richard Schmidt's magnum opus on Indian erotic literature, *Beiträge zur Indische Erotik*, or *Contributions on Indian Erotics*, which had been published in Berlin twenty years previously.

No more respectable was the edition disgorged by the so-called Medical Press of New York, in 1936. This was yet another semi-pornographic affair, issued this time by Sam Roth's chief collaborator, Jack Brussel — the forty-page introductory essay on 'The Doctor as Marriage Advisor' was simply lifted from an Austrian publisher's edition of Richard Schmidt's translation. But the Medical Press was not totally without imagination. In the same year, it issued the first *Kamasutra* to offer what would afterwards become the obligatory accompaniment to Vatsyayana's text: illustrations. These were not actual reproductions of erotic miniatures, but the artist, Mahlon Blaine, a bohemian figure who had acquired a steel plate in his head during World War I, was clearly extremely familiar with Indian erotic art. (His work was also heavily influenced by Aubrey Beardsley; tantalizingly, if Richard Burton had lived a little longer, Beardsley himself might well have ended up illustrating the *Kamasutra*, as the two men shared a publisher and a friend, Leonard Smithers.)

There was little sign of the *Kamasutra*, on either side of the Atlantic, in the late 1930s and 1940s, although a horse named Kama Soutra did finish as an also-ran at the Hyde Park Handicap of September 1937. After the hiatus of World War II, the flow of pornographic material from Paris to London was resumed. Les éditions de la Fontaine d'Or, or 'Golden Fountain Press', kept up the city's eroto-bibliophilic traditions by issuing a veritable stream of editions of what it called the 'Love Precepts of the Brahmans' from 1952

onwards. But the best-selling version of the *Kamasutra* belonged to
the notorious Olympia Press, again based in Paris. Issued in 1958,
with the dirty-green paper cover of the Traveller's Companion
series, their edition masqueraded under the authoritative-
sounding title of *Classical Hindu Erotology* and bore the spurious
imprimatur of one 'Swami Ram Krishnanada', a travesty of the
name of Swami Krishnananda, the Rishikesh-based leader of
the yogic Divine Life Society. Pornography, as ever, was slipping in
under the wrapper of Indology.

The Olympia edition sold in the tens of thousands, but it was
still forced to live in the semi-darkness of brown-paper packaging
and the backs of closets – a fact that only contributed to its reputation as potent pornography. Then, in 1961, the *Kamasutra* was
finally thrust into the sunlight. The force behind the shove was the
publication, on both sides of the Atlantic, of D.H. Lawrence's *Lady
Chatterley's Lover*. In the US, Federal Judge Frederick van Pelt Bryan
ruled in July 1959 that Grove Press's unexpurgated book-club
edition of the novel was not obscene, stating that 'the sincerity and
purpose of an author as expressed in the manner in which a book
is written and in which his theme and ideas are developed has a
great deal to do with whether it is of literary and intellectual
merit'. In the UK, on the basis of the reformed Obscene Publications Act of 1959, and Grove Press's success in the US, Penguin
Books dared to publish *Lady Chatterley's Lover* in August 1960. The
case came to trial in October and the jury returned a landmark
verdict of not guilty.

In publishing terms, Pandora's box was suddenly wide open.
Chatterley sold 2 million copies within a year. But publishers in the
United States were still faced with powerful conservative forces.
Boston's censorious Deputy Collector of Customs singled out the

Kamasutra for criticism. He was particularly horrified by its love slaps, scratches and bites, testifying in 1962 that 'the human mind is scarcely able to withstand the impact of the overwhelming obscenity and sexually-based desire for torture' in the book. The stakes were indeed high: facing the *Kamasutra* on the table was nothing less than sanity. Notwithstanding such rearguard actions, by 1962 a number of American publishers had staked their own claims in the Great Sex Rush.

The new fashion was for the *Kamasutra* to be prefaced by serious-minded essays from celebrity contributors, preferably with an Indian background. The latest production of the Medical Press of New York came with an approbatory introduction by the Indian novelist Mulk Raj Anand, who had published his *Homage to Khajuraho* two years earlier. E.P. Dutton, meanwhile, rushed out their own *Kamasutra* with a foreword by the Indian travel writer, Santha Rama Rau. She somehow assumed that Vatsyayana was describing the sex lives of contemporary Indians – an assumption based, presumably, on the old, patronizing hypothesis that India was primitive and unchanging. Accompanying her foreword was an essay by John W. Spellman who, unlike Rau, was an authority on ancient India. Unwittingly, Spellman gave a fillip to a no less misleading tradition by discussing the sexual aspects of Tantric belief and practice as part of the *Kamasutra*'s cultural context. Tragically, the spurious link between the *Kamasutra* and Tantra was made, and would prove almost impossible to untie. Over the next forty years, endless pulp sex books naively portraying the wonders of 'Indian sexuality' would roll the *Kamasutra* and Tantrism into one.

In London, William Kimber's 1963 edition tried to frame the *Kamasutra* in a more interesting context. This time, Vatsyayana's book of love was accompanied by a new translation of the *Phaedrus*, as if to suggest that these two Classical texts on erotic love were somehow in conversation – and that Vatsyayana could fight his corner with Plato, no less. Kenneth Walker's learned introduction even speculated on the Indian origins of Greek thought. Courtesy of the erotic pull of the *Kamasutra*, the idea that the West might have something to learn from it – something other than extreme sexual positions, that is – was finally reaching mass audiences.

As curator for their rival London edition, the respected house of George, Allen and Unwin chose W.G. Archer, the renowned Keeper of the Indian Section at the Victoria and Albert Museum. Like Arbuthnot, Bill Archer had worked as a British civil servant in India; like Burton, he had travelled extensively in the country with his wife – herself an acclaimed scholar of Indian art. In India, Archer had been no friend to the bridge-and-tiffin lifestyle of the Raj. He later recalled that he had been at his happiest when travelling in the Indian countryside, campaigning for village welfare as a district officer. He was that rare thing in the Indian Civil Service: a left-winger. He had been 'warmly friendly with Indians' and had even campaigned for independence. In a letter to a friend, he explained that his motivations had been emotional as much as political. 'I had found fulfilment in merging myself with the local people,' he wrote, in going 'deeper and deeper into Indian life and customs'. He had been, he confessed, 'the very opposite of aloof'. On returning to England in May 1948, Archer tried to settle in Oxford but found himself lost and unhappy. He missed the 'voluptuousness in the climate of India', the 'indescribable softness which soothes the mind and gives it up to the most delightful sensations'. He had, he said, 'acquired a sense of Indian identity'.

Editing the *Kamasutra*, then, was about more than scholarship.

Archer was convinced of the 'vital importance of the Introductory essays'. Following Arbuthnot's lead, he realized that they had the power to turn pornography into Indology, and Indology into politics. Which, of course, also made them a convenient shield against prosecution – and the risks were still very real. In December 1964, the Edinburgh magistrate Norman McQueen declared that the *Kamasutra* and *The Perfumed Garden* 'were capable of promoting and encouraging immoral practices and of inviting an unhealthy disregard for the proper limits of sexual behaviour'. Fortunately, Bailie McQueen's powers to set those limits were themselves somewhat limited. He 'admonished' a local bookseller, James Paterson, and confiscated his modest stock. Paterson promptly appealed, his advocate arguing that 'there is nothing shameful or indecent about love'.

Archer's introduction was not just window dressing. It was magnificent. He uncovered (most of) the story of the Kama Shastra Society, capturing the sense of risk and excitement felt by Arbuthnot and Burton – and pointing out that Burton had done little of the actual translation work. (Though nobody, apparently, was listening.) Unlike his rival American editors, Archer also knew a vast amount about the erotic in ancient India and could begin to place the *Kamasutra* in its real context. For Archer, the *Kamasutra* was fascinating not as a sex manual but as a monument to Indian civilization. The discovery of the *Kamasutra*'s existence, he wrote, 'revolutionised the Western approach to Indian culture. It showed how central and natural to Indian thought and life was sex... It is not too much to claim that from this classic translation in 1883 the modern understanding of Indian art and culture derives.'

Less than a hundred years after Bhagvanlal Indraji's search for a rare manuscript of the *Kamasutra*, Vatsyayana's book of love had finally become ubiquitous. It had not only recovered its place as *the* authority on sex in India, it was being hailed as one of the great Indian classics. Of course, not all readers agreed with Archer's judgement. Some preferred to continue to think of the *Kamasutra* as smut. In the *Saturday Review*, Robert J. Clements sneered that by pushing the book into the mainstream publishers had taken away all the thrill of the chase. The *New York Herald Tribune*'s reviewer, by contrast, was glad to assert that proper publication of the *Kamasutra* would 'do much to dispel this harem reputation and put it in its proper place as a fascinating – and still in many ways useful – classic of erotic and social psychological and cultural history'. The aside about the *Kamasutra*'s usefulness is telling. Most reviewers were struck by the book's dual status as both erotic manual and Oriental artefact – just as Arbuthnot and Burton had been, eighty years before. Curt Gentry, in the *San Francisco Chronicle*, considered Vatsyayana's book of love to be quite redundant as a sex guide, suspecting that most readers would find it 'a strong stimulant, but only to laughter'. He admitted, however, that it might act as a useful corrective to the prevailing cliché of India as a land of asceticism. Mary Barrett, in the *Library Journal*, was evidently confused about where librarians should shelve this book of love. Vatsyayana's wholesome criticisms of adultery led her to believe that it could comfortably sit alongside contemporary marriage manuals; but then again the *Kamasutra* was by no means an uncontroversial text, so Barrett suggested that librarians might prefer to hide it away in Special Collections, or Indian History. This ruse, she felt, might also protect the book from being stolen. Quite ignoring the glaring example of Arbuthnot and Burton, she seemed to assume that students of Indian history would not be drawn to the book's sexual content.

In the publishing frenzy of 1962 and 1963, half a dozen main-stream editions of the *Kamasutra* were published in the UK and US alone. George, Allen and Unwin swiftly followed up their success with the *Kamasutra*'s greatest successor in the Indian erotic tradition: Kokkoka's *Ratirahasya* or *Koka Shastra*. Again, Bill Archer wrote a preface, but the editor, translator and chief motivator was Dr Alex Comfort. At the time, Comfort was best known as a gerontologist, but he was also an acclaimed novelist, an accomplished poet and the author, some fourteen years previously, of two landmark works of sexology. Like Richard Burton, he was a polymath. And like Foster Fitzgerald Arbuthnot, he was committed to social radicalism under the banner of personal sexual liberation. In his novels and sexological works, published in the 1940s and 1950s, Comfort developed his belief, based on a passionately held pacifism, that aggression, including political aggression, had its roots in the stress of sexual constraint and could be safely discharged only by sexual play.

In 1962, two events affected Comfort profoundly: he travelled to India, and he read the *Kamasutra*. The following year, he was arguing for 'a literature of sexual enjoyment which treats the elaboration of sexuality as Indian and Arabic works have treated it – at the level of ballroom dancing'. Comfort complained that 'there are virtually no European works of this kind, for the tradition has not, until recently, permitted them – there are plenty of marriage manuals, certainly, but of a Stopesian squareness which is enough to make one abandon the project before the banns are up.' Comfort's first response was his edition of the *Koka Shastra*. His reply to a complaint published in the *New Statesman* magazine summed up his sense of mission: 'Mr Simon Raven finds sex "an overrated sensation which lasts a bare ten seconds" – and then wonders why

anyone should bother to translate the erotic textbooks of Medieval
India. One good reason for doing so is that there are still people in
our culture who find sex an overrated sensation lasting a bare ten
seconds.' But Comfort was unhappy with Kokkoka's original text,
protesting that it represented 'the dilution of Vatsyayana's astute
scholarship with nonsense'. He was also troubled by the use of
ancient or medieval writings as practical guides for modern living.
'Sex doesn't change an awful lot,' he later commented. 'Attitudes,
however, do.'

The solution of writing his own, contemporary *Kamasutra* arose
in a single phone call with a psychiatrist at a London hospital.
The astonishing result, in 1972, was *The Joy of Sex: A Gourmet Guide to
Lovemaking*, which went on to sell more than 12 million copies
worldwide. The original back cover claimed that it was nothing less
than 'the *Kama Sutra* brought up to date'. Indian erotic techniques
permeated the book. 'A surprising number of girls cannot initially
be got there at all without prolonged genital kissing,' Comfort
wrote, 'a fact which Indian love books recognize.' Referring to the
art of biting, he noted that 'Hindu eroticians classified these at huge
length.' Comfort even concocted his own quasi-Oriental style of
lovemaking. Under the heading 'Indian style', readers were assured
that this manner was 'now widely familiar from the *Kama Sutra*, the
Koka Shastra and so on. Intercourse on a bed or on cushions, fully
naked, but with the woman wearing all her ornaments. Many
complicated positions, including some derived from yoga which
aim to avoid ejaculation.' Sadly, the promised 'complicated positions' failed to find elbow-room in the *Joy of Sex*, Comfort
dismissing them as a mere 'human classificatory hobby' and regret-
ting only 'the loss of the fancy names, Arabic, Sanskrit or Chinese,
which go with them'.

Tantrism found a place in the *Joy of Sex*, however, as did the 'Hindu' positions 'where he picks her up'. Comfort advised his joyous readers that 'Indian erotology is the only ancient tradition devoid of stupid patriarchal hangups about the need for her to be underneath.' In this statement lies the secret of the *Kamasutra*'s new-found fame. Its very distance from contemporary Western culture meant that it could be used not only as a relative standard by which modern sexual ethics could be judged, but also as a measure against which the repressive sexual attitudes of Judaeo-Christian patriarchy could be found excessively burdensome. Looking back at the West's authoritarian sexual heritage, radicals and liberals might despair, but in the *Kamasutra* they were suddenly presented with what could be read as the founding document of an alternative, sexually liberated tradition. The *Kamasutra* was not just a weapon to brandish against patriarchy; it could be used to challenge the core idea underlying Western paternalism, the idea of cultural superiority based on a more 'masculine', energetic progressivity. If the *Kamasutra* represented a healthier, more sophisticated sexual civilization than the West's, where had the West gone wrong?

Indian liberals were asking themselves a similar question about modern India, and with even greater urgency. If the erotic ideal had dominated Indian courtly culture until well into the seventeenth and eighteenth centuries, it seemed obvious that, from the nineteenth century onwards, the ascetic had gotten very much on top. Indian intellectuals began to question what had caused the wheel to turn so dramatically. The simplest and easiest answer was power and patronage. Erotic literature had been the creation of poets and princes, the argument ran, and as 'lascivious' Hindu despots had given way to 'fanatical' Mughal overlords, the patronage on which erotic literature depended had withered and died. The small problem of Mughal enthusiasm for the erotic arts could be neatly turned by claiming that the spectacular erotic creativity of that era was merely the last, valedictory flourishing of a tragically deracinated tradition. As for the British, their role in the rediscovery of India's heritage was simply dismissed. They were remembered not for translating the *Gitagovinda* or the plays of Kalidasa — still less for their painstaking work tracing *kama shastra* manuscripts in decaying libraries — but for the stiff moralism of Raj-era colonial clubs.

Among liberal nationalists, India's sexual conservatism could be blamed on an unholy combination of imposed Muslim religiosity and imported British 'Victorianism'. As always, there is some truth in the cliché, but prudery was not simply an exotic attitude forced on an innately sensual subcontinent. The sexual economics of empire were no less complex than any other form of colonial exchange. The Indian Penal Code of 1860 admittedly defined all non-procreative sex as criminal; Section 497 even threatened men who have 'sexual intercourse with a person who is and whom he knows or has reason to believe to be the wife of another man' with five years in prison. While the Code was one of the first acts of the newly established British Raj, it does not follow that it reflected purely British attitudes. In fact, it had something to do with Manu as well as Her Imperial Majesty, given that the British had used Manu's *Laws* as a guide in shaping it. Nevertheless, as soon as nationalists could compare such Raj-era strictures to Vatsyayana's hymn to the joys of 'Other Men's Wives', the result would be painfully glaring. The fact that there was no ancient, Western 'book of love' of standing comparable to Vatsyayana's only reinforced the apparent gulf between the two cultures.

For the first few years of the twentieth century, the *Kamasutra* remained in the hands of traditional Indian scholars. Not all were *pandit*-published efforts, like Durgaprasad's 1891 edition; some simply chose to remain cautiously cloaked in Vatsyayana's original Sanskrit, much as Richard Schmidt's translation had modestly disguised itself in Latin. It was not long, however, before Vatsyayana's book of love began to shed its Sanskrit clothing. A Bengali edition was the first to reveal itself, in Calcutta, in 1909, and a bilingual Hindi–Sanskrit text popped up in Bombay two years later. Then, in 1921, K. Rangaswami Iyengar, the librarian and 'First Pandit' of Mysore's Government Oriental Library, published his own English translation in Lahore – albeit only with the assurance of 'the great precautions which the reputed publishers have promised to take in the matter of its circulation'.

The *Kamasutra* was slowly insinuating itself into the consciousness of modern India – very slowly, if Iyengar's publishers were true to their word. It was not welcomed universally; far from it. As the British prepared to leave India, the retaining grip of Hindu asceticism only grew tighter. The quintessential exemplar of this ascetic ideal was Mohandas K. Gandhi, the founding father of Indian independence. For Gandhi, realizing the potential of the self and the nation alike required renunciation and discipline. Epitomizing his own ideal of *swaraj*, or self-governance, he chose to become celibate in 1906, at the age of thirty-six. If Gandhi could be said to represent the traditional Hindu goals of *dharma* and *moksha*, or duty and liberation, and Jawaharlal Nehru, India's first Prime Minister, represented *artha*, or politics and wordly success, who would stand up for *kama*? Certainly not Pandit Madhavacharya, whose 1911 Hindi–Sanskrit *Kamasutra* acquired an extraordinary introduction in 1934 that managed to interpret the text as prescriptive and

moralistic. Taking Vatsyayana at his word — that is, that the techniques of adultery were described only so as to warn honest
husbands what they might face, Madhavacharya argued that the
Kamasutra should be read by young people specifically in order to
dissuade them from philandering, and to arrest any 'improper
tendencies in desire'. Citing the holy example of Shri Rama,
Madhavacharya held up sex within marriage as the only ideal — and
procreative sex, at that. Iyengar's 1921 translation pulled a similar
stunt, apologizing for the *Kamasutra*'s coverage of adultery, the
tricks of prostitutes and oral sex between men. If Vatsyayana mentioned such 'bad and immoral practices', Iyengar explained, it was
only for the sake of 'exposing those matters and putting righteous
people on guard'.

Even liberals who wished to reclaim India's erotic heritage were
touchy about any suggestion of personal depravity. In his landmark
1929 study, *Social Life in Ancient India*, the historian Haran Chandra
Chakladar could not refrain from making the aside that oral sex is
'a very filthy practice'. He interpreted the *Kamasutra*'s account of
the 'social sore' that is sex with other men's wives as 'a masterly
analysis of the psychology of the man who seeks such love — the
jealousy, anger, hatred, passion, greed, selfishness that working
with the brain of the human animal, cloud his judgment and
pervert his tastes'. Despite his moral reservations, Chakladar was
one of the first Indian commentators to claim the *Kamasutra* as a
national treasure. For him, it was a trove that could be plundered
for its priceless gems of socio-historical detail. After all, no culture
except India had ventured to produce — and somehow preserve
over the centuries — a work describing the intimacies of daily life in
such rich detail.

Chakladar was rare in daring to discuss the *Kamasutra* openly, but even he was not advocating readership of the text by the masses. He was, after all, a historian, one of Arbuthnot's 'small portion' of the public 'which takes enlightened interest in studying the manners and customs of the olden East'. As in the West, the *Kamasutra* in India was discreetly nudged into specialist arenas, notably into the not-so-sterile hands of the medico-sexologists whose literature blurred into semi-pornography at its fringes. In 1930, H.S. Gambers, the author of an amazing range of Indo-sexo-medical booklets including *The Sex Organs (Illustrated)*, *Self Pollution*, *Yoga Exercises for Seminal Disorders* and *Onions for Health*, openly reprinted the 'Burton' translation in Amritsar, while the Medical Book Company of Calcutta published a new English translation by B.N. Basu in 1943. Despite the supposedly specialist nature of these publications, Vatsyayana's work started to attract serious numbers of domestic book-buyers. Within three years the Basu version was in its seventh edition, and it kept on selling for many years after-wards – not, it may be assumed, to medical students only.

When another new, English *Kamasutra* was published in Bombay, in 1961, it came with the same self-applied restrictions. S.C. Upadhyaya's edition carried an apologetic prefatory note announc-ing that the book was intended 'for members of the medical and legal professions, scholars and research students of Indology, psychology and social sciences'. A foreword by the scholar of Indian painting and ancient history, Moti Chandra, stressed Vatsyayana's 'cold scientific thoroughness', and the 'precision' and 'scientific viewpoint' of his treatment. The four pages of introductory quota-tions, however, told a very different story. Worthies ranging from Gandhi and Rabindranath Tagore to Havelock Ellis and Richard

Burton were all quoted as approving the importance of love. Reading between the lines, it was clear that this *Kamasutra* was not, in fact, intended for specialists only; it was for anyone who could experience love. Somehow, the awkward fact that almost all these quotations referred to ethereal or transcendent love, and almost none had any relation whatsoever to *kama* and the rampantly libertine world of the *nagaraka*, was sidestepped – as was the question of the relation between the text of the *Kamasutra* and the fifty black-and-white photographs of Indian temple sculptures and erotic miniatures that accompanied it.

Upadhyaya's *Kamasutra* was such a beautiful production that Western publishers eager to cash in post-*Chatterley* scrambled to import it, notwithstanding the strenuous efforts of UK Customs to stop them. It was a truly landmark publication. Not only was it the first post-*Chatterley Kamasutra*, it was also the first original translation into English to appear in the West for eighty years. Astonishingly, it remained the only alternative to the 1883 version for another quarter-century. Despite the excitement of the rediscovery of Vatsyayana's book in the 1960s and 1970s, and the tens of thousands of versions of the 'Burton' translation sold in that time, no Westerner seemed inclined to attempt a new translation of their own. Serious Sanskritists were hardly encouraged to involve themselves with a book that was retreating ever further into the semi-pornographical twilight of the shelf under the coffee table. Liberals and radicals, on the other hand, just didn't have the Sanskrit – and the *Kamasutra* was a notoriously difficult text.

Finally, in 1987, an eminent German Sanskritist, Klaus Mylius, put his head above the parapet with a new translation; and three years later, Cinzia Pieruccini's Italian version followed. Astonishingly, these were the first translations by Western scholars since Richard Schmidt ninety years earlier. Both were serious, considered works and both managed to access popular audiences to boot – the full-colour, coffee-table version of Mylius's translation helped it sell 100,000 copies in Germany – but they could not match the 1883 text for notoriety. To compete with Burton, the late-twentieth century would require a character of equivalent complexity and colour.

The 'new Burton' finally appeared in 1992, brandishing his *Kâma Sûtra* in one hand and pointing the finger accusingly at Western society with the other. His name was Alain Daniélou, and his path to the *Kamasutra* was a surprising one. As an artist friend of Jean Cocteau and Max Jacob, international playboy, student of Rabindranath Tagore, popularizer of Indian Classical music, Hindu proselyte and, ultimately, translator of the *Kamasutra*, he tried on even more disguises than Richard Burton. Throughout the 1940s and into the early 1950s, Daniélou lived in a crumbling but elegant riverside palace in Varanasi with his lover, Raymond Burnier, studying Hinduism, Sanskrit and Indian music – like Vatsyayana's *nagaraka*, he learned to play the *vina* lute. Daniélou took the name Shiv Sharan and succeeded in underpinning his dilettante lifestyle with serious scholarship. On his return to France, he became a prolific writer on Hinduism and a proselytizer for 'traditional' Indian culture. He paid particular attention to its sexual aspects. The worship of the 'primordial' god he called Shiva-Dionysus was, he claimed, the only path to salvation. 'Only those who faithfully practice phallus-worship will be saved,' he wrote in one book; 'eroticism may become the means, and perhaps the only means, of

attaining Liberation,' he declared in another. He was known for
wearing a little golden *lingam* on a necklace, hanging outside his
shirt. At least he was no exponent of what he derisively termed
'drawing-room yoga'.

Daniélou turned to the *Kamasutra* in the last years of his life,
working on deciphering the Sanskrit for four whole years. When
his translation appeared in 1992, two years before he died, he gave it
the subtitle *Le Brévaire de l'amour*, or 'the breviary of love'. The title
owed much to France's distinctive relationship with India and the
Kamasutra. Where Indology in Germany was a professional affair
founded on philological principles, French students of India had
tended to conjure it as a place at once more mystical and sensual.
In 1891, Pierre Eugène Lamairesse, the publisher of one of the earliest pirated, Parisian printings, had even described Vatsyayana's book
as a '*Théologie Hindou*'. Daniélou shared this notion that the
Kamasutra was a religious tract, calling it a *traité* and bemoaning the
fact that Western books that reproduced secular Persian miniatures
as accompaniments to the text ran completely counter to the spirit
of this '*texte sacré*'.

Daniélou was determined to position India as the natural home
of sexual liberation, in militant contrast to the repressiveness of the
West. 'The persecution of sexuality — the essential element of happiness,' he wrote, 'is a characteristic technique of all patriarchal,
political or religious tyrannies.' The *real* India, Daniélou believed,
existed in a state of Rousseau-like perfection, where sexuality was
'presented and taught like one of the Fine Arts'. 'In traditional
India,' he claimed, 'a six-year-old schoolboy has already studied
texts of the *Kamasutra* which explain all the secrets of loveplay and
its variations.' Vatsyayana, of course, had recommended that the
text be taught to the young. The West, it was implied, dissipated its

efforts in sexual instruction by, say, merely training their six-year-olds not to masturbate.

Daniélou's idealized vision of the place of the *Kamasutra* in Indian sexual culture owed more to his disgruntlement with the West than to his knowledge of Indian six-year-olds. The *Kamasutra* may have been published in numerous Indian editions, but it was by no means to be found beside the bed in every village household. As had been the Orientalist habit for centuries, Daniélou somehow elided the centuries between the society described in the *Kamasutra* and contemporary Indian culture. Just like the early colonists, he still saw India as an inchoate mass of ancient practices – even if personally he found those practices more attractive than those of the 'advanced' and ever-advancing West.

Daniélou's *Kamasutra* was quickly retranslated into English, where it found an eager market as *The Complete Kama Sutra: the First Unabridged Modern Translation of the Classic Indian Text* – a title that cleverly incorporated both a twist on the old pornographers' trick of promising, this time, the real deal, uncut, and an indication that this was not mere pornography: it was a *text*. The incorporation of not only Yasodhara's thirteenth-century *Jayamangala*, but also the 1960s Hindi commentary by Devadatta Shastri, the *Jaya*, really helped reinforce the notion that the book was weightily authoritative; at over 500 pages, it truly looked the part.

The book became a landmark in its own right. It never surpassed the 'Burton' version for ubiquity but was nevertheless to be found on tens of thousands of bedside bookshelves on both sides of the Atlantic. Unfortunately, the translation was distinctly quirky. In the long tradition of writers and translators of the *Kamasutra*, Daniélou had a number of agendas. First and foremost was his passionate espousal of Hinduism. If the *Kamasutra* did not fit

comfortably into Hindu tradition, Daniélou would bend over backwards to make sure that it could be interpreted in such a way that
it did. The object of eroticism, according to his introduction, may
be 'firstly a search for pleasure', but the *ultimate* 'goal of the techniques of love is to attain a paroxysm considered by the Upanishads
as a perception of the divine state, which is infinite delight'.
Similarly, for Daniélou, 'a magical significance' apparently lurks
behind the sexual positions which, 'if they are used in erotic ritual,
correspond in their psychological and physical effects to the postures of yoga'. There is, of course, no Tantric or yogic ritual in
Vatsyayana's book, even if the positions do recall yoga's *asanas*, or
postures.

The *Kamasutra* had been wielded on behalf of many causes before
Alain Daniélou picked it up, but it is fitting that its chief use in the
1990s was as a weapon in the campaign for the political legitimiza-
tion of homosexuality. A hundred years earlier, just as Victorian
society was beginning to question many of its sexual values,
Arbuthnot had held the *Kamasutra* up to the West as an example of
sexual sincerity and rationality; now, as gay rights were being
asserted across much of the world, Daniélou would do the same for
the homosexual-focused material. His prime target, however, was
India. Daniélou wrote that 'true love, pure love can only be aberrant and illegitimate'. This was an orthodox point of view in the
bhakti tradition, which viewed Krishna's relations with the cow-girls
to be adulterous and therefore necessarily all the more passionate.
But for Daniélou, as a Hindu convert and the rogue scion of a traditional French Catholic family – his brother was a cardinal, albeit
one who died of a heart attack on the stairs of a prostitute's house
– aberrance and illegitimacy had a different meaning. He was 'out'
at a time and in a place when it was rare to be openly gay, and the

conviction that drove him to be open about his sexuality also motivated his publication of the *Kamasutra*.

Mainstream Indian society in the 1940s and 1950s certainly
frowned on homosexuality, and traditional Hinduism hardly
approved of it either, although the ancients were not in fact overly
troubled. While the *Laws of Manu* saw anal sex between men as an
offence that technically meant losing caste, in practice it recommended a ritual bath as sufficient penance. The *Arthashastra* simply
stipulated fines for men having sex with other men, and set the
rate at 48 to 96 *panas*, or 24 *panas* for lesbian women. (A fully trained
soldier or top spy was paid 500 *panas* a year.) The *Kamasutra*, as ever,
had a more liberal approach. Vatsyayana described two kinds of
men who have sex with men (or, more specifically, 'people of the
third nature' who give *nagarakas* sexual satisfaction) without con-
demnation. There was the person 'in the form of a woman', who
would imitate women's behaviour, their 'dress, chatter, grace,
emotions, delicacy, timidity, innocence, frailty and bashfulness';
there was also the person 'in the form of a man'. One might call
them 'femme' and 'butch', though Vatsyayana differentiated the
two types by profession, not by sexual style: the 'femme' lived like
a courtesan, whereas the 'butch' worked as a masseur. Fascinatingly, Vatsyayana used the feminine pronoun 'she' for both. This
may simply reflect the fact that the Sanskrit word for 'nature',
prakriti, is feminine, but it also suggests that gender was seen as
dependent on sexual role: both kinds of men were significant to the
nagaraka only in that they might give him a blow-job or jerk him
off. This was not an entirely one-sided sexual service. Vatsyayana
described the femme as getting 'her sexual pleasure and erotic
arousal as well as her livelihood from this', while the butch would
conceal 'her desire when she wants a man'.

People who were not of 'the third nature' were also known to enjoy homosexual encounters. The verses at the end of the *Kamasutra*'s chapter on oral sex described how 'young men, servants who wear polished earrings indulge in oral sex only with certain men'. They were evidently choosing their partners on the basis of attraction. 'And, in the same way,' the verses continued, 'certain men-about-town who care for one another's welfare and have established trust do this service for one another.' Vatsyayana also reported the opinion of 'some people' who held that the person of the third nature counts as another 'sort of woman who can be a lover', on the grounds that 'there is no difference in the purposes for which they are used'.

Daniélou was not the first commentator or translator to read the *Kamasutra* and be struck by its depiction of sex between men, but he was one of the first to be publicly comfortable with it. Yasodhara squeamishly decided that the *nagarakas* who service each other must equate to 'the ones who are practically women'. He did imagine, however, that this oral sex must feel good. When the *nagarakas* go down on each other simultaneously 'by turning their bodies head to foot', he observed that they lose 'all sense of time because of their passion'. In 1911, Pandit Madhavacharya here footnoted that 'such boys do not engage solely in oral activity, they also engage in another kind of unnatural fornication' – presumably the misuse of what he described as the 'bad path'. The *pandit*'s readers were further warned that 'people involved in theatre commonly are puppets of that type of vice'. Even fifty years on, the Hindi commentator, Devadatta Shastri, was remarking frowningly that the 'extremely base' act of oral sex between men was evidently 'not a new but an old and wicked deed in our tradition'. It can only have been included, he assumed, 'because a *shastra* is a

reference book on sex, and fellatio is a sexual act'. With similar
unease, the 1883 *Kamasutra* described the people of the third nature
as eunuchs. More shockingly, it entirely expurgated the sentence in
which 'some people say' that the person of the third nature is
another sort of woman who can be a lover. (This must have been
the work of Arbuthnot and the translating *pandits*. It's a safe bet
that if Burton had ever seen the original Sanskrit, the sentence
would have stayed.)

In edition after edition, the *Kamasutra* had been deliberately de-
queered. Alain Daniélou made the mistake of over-compensating.
He changed all the pronouns in the chapter on oral sex from 'she'
to 'he', referred to the person performing oral sex as 'the boy' and
construed the reference to mutual oral sex between *nagarakas* as
'there are also citizens, sometimes greatly attached to each other
and with complete faith in one another, who get married
together'. He also translated the *svairini*, or independent, sexually
unrestrained woman, as 'lesbian', when Vatsyayana mentions sex
between women only once, and in a distinctly un-lesbian context —
the women of the harem are imagined as dressing each other up as
men and using dildos to give each other pleasure.

But Daniélou's most overt 'queering' of the *Kamasutra* was his
introduction, which used the text to appeal for sexual tolerance
not just in the West, but in modern India. He contrasted the way in
which 'male homosexuality forms an integral part' of the sex life of
the *nagaraka* with the penal code promulgated by Nehru's government, which, under article 377, prohibits 'sexual relations against
nature with a man, woman or animal, whether the intercourse is
anal or oral'. (Daniélou quoted Nehru as pronouncing that 'such
vices in India were due to Western influence', an unusual riff on the
common conservative-nationalist claim that Muslim invaders

were to blame. Fascinatingly, this belief can be traced back to none other than Burton, who observed in one of his footnotes to the *Kamasutra* that oral sex 'does not seem so prevalent now in Hindustan, its place perhaps is filled up by the practice of sodomy, introduced since the Mahomedan period'. Anal sex, in the *Kamasutra*, is in fact mentioned only as an 'unusual' practice between men and women 'in the South'.) Thanks to its illiberalism regarding homosexuality, 'the country of the *Kama Sutra*', Daniélou protested, has 'been relegated to the level of the most backward countries in the sphere of liberty'. Fortunately for Daniélou, on a personal level the traveller could apparently 'find amorous adventures that show that the people of India have forgotten nothing of the teachings of the *Kama Sutra*'.

The *Kamasutra*'s many translators and popularizers all sought to use the book of love in the service of an agenda, and Alain Daniélou was no exception. But in spite of his efforts, and those of Arbuthnot, Burton, W.G. Archer and Alex Comfort, the *Kamasutra*'s afterlife has not centred on Indology, anthropology, pornography, sexology or indeed gay rights. Not in the West, at least – though in India the *Kamasutra*'s resurgence continues to bring all those issues into focus. In the West, by contrast, the book of love has become a mere manual for sex instruction; the very word '*Kamasutra*' is now a synonym for advanced fucking. If this was not what the earnest patrons of the book of love thought the West needed, it was what the West would prescribe for itself in the twenty-first century.

*I*F YOU COAT your penis with an ointment made with powdered white thorn-apple, black pepper, and long pepper, mixed with honey, you put your sexual partner in your power. If you make a powder by pulverizing leaves scattered by the wind, garlands left over from corpses, and peacock's bones, it puts someone in your power. If you pulverize a female 'circle-maker' buzzard that died a natural death, and mix the powder with honey and gooseberry, it puts someone in your power. If you cut the knotty roots of the milkwort and milk-hedge plants into pieces, coat them with a powder of red arsenic and sulphur, dry and pulverize the mixture seven times, mix it with honey, and spread it on your penis, you put your sexual partner in your power. If you burn the same powder at night, you can make the moon, viewed through the smoke, appear golden. If you mix the same powder with monkey shit and scatter the mixture over a virgin, she will not be given to another man.

Kamasutra
Book Seven: Erotic Esoterica
Chapter One: Putting Someone in your Power
translated by Wendy Doniger and Sudhir Kakar (2002)

CHAPTER SEVEN

Kama Commodified

Lovers today can choose between the *Modern Kama Sutra, New Kama Sutra, Essential Kama Sutra, Pocket Kama Sutra, Cosmo Kama Sutra, Everything Kama Sutra, Real Kama Sutra, Complete Kama Sutra, Illustrated Kama Sutra, Complete Illustrated Kama Sutra, Little Book of the Kama Sutra, Bedside Kama Sutra* and, just occasionally, *Vatsyayana's Kama Sutra*. 'Advanced' couples can reach for *Beyond the Kama Sutra, Kama Sutra for Life, Red-Hot Sex the Kama Sutra Way, Kama Sutra Tango* and *Pure Kama Sutra* — presumably while they wait for the 'impure' sequel. Exhibitionists can furnish themselves with the *Office Kama Sutra*, 'Being a Guide to Delectation and Delight in the Workplace', or the *Outdoor Kama Sutra*. Women can opt for the *Kama Sutra for Women, Women's Kama Sutra* and the French *Kama Sutra revu et corrigé par les filles*, which is 'a playful way to discover 77 previously unseen and rare positions'. Gay men are well provided for, with the *Gay Kama Sutra, Gay Man's Kama Sutra* and the *Kama Sutra of Gay Sex*, while gay women have, as yet, only one dedicated publication, the *Lesbian Kama Sutra*. Men going solo have the *Kama Sutra for One*, billed as 'the single man's guide to self-satisfaction' and authored by a certain

Richard O'Nan and Pamela Palm. Playful readers may appreciate the *Kama Sutra Illuminated*, the sketchy *Purple Ronnie's Kama Sutra*, the irreverent *Kama Sutra of Pooh*, the grotesque *Viz Fat Slags Kama Sutra*, the boggling *Kama Sutra in 3D*, the intriguing *Kama Sutra for Cats* and no less than two versions of a *Pop-up Kama Sutra* – sadly, neither of which capitalizes on the most obvious pop-up opportunity.

Sex writers have built whole sub-careers around the *Kamasutra* brand. Dorling Kindersley, the publisher of glossy illustrated books, offers an entire range of *Kamasutra*-branded sex manuals by the veteran sex therapist and writer Anne Hooper. Many less well-informed writers simply use the *Kamasutra* to add a dash of exotic spirituality to sex, as if adding a spoonful of curry powder to fast food. Tantrism is a favourite combination flavour, in spite of the lack of any authentic relation between Tantra and Vatsyayana. Witness *The Kama Sutra of Sexual Positions: The Tantric Art of Love*, *The Kama Sutra of Erotic Massage* – billed as 'the Tantric art of touch', *Sex and the Perfect Lover: Tao, Tantra and the Kama Sutra*, *Sextasy: Master the Timeless Techniques of Tantra Tao and the Kama Sutra to Take Lovemaking to New Heights*. In 2006, New Age 'holistic healer' Deepak Chopra and Virgin Books launched *Deepak Chopra's Kama Sutra: the Seven Spiritual Laws of Love*. Chopra is the sort of sexpert who can unctuously murmur that 'in Ancient India we didn't distinguish between spirituality and sexuality'. The true spirituality of his 'version' can best be judged by its press release, which announced the highly saleable marriage of 'two of India's most well-known and established brands' – Deepak Chopra and the *Kamasutra*. Chopra hoped his 'interpretation' would be 'a rebirth for a classic text that understands human sexuality in the context of a meaningful life'.

Of course Chopra is an *Indian* writer – albeit one based in California. As a non-Westerner writing on the *Kamasutra*, he is a relatively rare quantity, for the book of love today is still what it was in the nineteenth century. It is a classic imperial commodity – an exotic product that the West imports raw, processes and feeds to itself in a more easily swallowed form. Sexual gourmands can actually feast on the *Kamasutra* in the shape of Kama Sutra Chocolates decorated with pictures of positions. Lovers with stamina can apply Kama Sutra Lubricants, which promise to smooth and soothe otherwise painful-sounding 'unlimited hours of passion'; afterwards they might want to soak in Kama Sutra Bath Oils. Couples lacking inspiration can play Kamasutra The Game, which allows lovers to 'get carried away in the sensual and romantic world of the oriental love mysticism'. The Kama Sutra Spinner Game, on the other hand, will let them simply 'discover the joys and pleasures of each other'.

Whether or not Vatsyayana's third-century book of love is actually any use as a modern sex manual – still less as the inspiration for a board game – is questionable. The original subscriber's prospectus for the 1883 edition advertised that many of Vatsyayana's remarks 'are so full of simplicity and truth that they have stood the test of time, and stand out still as clear and true as when they were first written, some eighteen hundred years ago'. True; but the *Kamasutra* has nothing whatsoever to say about contraception or, Kama forbid, conception. Its recipes for aphrodisiacs, even where they are intelligible, are of dubious utility. In terms of technique, Burton's early biographer, Thomas Wright, was right to say that 'a man who could not kiss properly after reading the *Kamasutra* would be a dullard indeed', but a man seeking to bring a woman to orgasm could be excused for being in more doubt. Vatsyayana never mentions the clitoris. He does vaguely describe how a man touches a woman 'here and there' and 'caresses her between her tightly closed thighs', and he states that before a man enters a woman, 'he puts his hand, like an elephant's trunk, inside her and agitates her until she becomes soft and wet'. When 'her eyes roll when she feels him in certain spots', Vatsyayana adds, the man should press her in precisely those places. These 'certain spots', according to the sage Suvarnanabha, are 'the secret of young women'. And yet the *Kamasutra* does not exactly unveil the mystery. As for cunnilingus, Vatsyayana fails even to give it a name, acknowledging only, and reluctantly, that 'Sometimes men even perform / This act upon women'.

The *Kamasutra* was evidently not written for women. While fellatio is described in no less than a dozen energetically descriptive *sutras*, the technique for going down on a woman is skimmed over as being a matter merely of 'transposing the procedure for kissing a mouth'. (Vatsyayana is under no illusions about the incredible sexual potency of cunnilingus, however. It is for this, he says, that courtesans 'reject virtuous, clever, generous men, and become attached to scoundrels, servants, elephant-drivers, and so forth'. Modern scoundrels and elephant-drivers may take heart.) Women are seen as potential sexual partners who may have to be aroused but somehow never need to be seduced. Their availability and compliance is assumed. The chapter on 'devious devices for weddings' even covers the practices of slipping virgins intoxicating drinks, having sex with them while they are sleeping, and carrying them off by force with the help of a gang of murderous helpers. Of course, Vatsyayana is describing as much as he is prescribing, and in fact he recommends the 'love-match' as far superior to this kind of skulduggery, 'since mutual love is the fruit of wedding rites'. Modern, liberal readers may breathe again. A woman's perspective is presented only in the books on 'Wives' and 'Courtesans'. The emphasis

of the former, however, is on wifely duties, while even the courtesans' guide that is Book Six focuses on how a prostitute can keep
her favoured male clients, not on how she herself can achieve
sexual pleasure.

Men are unequivocally the heroes and principal audience of the
Kamasutra. Even when Vatsyayana recommends that women study
his text, as well as men, it isn't entirely clear whom this is designed
to benefit. Nevertheless, modern women need not entirely reject
the book of love. Almost uniquely among ancient writers, from
any culture, Vatsyayana champions women's right to sexual pleasure. Because men and women are 'not of different species', he
suggests, their goal – orgasm – is the same. Sex, therefore, is just
like 'when two rams batter one another', or when 'two wrestlers
are locked together in a fight'. It may be combative, but mutuality
is the key. Vatsyayana theorizes that a woman is the 'passive locus',
while a man is the 'active agent', but in practice, a surprising
number of the 'ways of embracing' described in the *Kamasutra*
reverse the roles. In the 'close embrace of the pelvises', the woman
really cuts loose. With her hair flying, she 'leaps on top of the man
and presses his pelvis with her pelvis, to scratch, bite, slap and kiss
him'. And when confronted with a man who delights in the
Kamasutra's many varieties of love bites and fingernail marks, the
woman is advised to up the ante. She should return bite for bite,
and with twice the force. Playing at quarrelling,

> She grabs him by the hair
> and bends down his face and drinks from his mouth;
> she pounces on him and bites him
> here and there, crazed with passion.

In the aftermath of this wild, tooth-and-nail eroticism, the lovers find their shared secret binds them together. They playfully display their marks to each other and, although they pretend to rebuke each other, they are in fact showing 'modesty and concern for one another's feelings'. As a result 'their love will never wane, not even in a hundred years'.

The West has chosen not to enquire too closely into the ways in which the *Kamasutra* treats women, still less the orgasmic efficiency of its techniques. What has loomed largest in the popular imagination is the sheer scale of the book's imaginative variations on the sexual act, a brazen creativity most obviously made flesh in its infamous sexual 'positions'. These 'postures' are the chief source of the *Kamasutra*'s modern fame. They are what has distinguished it in the Western imagination from potential rivals such as Chinese pillow books – some of which are more ancient than the *Kamasutra*, but none of which conceive of more mind- and body-bending ways in which two people can arrange their limbs around an interlocked vagina and penis.

For over 2,000 years, the West has been primed for the arrival of just such a book. Ever since the demise of Rome there has been a gap on the shelves that only the *Kamasutra*, with its ambitious sexual positions, could adequately fill. The West, it seems, was even more careless with its erotic inheritance than India had been prior to Vatsyayana's rescue mission. Martial's epigram 12.43, the 'Wanton Verses of Sabellus', mentions 'the little books of Elephantis', which apparently described a number of 'radical positions for lovemaking, such as a dissolute fucker would dare'. But Elephantis's books are lost. Ovid's *Ars Amatoria*, meanwhile, proclaims that 'there are a thousand fun-filled ways for sex'. But Ovid, rather bathetically, troubles to list only a few simple positions (including one 'of no great effort', in which 'she lies semi-reclined on her right flank' and one for men who are unusually tall, whom Ovid advises to 'kneel with your head turned slightly sideways'). Friedrich-Karl Forberg's 1824 collection of obscene epigrams, *De Figuris Veneris*, listed no less than ninety sexual postures supposedly known to the ancient world – but Forberg was widely suspected of making them up. All that remains are little worn-out medals or *spintriae* that depict interlaced couples, without explanation. The rest of ancient Rome's sexual wisdom, if wisdom it was, has disappeared.

Nevertheless, the myth of sexual positions survived the fall of Classical civilization. Ironically, this was partly thanks to the Church, which had long taken the view that any positions in which the man was not on top were actually sinful. A woman driving the sexual act was thought to violate natural laws of male supremacy, and some argued that having sex in this diabolical fashion actually counted as sodomy (the exact nature of which was much debated). Sex 'from behind', meanwhile, was uncomfortably reminiscent of the base, animal nature of sexual intercourse. The early fourteenth-century treatise *De Secretis Mulierum*, or *The Secrets of Women*, even gave room to the notion that unnatural postures were responsible for birth defects. Experimentation of any kind was strongly discouraged, and a man who loved his wife 'immoderately', as Thomas Aquinas coyly put it, was deemed to be an adulterer.

Of course, the more that sexual positions were demonized, the sexier they became, and the positions were celebrated in countless bawdy tales, satires and poems. Most notorious of all these scurrilous works of literature were the sixteen 'luxurious' sonnets by the Italian Renaissance satirist Pietro Aretino, the so-called 'scourge of princes'. Composed to accompany drawings of sexual

positions by Raphael's pupil, Giuliano Romano, they included
deliberately shocking lines such as 'Open up your thighs, then, so
I can clearly see / Your pretty arse and cunt, full visible to me.'
Known as the Sedici Modi, the poems – and the positions – were
infamous. All known copies of the actual pictures however, were
destroyed. The resourceful Fred Hankey could find only substitute
engravings by Agostino Carracci to offer Richard Monckton
Milnes. In 2006, however, a surviving book of the sonnets with
accompanying woodcuts turned up unexpectedly in a Christie's
sale in Paris. It fetched £227,000.

Milnes would have been interested in the book as a bibliophile,
but not as an erotomaniac. By his, and Hankey's, time, knowledge
of a mere sixteen positions was nothing to boast of. Burton himself
added over two dozen to his translation of *The Perfumed Garden*. The
apocryphally French *quarante façons de faire* were well known – by
name if not in practice – and, by 1899, *The Horn Book: A Girl's Guide to
Good and Evil*, published in London by the 'Erotica Biblion Society',
was listing sixty-two positions, among them the 'baker', the 'stork',
the 'view of the low countries', the 'elastic cunt', the 'wheelbarrow', the alarming-sounding 'wheelbarrow reversed' and the
'St George' – the last-named being the standard term used by
nineteenth-century pornography for the woman 'riding' on top.

As long as they dwelled on positions, sex writers were locked
into a kind of arms race: each new book had to have a greater
number than the last. The absurd conclusion of this contest was
Joseph Weckerle's Viennese *Golden Book of Love*, of 1907. It listed precisely 531 positions in its second volume, which dealt with what it
called the *Gymnoplastik* of love. Theodore van de Velde's remarkably
frank 1928 manual, *Ideal Marriage*, could not match this number,
but it could surpass its rival in systematization. Like Vatsyayana

(and like Burton), van de Velde risked publishing a book on sex only in the closing years of his life. What he wrote, however, was astonishingly daring and thorough. He incorporated a flabbergasting 'Systematised Table of Attitudes Possible in Sexual Intercourse', with 'Indications' and 'Contra-indications' noted for various kinds of men and women.

Neither Weckerle nor van de Velde seemed to have read the *Kamasutra*. Nevertheless, the idea that India held the secret to the ultimate teachings of sexual prowess was becoming ever more widespread. Van de Velde himself referred to 'the habitual exaggeration of prolonged coitus by the Hindoos, Javanese and other Orientals', while Helena Wright's *The Sex Factor in Marriage*, published in London in 1930, acknowledged that 'the Indians and the Arabs gradually discovered and wrote down probably all there is to know about perfection in the sex-life'. (Unfortunately, she did not trouble to describe exactly what this supreme knowledge was, and restricted herself to five positions, saying 'these attitudes are sufficiently varied for adoption at the beginning of married life'; thereafter, the couple would apparently 'need no further directions'.) When Eustace Chesser published his sex manual, *Love Without Fear*, in 1941, he too regretted that he would not 'endeavour to indicate all possible positions' even though 'some "love manuals", both Oriental and Continental, have listed over a hundred'.

When the *Kamasutra* made its 'official' debut in the West, in 1962, it was immediately co-opted as the latest in the long lineage of position-based erotic books. It hardly seemed to matter what was actually *in* the book of love – as long as it fulfilled the role that the West expected of it. The magical number sixty-four, being the tally of both the 'arts' and 'techniques' of love in the *Kamasutra* – in addition, Vatsyayana tells us, to being a nickname for the book itself — was widely assumed to refer to the number of sexual positions. But the *Kamasutra*'s modern fame doesn't so much rest on the quantity of postures it includes as on the fact that they are supposed to be so advanced that only a black-belt yogi, if there was such a thing, could achieve them.

The legend of impossibility originated with Burton himself, who added a footnote to the *Ananga Ranga* to the effect that many of 'the various postures... would seem to be impossible of accomplishment by stiff-limbed Europeans'. In his introduction to Hamilton's 1963 edition of the text, the Indian writer Dom Moraes picked up the old canard, put it under his arm and ran with it. He speculated that 'though some of the postures recommended by Vatsyayana require not only a high degree of credulity but an unusually fevered imagination to envisage, it seems important to remember that the human race has undergone certain physical changes over the last thousand years'. In 1975, the Marxist historian Narendra Nath Bhattacharya was able to state definitively that most of Vatsyayana's 'acrobatic techniques' were impossible.

The myth is only more established today. Linda Sonntag, author of the *Photographic Kama Sutra: Exotic Positions Inspired by the Classic Indian Text*, recalled that her art directors had been obliged to find replacement models for the shoot, as the original pair had been insufficiently flexible. *FHM* magazine's boisterously demotic 'Kama Sutra 2' chose to give each of its positions — including 'the sure-footed shower' and 'the defiling of the alleyway' — a rating out of ten for difficulty, as if this was the whole point. 'If she's not very supple,' the strapline warned, 'this might hurt, so only attempt it with ballerinas, gymnasts and girls who did well in gym class.'

Most revealingly, the British comedian Sanjeev Bhaskar named his TV series, based on the history of the *Kamasutra*, 'Position Impossible'. He described how whenever someone mentioned the book to him in conversation he'd instantly know 'they were trying to check me out as some sort of sexual gymnast'. Awareness of yoga, which in the West has tended to focus on static *asanas*, or named positions, may have contributed to the preconception that the *Kamasutra* was about postures. It may also have reinforced the myth of their difficulty. Earnest Westerners who struggle to achieve a 'downward-facing dog' in their yoga evening classes, might well imagine Vatsyayana's 'crab' or 'mare's trap' to be even more demanding.

But above all, the myth that the *Kamasutra* was a book about sexual positions was created by the use of Indian erotic art to illustrate it. Arbuthnot and Burton used white vellum to underscore the luxuriousness of their product; later publishers chose to employ glossy images instead. The small problem that the *Kamasutra* had never been an illustrated book was easily circumvented. Medieval India provided a wealth of erotic images to draw on, and the fact that they bore little relation to Vatsyayana's era did not seem to matter. The West had a long tradition of setting its own Bible stories in contemporary dress, after all, and while illustrating Ovid with, say, Hogarth's *Rake's Progress* might have raised eyebrows, no one had the same range of historical reference to draw on in relation to India. And in any case, India was widely supposed to be profoundly unchanging, as generations of writers and travellers had observed.

Raymond Burnier, a fine photographer and the lover of Alain Daniélou, was one of the first to exhibit images of temple carvings in the West, but picture books of Indian erotic art became available only in the late 1950s. The first to add images to the *Kamasutra* itself was S.C. Upadhyaya, whose 1961 edition used photographs of temple sculptures. These, however, had proved disappointing. Firm-breasted *apsara* nymphs and copulating couples were all very wonderful, but their sheer stoniness made it hard for many modern readers to imagine themselves in those positions. And after a thousand years of weathering, the statues were also tamely monochrome. *The Love Teachings of Kamasutra*, a London production of 1980, remediated all these faults by lavishly illustrating the text with erotic images drawn from miniature paintings. Still more resplendent was a *Kamasutra* co-created in New Delhi by the writer, Mulk Raj Anand, and an avid and knowledgeable collector of erotic artworks, Lance Dane. Anand had first had the idea of producing an illustrated *Kamasutra* as a graduate philosophy student at Cambridge. He discussed it with none other than Havelock Ellis, who agreed that the text needed artworks in order to fully communicate Vatsyayana's meaning. But only when Anand teamed up with Lance Dane and his superb art collection was the project made possible. This latest east–west cooperation was supposedly 'aimed at academicians', but it was no less influential than Arbuthnot's and Indraji's work had been. The art-tome format and use of illustrations from right across the Indian artistic tradition won awards and set the standard for hundreds of editions to come. Henceforth, the *Kamasutra* of the modern imagination would be inextricably linked with medieval erotic art.

Even if the temple-nymphs and the lovers of Persian miniatures hadn't actually illustrated the *Kamasutra* in their day, they did now. Western readers were soon buying the *Kamasutra* for the gorgeous erotic miniatures that accompanied the text as much as for the book of love itself. The paintings revealed a side of sex that the West had never before seen, or certainly not in such stunning, vivid detail. Indian sex was luxurious, aristocratic and artful, it was splendidly self-aware without being self-conscious. It was gorgeous and possibly even admirable. A new audience, one that would have been less inclined to wade through a book dedicated to the manners and customs of the olden East, became aware of India's erotic civilization.

Unfortunately, understanding of the actual *Kamasutra* suffered. Many readers came away with the impression that the images and text had always been one and the same, to the extent that the Kamasutra was even understood to *be* a set of images rather than a book. In 2001, a disgruntled customer of Amazon.com even complained in his review that 'this book is not a Kama Sutra. There are no illustrations.' The almost ubiquitous use of the 1883 translation was another problem. Readers who had once thrilled at the incredible immediacy of the *nagaraka*'s world were now more likely to find it quaint and antiquated, if not outright confusing. What, they wondered, could it mean to 'shampoo' the joints of someone's thighs? And what exactly might 'congress' involve? As edition followed edition, increasingly savage cuts were made to the actual text. If the *Kamasutra* wasn't a list of sex positions, it could easily be edited to look like one. Erotic images suffered equally drastic cropping. Any context – courtyards, palaces, gardens, rivers, forests – was all too often excised, leaving simple images of interlocked lovers in full, pornographic close-up. The most extraordinary scenes of acrobatic lovemaking or mass contortion were favoured above all others. The result was to illustrate not the *Kamasutra*, but the West's own preconceptions of how exotic sex should look.

The coffee-table *Kamasutra* was all about positions – and the more fantastical the better. The real *Kamasutra*, unfortunately, falls far short of the myth. There are 'just' eighteen sexual positions proper, plus three 'unusual sexual acts' that could be described as positions, ten 'sexual strokes' for men, and three postures for the woman who 'plays the man's part'. Most are descriptions of fairly straightforward sex acts designed purely to compensate for disparities between the sizes of the lovers' genitals. The 'squeeze', for instance, involves the cavernous 'elephant' woman squeezing her thighs together, while the 'yawning' posture requires the narrow 'doe' woman to spread her thighs wide apart while keeping her legs suspended. Few positions are much more ambitious. The notorious 'impaling on a stake', which requires the woman to have one of her legs athletically raised above her head while the other is stretched out, is a rare exception. And Vatsyayana himself advises when a posture, such as this one, 'can only be done with practice'. As generations of readers have been disappointed to discover, the *Kamasutra*'s positions are notable for their simple efficacy rather than for their spectacular effect. Far more splendid variations can easily be found in modern sex manuals, many of which are more obviously addressed to twenty-first-century audiences: perhaps incorporating advice on contraception and sexual health – or, indeed, mention of the clitoris.

If contemporary inventiveness has made the *Kamasutra*'s sexual positions look tame, and modern anatomy has rendered its sexual anatomy redundant – not to mention the fact that Western sexual politics have called into question its attitudes to women – what future, then, remains for the book of love? Two recent novels suggest that it exists as a fantasy of unattainable sexual perfection, as if the story and the idea of the book has superseded the *Kamasutra* itself. *The Revised Kama Sutra* (1998), by Richard Crasta writing as 'Avatar Prabhu', explores the sticky mess of ideas and counter-ideas about sex fighting for control of the id of the hero, a Goan Catholic who dreams of America, where he imagines 'millions of ravenous women are waiting for him'. Where Crasta satirizes naive, Indian ideas about Western sexuality, Lee Siegel's brilliant, Sterne-esque tragicomedy, *Love in a Dead Language* (1999), sends up Western fantasies about India. He charts the downfall of an American professor of Indian studies who lusts after one of his students, the beautiful, facile and Californian Lalita Gupta. 'I've dedicated my life to studying Sanskrit, to learning about India,' Professor Roth complains, 'yet I've never made love to an Indian woman.' Roth sets about inveigling his 'Lalita' to go on a solo study tour of India and he begins producing his own translation of the *Kamasutra* as a gift of love. He is eventually murdered with a Sanskrit dictionary: hoist with his own petard, one might say.

In India, by contrast, the *Kamasutra* has not yet entirely succumbed to this kind of postmodern treatment. Liberals are still using the book to argue against India's prevailing anti-sensual culture — a culture that defines itself as traditionally Indian, in opposition to modern, Western permissiveness; a culture that forced Lee Siegel to make cuts and changes for the Indian edition of his novel, including deleting the sex scene set in a temple and giving the second part, entitled 'fucking', the more demure heading of 'sexual union'. In the face of this kind of prudery, Indian liberals want the *Kamasutra* to have the same corrective impact at home that it had during a century of adventures abroad.

Back in 1963, the left-wing novelist Mulk Raj Anand bitterly compared the West's enthusiastic reception of the *Kamasutra* with the relatively stony ground on which the book had fallen at home, bemoaning the fact that 'while the younger intelligentsia of the West turns in admiration to our monuments, the false shame of our new bourgeois parades itself in the most abject apologies about the decadence of our medieval art, and prohibits even husbands and wives to hold hands on the seashore'. Anand's analysis was rather confirmed the following year, when Devadatta Shastri published his Hindi 'Jaya' commentary on the *Kamasutra*. It somehow managed to gloss the purpose of the text as essentially asexual. The book 'describes a moral eroticism leading to spiritual realization', Shastri concluded, 'and not the sating of the passions or the encouragement of pleasure seekers'.

Almost fifty years later, little has changed. At least, liberals make the same complaints. In 1993, Dr Indira Kapoor, then director of the South Asian Regional Office of the International Planned Parenthood Federation, claimed that 'Although the evidence of the *Kamasutra* and erotic temple carvings shows an open attitude to human sexuality in South Asia in the distant past, today ignorance and embarrassment cause much unhappiness.' In 2004, HarperCollins India published *Love and Lust*, an anthology of sublimely erotic ancient and medieval literature. Sounding strangely like Arbuthnot and Burton addressing the West in 1883, the editors warned that 'In India today, the philosophical acceptance of desire and the erotic sentiment has been asphyxiated by a hypocritical morality that has for much too long equated sex with sin and desire with guilt.' Pavan K. Varma and Sandhya Mulchandani hoped their anthology would provide 'evidence of an alternative vision, so that readers can get a glimpse of the sense of maturity and honesty that animated our ancestors'.

It's curious that a country with thousands of years of erotic civilization could be seen to lack 'maturity' concerning matters sexual. But an India where love marriage — as praised by Vatsyayana — is rare in most sections of society; where young couples in Calcutta feel obliged to march against police harassment for the crimes of meeting, talking and just occasionally kissing in public; where the vaginal 'touch-hole' of a sculpture at Ellora was cemented over; where a Hindu-nationalist Health Minister can insist that the 'Indian traditions' of abstinence and fidelity are more effective barriers against HIV than condoms; and where the 1860 Penal Code defines all extramarital sex as criminal – this is an India that has moved far away from the easy sensuality of Vatsyayana and his *nagarakas*.

There is, however, another India – as there always has been. Just as Vatsyayana's book of love existed alongside the *Laws of Manu* and the ascetic ideal, so the Bharatiya Janata Party and the Penal Code exist alongside a reported two thirds of young adults who would have casual, pre-marital sex before an arranged marriage; alongside plastic-wrapped, yellow-jacketed copies of *Kok Shastra* and *Old Kam Sutra* sold furtively at streetside bookstalls, and, since 1991, alongside the KamaSutra condom. If any prophylactic sheath could be said to encapsulate the conflicting attitudes to sex in modern India, it is the 'KS' condom. It was designed to replace the despised government-subsidized product, a sturdy, yellow, unlubricated length of misery that took its name, tellingly, from the Sanskrit word for 'restraint' or 'control'. The Nirodh, however, did little to stem India's awesome birth rate or its terrifying rate of HIV infection and, thanks to the governnment's health campaigns promoting its use, condoms had become associated with seedy, risky and illicit sex. The new KamaSutra condom was designed to project a very different image: to ride on the aristocratic coat-tails of the *Kamasutra* in order to sell itself to a pleasure-seeking, wealthy and urban demographic – to the *nagarakas* of modern India.

In the 1990s, it seems, *Kamasutra* meant 'sexy'. Alyque Padamsee of Lintas, the advertising agency responsible for the marketing campaign, described *Kamasutra* as 'universally recognized as a code for eroticism'. Smart Bombay college girls, he said, would even describe an attractive man as 'quite KS'. As a brand name, *Kamasutra* 'telegraphed sex without actually mentioning the forbidden word', he said. 'It was daring, yet culturally it was wholly acceptable.' Except that it was not. Adverts broadcasting the notion: 'It's your revolution. It's your condom. It's KamaSutra,' accompanied by eye-wateringly sexy photographs of the actress Pooja Bedi, were deemed 'vulgar and indecent in the context of an Indian morality' by the Press Council of India. Conservatives were determined to rewrite the *Kamasutra* out of Indian history. Somewhere between authoritarian hostility to sexual expression and the percolation of 'Western' sexual mores among the upper-middle classes, India's erotic heritage seemed once again in danger of being lost. Eighteen hundred years after Vatsyayana, someone would have to begin another rescue mission.

The highest-profile candidate to date has been film-maker Mira Nair. Her lavishly sensual feature of 1996, *Kama Sutra: A Tale of Love*, looked back misty-eyed to the last days of a Hindu kingdom ruled by the erotic ideal. The *Kamasutra* is a potent presence, especially among women: a group of wives gives a princess bride sex tips from the *Kamasutra* as she prepares for her wedding; the sensual heroine, meanwhile, studies Vatsyayana's *sutras* at a female-run school of love. Thanks to male sexual jealousy, however (and the black-clad Muslim hordes that, rather disturbingly, overrun the kingdom at the finale), all this learning is about to be tragically lost. 'I feel that sexuality in our country is so repressed and so twisted,' Nair commented in an interview. Looking around her with disbelief, she asked: 'Could this be the country that created the *Kamasutra*?' Given that the cast and crew were harassed and even threatened with arrest during filming, and that India's Board of Censors asked for a fifteen-minute cut before finally banning the film altogether as pornographic, her question was answered for her.

Mira Nair claimed she wanted to conjure a distinctively *Indian* approach to sexuality in her film. 'In India we now have so little of our history,' she complained. 'The only views of female sexuality we see – *Elle*, *Cosmopolitan*, television – are totally Western, and they have nothing to do with our reality.' She was not the first to say as much. In his 1985 book, *Kamasutra: Its Relevance Today*, the doctor and writer Girija Khanna pitched the *Kamasutra* as representing a middle road between asceticism and eroticism that was quintessentially Indian. Did it not call for a respect for *kama* within the framework of the *trivarga*, or triple path, after all? 'We cannot accept as our pattern,' Khanna protested, 'an absolutely decadent sensualism which results in a lopsided notion of human nature – i.e. Western permissiveness.'

The prominent Indian psychoanalyst and writer, Sudhir Kakar, has taken a nuanced version of the same stance. Inspired by the *Kamasutra* itself, which opened for him 'a window on our heritage, an ancient Hindu heritage very different from the one conveyed in most philosophical, historical and religious discourse', Kakar has led a thoughtful professional campaign against sexual repression. For him, the book of love held out the hope that the 'ideal of a balance between Eros and spirituality may indeed once again become our own' – in contrast to what he called 'the icy frost that threatens it from, what I hope, are the fringe elements of Hindu culture'.

The book of love itself is chief among Kakar's resources. In 1998, he published *The Ascetic of Desire*, a naturalistic novel set in Vatsyayana's own time. It dramatized the adventures of a Vedic student who is drawn to the 'subversive intent' and 'self-assertive' voice of the *Kamasutra* and decides to learn from the master himself. The student sometimes seems to stand in for Kakar, sometimes for Vatsyayana – and sometimes for the sexual soul of India, exposed as if on an analyst's couch. 'I did not have a natural gift for what I was trying to become,' the student confesses. 'My inner irreverence could not breach a painfully correct exterior; the spontaneity I often felt, even intimations of a passionate nature inclined towards excess, did not undermine the stilted movements of my body and my terse, much too deliberate speech.'

Kakar believed that the *Kamasutra* did not have a message for India alone. In Europe and the US, the book's task was 'the rescue of the erotic from the clutches of raw sexuality'. 'Eros, that divine creation of human beings,' he added, 'is always in danger from both the moral and the instinctual.' To help fight those twin enemies, he worked with the revered American Indologist Wendy Doniger on a landmark edition of the *Kamasutra*, published in 2002 by Oxford University Press. It was yet another east–west partnership, as now seems almost obligatory. Kakar provided psychological insights and translations of the Hindi commentaries. Wendy Doniger handled the Sanskrit.

Doniger was thus the first professional, Western Sanskritist ever to translate the *Kamasutra* into English. This, then, was the first time many English speakers would hear Vatsyayana's *sutras* without the distorting layers contributed by Indraji, Bhide, Arbuthnot and Burton – or their later, amateur rivals. Such, at least, was Doniger's own argument. She acknowledged that Burton had 'managed to get a rough approximation of the text published in English in 1883, nasty bits and all'. 'His' translation 'remains precious', she wrote, 'like Edward FitzGerald's *Rubaiyat*, as a monument of English literature, though not much closer to Vatsyayana than FitzGerald was to Omar Khayyam'. The claim – a gross misrepresentation of Indraji's and Arbuthnot's careful translation, if not of Burton's own, solo Arabic efforts – echoed its way through the press.

Reviewing Doniger's translation in the London *Guardian*, the writer Maureen Freely referred to the text's 'moralistic mistranslations'. The doyenne of South Asian queer studies, Ruth Vanita, fantasized that 'Burton's' translation was not only 'inadequate' but also 'skewed by his tendency to exoticise Asian sexuality as more "primitive" than European sexuality'. Sex journalist Michael Castleman, in the online magazine *Salon*, went further: Burton was 'the editor from hell', he wrote. 'He altered the text considerably to shoehorn it into Victorian views about sexuality, notably the then-popular notions that only men experience sexual desire and pleasure, and that women are nothing more than the passive recipients of men's lust.'

The charges laid against Burton seemed to stem from the assumption that the Victorian translation over which he presided must have somehow been 'Victorian'. Of course, Castleman's 'then-popular notions' were actually fairly unusual in the Victorian era, and Burton was perhaps the least likely person in England to shoehorn any text anywhere in their service. The 1883 translation, in fact, is regarded by the philologist Chlodwig Werba as coming second only to Richard Schmidt's academic, German–Latin text. Certainly, it is astonishingly accurate given the circumstances of its creation. But Arbuthnot, Indraji and their collaborators did make one arguably misleading decision. They chose to use the word 'should' to translate the *Kamasutra*'s original optative mood. This optative was a grammatical form long lost in European languages which, in Sanskrit law books, could indeed mean 'shall' or 'should'. But in plays and poetry it was often used with a more open sense, to indicate what might happen – as in 'the train should arrive in half an hour'. Wendy Doniger, therefore, chose to use the present tense throughout her translation, on the grounds that this better conveyed 'the flavour of a novel or a play'. Even if the *Kamasutra* is closer to a book of rules, she said, 'when a woman gives you a recipe on how to make potato soup, she doesn't say "you should take the potatoes", she says "you take the potatoes, and then you peel them."'

Rightly or wrongly, Doniger's translation captured a renewed sense of immediacy, a feeling that the *Kamasutra* was about 'people like us'. She asserted that the book had plenty to teach modern lovers. 'Americans in particular have made a cult of pleasure without any of the constraints that the *Kamasutra* teaches,' she frowned. 'They have turned sex into pornography and food into an occasion for unhealthy gorging'. Her book's introduction described pleasure as a 'legitimate goal' but one that 'must not be indulged in a thoughtless, brutal way.' Or, as the *Kamasutra* put it (in her own English words), 'Pleasures are a means of sustaining the body, just like food, and they are rewards for religion and power. But people must be aware of the flaws in pleasures.'

From Arbuthnot and Burton through to Comfort and Daniélou, the West has looked into the book of love and found sexual liberation. Should it now open the *Kamasutra* and discover sexual discipline instead? Vatsyayana's final verses conclude, after all, that 'a man who knows the real meaning of this text' is ' a man who has truly conquered his senses'. This does not mean overcoming the senses by strangling them, however. The *Kamasutra* is clearly not advocating passionless celibacy. Nor does it mean acquiring control over one's own and one's lovers' orgasms – though this is important. It means cultivating the raw material of sexual desire and, ultimately, turning it into art. Between lovers who have conquered their senses, sex becomes a sophisticated communication, a performance with the partner as the cherished audience. And beyond the act of lovemaking, sex in a wider sense becomes a microcosm of civilization. In the *Kamasutra*, sex is mannered, moral, social and, above all, civilized – precisely because it is an integral part of civilization.

Vatsyayana wrote his book of love because he feared that sexual learning had become so dangerously fractured it risked being lost. He succeeded in rescuing that learning – the *Kamasutra* still exists today, after all, as the pre-eminent monument of a civilization that attempted to turn the passions into art. Vatsyayana did not succeed, however, in defending erotic culture from its own tendency to fragment. The monument that is the book of love now stands like a crumbling palace on a faraway hilltop: marvellous but uninhabitable. Even as the *Kamasutra*'s many translators, publishers and commentators have sought to build new sexual civilizations by quarrying that palace for foundation stones, they have only contributed to its ruin, to the very fragmentation that Vatsyayana struggled against. To seek lessons in the book of love inevitably involves excising them from the context in which they were written; and to take the sex out of a civilization means taking the civilization out of sex.

If a moral must be drawn from the book of love it surely lies not in Vatsyayana's *sutras* – no matter how high his meditation when he composed them or how perfect his chastity – but in the story of how they were read. It is the story of how the palace of pleasures that is the *Kamasutra* was occupied by decadent descendants of the original owners who used its walls as backdrop for their exquisite dramas and cavorted in its bedchambers before abandoning it and leaving it to the jungle; of how, after hundreds of years, it was redis-covered by foreign explorers who fought their way to it through thickets, then stripped its fine interiors, carted off its antiquities to Indological museums, and sold its choicest furnishings on the pornographic black market; of how it is visited today by millions of admiring tourists – most of whom see only its splendid bedroom.

Note on Sanskrit Spelling and Pronunciation

This book follows the usual popular forms for transliterating familiar Sanskrit words and names into English, rather than the scholarly system. It describes, therefore, the god Shiva, not the more technically correct Śiva, and refers to *shastras* not *śastras*. Indologists, it is felt, will know where the accents belong.

काम, the Sanskrit word for 'desire' or 'sexual pleasure' is given as *kama* not *kāma*. *Sutra*, meaning 'thread' or 'aphorism', is rendered as *sutra* not *sūtra*. (The macron is properly used to indicate a long vowel sound.) It means, confusingly enough, that in BBC English at least *kama* is pronounced in much the same way as the even better-known Sanskrit word *karma*, meaning 'action' or 'result'. The first syllable of *sutra* is pronounced like 'hoot', not 'nut'.

Similarly, the author of the *Kamasutra* appears as *Vatsyayana* not *Vātsyāyana*. Note that in spoken English the stresses in the name fall more in the pattern of *O'Flaherty* than, say, Richard *Burton*. The two-word English title, *Kama Sutra*, is used only for the proper name of the 1883 translation — *The Kama Sutra of Vatsyayana*, in full — or for other, later English editions, which also chose to split the word into its two constituent parts.

Bibliographical Essay

The most accessible English translation of the *Kamasutra* is the recent one by Wendy Doniger and Sudhir Kakar (Oxford: Oxford University Press, 2002). The English is clear and nicely phrased, and the notes superb. It also has a very good bibliography. The 1883 *Kamasutra*, aka the 'Burton' edition, is fascinating in its own right; Penguin Popular Classics do a useful, inexpensive edition, *The Kama Sutra* (Harmondsworth: Penguin, 1997). The full 1883 text, including footnotes, can also be viewed online at www.sacred-texts.com/sex/ kama/index.htm

Chapters 1 and 2: India

Readers interested in the key texts of ancient India may want to begin at the beginning with translations of the *Rig Veda*, by Wendy Doniger O'Flaherty (London: Penguin Classics, 1981), and of the major *Upanisads*, by Patrick Olivelle (Oxford: Oxford World's Classics, 1996). Arguably a more entertaining read than either is the epic poem, *The Mahabharata*; the translation of the critical edition begun by J.A.B. Van Buitenen (Chicago and London: The University of Chicago Press, 1973), and continued by other hands, is a recognized classic. An excellent alternative is the Clay Sanskrit Library's ongoing *Mahabharata* project, in which each of the original's books comes as a separate volume and has a different translator. The best guide through the maze of myths surrounding Shiva, in the Puranas and the *Mahabharata*, is undoubtedly Wendy Doniger O'Flaherty's *Asceticism and Eroticism in the Mythology of Siva* (Oxford: Oxford University Press, 1973), retitled *Siva: The Erotic Ascetic* (New York: Galaxy, 1981).

The *Kamasutra*'s siblings make for drier reading. Wendy Doniger and Brian K. Smith's *Laws of Manu* (Harmondsworth: Penguin Books, 1991) and Patrick Olivelle's *Manu's Code of Law* (Oxford, New York: Oxford University Press, 2005) are both excellent; the former has a livelier style. Penguin India currently publishes a 900-page paperback of L.N. Rangarajan's translation of Kautilya's *Arthashastra* (New Delhi: Penguin India, 1992), but the most accurate translation is that in the hard-to-find second volume of R.P. Kangle's three-volume critical edition (Bombay: University of Bombay, 1960–65). As an alternative, the text of the 1925 Shamashastry translation of the *Arthashastra* can be viewed at www.mssu.edu/projectsouth asia/history/primarydocs/ Arthashastra/index.htm

For an overview of ancient Indian history, *Daily Life in Ancient India: from 200BC to 700AD*, by the French Orientalist Jeannine Auboyer, translated by Simon Watson Taylor (London: Weidenfeld & Nicolson, 1961) is a splendidly evocative description of social, religious, political and economic structures of the era. The drawback is that Auboyer conjures a monocultural society from the various sources without too much critical reflection on their contexts. *Early India: From the Origins to AD 1300* (Berkeley, Los Angeles: University of California Press, 2002), by Romila Thapar, Professor Emeritus in History at the Jawaharlal Nehru University, New Delhi, takes a more nuanced, diachronic view. It is chiefly concerned with the emergence of political and economic structures, however, and as a consequence is a drier read than Auboyer.

The best survey of the world of the *shastras* is found in *Shastric Traditions in Indian Arts*, edited by Anna Libera Dallapiccola (Stuttgart: Steiner, 1989).

There is surprisingly little specific literature on Indian sexual culture. David Smith's *The Hindu Erotic: Exploring Hinduism and Sexuality* (London: I.B. Tauris, 2007) is a fascinating treatment of the topic. Smith is a genuine authority and writes stylishly. Not counting Wendy Doniger and Sudhir Kakar's landmark introduction to their Oxford edition of the *Kamasutra*, there are three key academic essays in English on the *Kamasutra*: Wendy Doniger, 'On Translating the *Kamasutra*: A Gurudakshina for Daniel H. H. Ingalls', *Journal of Indian Philosophy*, 29/1–2 (April 2001); Ludo Rocher, 'The *Kamasutra*: Vatsyayana's Attitude toward Dharma and Dharmashastra', *Journal of the American Oriental Society*, 105/3 (1985); A.Y. Syrkin, 'Notes on the *Kama Sutra*', *Semiotica* 11 (1974).

Other work on sex in ancient India is, for the most part, dated and flawed. Johann Jakob Meyer's magisterial *Sexual Life in Ancient India* (New York: Barnes and Noble, 1953) is in fact a detailed analysis of attitudes towards women and sexuality as expressed in the *Mahabharata*. Narendra Nath Bhattacharya's *History of Indian Erotic Literature* (New Delhi: Munshiram Manoharlal, 1975) is a Marxist thesis about how patriarchy displaced what the author imagines to be India's original matriarchal state – disguised as a survey of erotic literature. Haran Chandra Chakladar's *Social Life in Ancient India: Studies in Vatsyayana's Kamasutra* (Calcutta: Greater India Society, 1929) is a dated but nevertheless thorough analysis of the probable date and location of the *Kamasutra*'s composition, combined with a somewhat unreflective summary of social attitudes as expressed in the *Kamasutra*.

The classic translation of the *Natyashastra* is Manomohan

Ghosh's *The Natyashastra: A Treatise on Ancient Indian Dramaturgy and Histrionics ascribed to Bharata-Muni* (Kolkata: Manisha Granthalaya, 1995). It is in two volumes, and not easy to get hold of in print, though it can be read online at www.nadanam.com/general/ g_natyashastra.htm. Adya Rangacharya's translation of *The Natyasastra* (New Delhi: Munshiram Manoharlal, 2003) is easier to find in print, but it leaves a lot of Sanskrit technical terms untranslated and isn't, therefore, very readable.

To read Sudraka's superb play *Mrcchakatika*, or *The Little Clay Cart*, you'll have to hunt down a copy of J.A.B. van Buitenen's *Two Plays of Ancient India: The Little Clay Cart; The Minister's Seal* (New York: Columbia University Press, 1968). Two translations of Kalidasa's wonderful play *Shakuntala* are currently in print: *The Recognition of Sakuntala*, translated by W.J. Johnson (Oxford: Oxford University Press: 2001) is clear and well noted; but *The Recognition of Shakúntala, Kashmir Recension*, translated by Somadeva Vasudeva (New York: New York University Press/JJC Foundation, 2006), perhaps has the edge, as it is underpinned by adventurous scholarship and Vasudeva has a good ear for dialogue.

Key texts on Sanskrit drama include: Robert Goodwin, *The Playworld of Sanskrit Drama* (Delhi: Motilal Banarsidass, 1998); Rachel van M. Baumer and James R. Brandon (eds), *Sanskrit Drama in Performance* (Honolulu: University of Hawaii, 1981); and Barbara Stoler Miller (ed.) *Theater of Memory: The Plays of Kalidasa* (New York, Columbia University Press, 1984). Sushil Kumar De's *Ancient Indian Erotics and Erotic Literature* (Calcutta: Firma K.L. Mukhopadhyay, 1959) may be dated but it is a pithy and elegantly written introduction to the topic, and one of the few works to treat Indian literary eroticism as a subject in its own right.

For translations of Sanskrit poetry (and drama), look no further than the admirable Clay Sanskrit library, whose volumes come in an attractive, Loeb-style, mini-hardback format, each with a transliteration of the original Sanskrit and an introduction by a leading scholar. The CSL list seems to grow constantly; among the works discussed in this book are: *Love Lyrics by Amaru, Bhartri-hari & Bilhana*, translated by Greg Bailey and Richard Gombrich (New York: New York University Press/JJC Foundation, 2005); and Kalidasa, *The Birth of Kumara*, translated by David Smith (New York: New York University Press/JJC Foundation, 2005). For Kalidasa's *Raghuvamsa*, the best option currently in print is the worthy but somewhat unwieldy *The Raghuvamsa of Kalidas: With the Commentary of Sanjivani of Mllinatha*, edited by Moreshwar Ramchandra Kale (New Delhi: Motilal Banarsidass, 1998).

For secondary literature on Sanskrit poetry, Lee Siegel's *Fires of Love, Waters of Peace: Passion and Renunciation in Indian Culture* (Honolulu: University of Hawaii Press, 1983) is a fascinating discussion of the opposing themes of sensuality and asceticism in the poems of Amaru and the works of the eighth-century philosopher Sankara. Neils Hammer's *The Art of Sanskrit Poetry: An Introduction to Language and Poetics, Illustrated by Rasah, Dhvanih and Alankarah Analyses* (New Delhi: Munshiram Manoharlal, 2003) is a useful essay on the aesthetic theories behind the poetry. Viswanath K. Hampiholi's *Kamashastra in Classical Sanskrit Literature* (Delhi: Ajanta Publications, 1988) painstakingly traces the cross-influences between *kama shastra* literature and Sanskrit poetry and drama.

For books on Tantra, avoid the torrent of nonsense that floods most bookshops and go straight for David Gordon White's authoritative *Kiss of the Yogini: 'Tantric Sex' in its South Asian Contexts* (Chicago, London: University of Chicago Press, 2003). Gavin Flood's *The Tantric Body: The Secret Tradition of Hindu Religion* (London and New York: I.B.

Tauris, 2006) is more of a textbook. *The Roots of Tantra*, edited by Katherine Anne Harper and Robert L. Brown (Albany: State University of New York Press, 2002), is a good collection of academic essays on Tantra's earliest manifestations.

Michael Rabe's brilliant essay on Khajuraho's hidden *yantras*, 'Secret Yantras and Erotic Display for Hindu Temples', is found in *Tantra in Practice* (Princeton: Princeton University Press, 2000), edited by David Gordon White. On the link between Tantra and temples, see Vidya Dehejia, *Yogini Cult and Temples: A Tantric Tradition* (New Delhi: National Museum, 1986); and Devangana Desai, *Khajuraho: Monumental Legacy* (New Delhi: Oxford University Press, 2000). Desai's *Erotic Sculpture of India: A Socio-Cultural Study* (New Delhi: Munshiram Manoharlal, 1985) is the key general work on the topic, though a little coyly phrased and now somewhat dated. Alain Daniélou's *The Hindu Temple: Deification of Eroticism*, translated by Ken Hurry (Rochester, Vermont: Inner Traditions International, 2001) has a splendidly idiosyncratic over-focus on eroticism and is very readable.

The best translation of the *rasa lila* from the Bhagavata Purana is Graham M. Schweig's *Dance of Divine Love: The Rasa Lila of Krishna from the Bhagavata Purana, India's Classic Sacred Love Story* (Princeton: Princeton University Press, 2005), which comes with fine explanatory notes. My preferred translation of the *Gitagovinda* is found in Lee Siegel's enthralling book *Sacred and Profane Dimensions of Love in Indian Tradition as Exemplified in Gita-Govinda of Jayadeva* (Delhi, London, New York: Oxford University Press, 1978). A good – and more easily found – alternative is Barbara Stoler Miller's *Gitagovinda of Jayadeva: Love Song of the Dark Lord* (New Delhi: Motilal Banarsidass, 2003).

For a serious introduction to medieval India, Daud Ali's *Courtly*

Culture and Political Life in Early Medieval India (Cambridge: Cambridge University Press, 2004) is unrivalled; it does a superb job of putting Sanskrit aesthetics in historical context. If only there were books on *kama shastra* of similar quality. Ram Kumar Rai's *Encyclopedia of Indian Erotics* (Varanasi: Prachya Prakasan, Chowkhama Sanskrit Series Office, 1981) is a detailed A–Z of Sanskrit erotic terminology as found in *kama shastra* texts; it is hardly gripping, but perhaps has curiosity value for the non-specialist.

The model for translations of *kama shastra* texts ought to be the superb book on *rati shastra* by Kenneth Zysk, *Conjugal Love in India: Ratisastra and Ratiramana* (Leiden: Brill, 2002); sadly, no one has yet done a similar job for *kama*. Alex Comfort's translation of *The Koka Shastra* (London: George, Allen & Unwin, 1964) is widely available; an illustrated version of his text, meanwhile, *The Illustrated Koka Shastra: Erotic Indian Writings based on the Kama Sutra* (London: Mitchell Beazley, 1997), has some of the best reproductions of Indian erotic miniatures you can find and includes notes on lots of other *kama shastra* texts, with a full translation of the *Ratimanjari*. 'Burton's' *Ananga Ranga* is very widely reprinted; scandalously, given its many faults, exaggerations and additions, there is no other original English translation available.

There are endless coffee-table books devoted to Indian erotic art but few have accompanying text of any quality; the exception is Philip Rawson's *Erotic Art of India* (London: Thames & Hudson, 1977). Otherwise, *Love in Asian Art & Culture* (Seattle and London: University of Washington Press, 1998) includes excellent essays on Rajput painting, by Annapurna Garimella, and on the Khajuraho erotic sculptures, by Vidya Dehejia. *Le Kamasutra de Bikaner*, edited by Wendy Doniger (Paris: Gallimard, 2004), includes forty beautiful colour plates from the Fitzwilliam Collection as well as Doniger's introduction, but isn't currently published in English. Klaus Ebeling's excellent *Ragamala Painting* (Basel, Paris, New Delhi: Basilius Press, 1973) discusses the pre-Mughal tradition, the role of *nayakas* and *nayikas* in art as Krishna and Radha, and also the relationship between painting and later literary-erotic texts such as the *Rasikapriya*.

The only other option is to sift through general works on Indian art – the best are often museums' descriptive catalogues – for mention of the erotic. Anything edited or written by W.G. Archer is worth reading, but see especially *Indian Paintings from the Punjab Hills* (London and New York: Sotheby Parke Bernet, 1973). Other good, and more recent, works on Hindu court painting include *Pahari Masters: Court Painters of Northern India* by B.N. Goswamy and Eberhard Fischer (Switzerland: Artibus Asiae Supplementum XXXVIII, 1992) and *Indian Miniature Paintings and Drawings* by Linda York Leach (Cleveland Museum of Art, 1986). There are two good, one-volume introductions to Indian art in general: J.C. Harle's *The Art and Architecture of the Indian Subcontinent* (New Haven and London: Yale University Press, 1994); and Vidya Dehejia's *Indian Art* (London: Phaidon, 1997).

Chapters 3, 4 and 5: The Nineteenth Century

The two best biographies of Richard F. Burton are Dane Kennedy's *The Highly Civilized Man: Richard Burton and the Victorian World* (Cambridge, Mass.: Harvard University Press, 2005); and Mary S. Lovell's *A Rage to Live: A Biography of Richard and Isabel Burton* (New York and London: W.W. Norton, 1998). They couldn't be more different: the former brilliantly and succinctly places Burton in his intellectual context; the latter is an authoritative and engaging reconstruction of Richard and Isabel's lives based on meticulous examination of the sources. Fawn M. Brodie's *The Devil Drives, A Life of Sir Richard Burton* (New York: Ballantine, 1967) is an attractively written classic, but rather undermined by psycho-sexual speculation. For a more antique flavour, Thomas Wright's original *The Life of Sir Richard Burton* (London: Everett & Co., 1906) is available online at http://etext.library.adelaide.edu.au/b/burton/richard/b97zw/

There is just one academic essay on the cultural context of the 1883 printing of the *Kamasutra*, a thoughtful piece by Ben Grant, 'Translating "The" *Kama Sutra*', in *Third World Quarterly Special Issue: Connecting Cultures*, 26/3 (September 2005). Henry Spencer Ashbee's *Bibliography of Prohibited Books* was printed in three volumes under this title in 1962 (New York: Jack Brussel, 1962); a shorter version edited by Peter Fryer appears as *Forbidden Books of the Victorians: Henry Spencer Ashbee's Bibliographies of Erotica* (London: Odyssey Press Ltd, 1970). Ian Gibson's *The Erotomaniac: The Secret Life of Henry Spencer Ashbee* (London: Faber & Faber, 2001) is an excellent biography. It outs Ashbee as the sex diarist 'Walter', whose *My Secret Life* has recently been republished in separate volumes with the subtitle *The Sex Diaries of a Victorian Gentleman* (Bath: Chalford Press, 2006); a text can also be found online at www.my-secret-life.info

There is no biography of Bhagvanlal Indraji, though Virchand Dharamsey was preparing one at the time of writing, provisionally entitled *Bhagwanlal Indraji: First Indian Archaeologist and His Period*. All Indraji's works are out of print. No works by Foster Fitzgerald Arbuthnot are in print, either, nor are any of the Western works on sex cited by him in the Preface to the 1883 *Kama Sutra of Vatsyayana* — except Richard Carlile's *Every Woman's Book*, republished as *What is Love? Richard Carlile's Philosophy of Sex*, edited by M.L. Bush (London: Verso, 1998). Charles Knowlton's 1832 *Fruits of Philosophy* was last republished in 1981 (Berkeley: University of California Press, 1981).

The secondary literature on nineteenth-century sexuality is extensive and of high quality. The landmark is Peter Gay's monumental series, *The Bourgeois Experience from Victoria to Freud* (London and New York: Norton, 1993–9); the five volumes are entitled *Education of the Senses*; *The Tender Passion*; *The Cultivation of Hatred*; *The Naked Heart*; and *Pleasure Wars*. Steven Marcus's enthralling *The Other Victorians: A Study of Sexuality and Pornography in Mid-Nineteenth-Century England* (London: Norton, 1985) shows how sexual literature – and sex itself – thrived in the period. Michael Mason's twin books, *The Making of Victorian Sexuality* (Oxford and New York: Oxford University Press, 1994) and *The Making of Victorian Sexual Attitudes* (Oxford and New York: Oxford University Press, 1994), by contrast, assert that Victorian anti-sensualism was a powerful force. The first of the pair focuses on actual sexual behaviour and the medical and social beliefs about it; the second concentrates on the philosophical, religious and political ideas that underpinned sexual attitudes. *The Facts of Life: The Creation of Sexual Knowledge in Britain, 1650–1950* by Roy Porter and Lesley A. Hall (New Haven and London: Yale University Press, 1995) is an authoritative study incorporating key research on nineteenth-century sex manuals and medical-scientific literature on sex.

Among the more specialized books on nineteenth-century sex, Ian Gibson's *The English Vice: Beating, Sex and Shame in Victorian England and After* (London: Duckworth, 1978) is a well-researched study of sexual flagellation. James G. Nelson's *Publisher to the Decadents: Leonard Smithers in the Careers of Beardsley, Wilde, Parson, With an appendix on Smithers and the Erotic Book Trade by Peter Mendes* (University Park: Pennsylvania State University Press, 2000) gives a powerful taste of the world of pornographic publishing at the end of the Victorian period. Lisa Z. Sigel's *Governing Pleasures: Pornography and Social Change in England, 1815–1914* (New Brunswick, NJ: Rutgers University Press, 2002) is a good if somewhat swift treatment of the topic. James Pope-Hennessy's dated two-parter, *Monckton Milnes: The Years of Promise* (London: Constable, 1951) and *Monckton Milnes: The Flight of Youth* (London: Constable, 1951) is the only biography of Milnes; unfortunately, it gives short weight to his erotic preoccupations.

There is remarkably little literature on the West's discovery of India's literary heritage. John Keay does the job very engagingly for the discovery of India's monumental heritage, in *India Discovered: The Recovery of a Lost Civilization* (London: HarperCollins, 2001), but there is comparatively little on the discovery of Sanskrit literature in the book. Raymond Schwab's *The Oriental Renaissance: Europe's Rediscovery of India and the East, 1680–1880* (New York: Columbia University Press, 1984) has more detail, but the focus is on French Indology – and the book is out of print. Ronald Inden's impressive and serious *Imagining India* (Oxford, UK and Cambridge, Mass.: Blackwell, 1990) describes how India has been constructed in the Western imagination; as such, it covers a good number of nineteenth-century accounts – without touching on the erotic. Peter van der Veer's *Imperial Encounters: Religion and Modernity in India and Britain* (Princeton and Oxford: Princeton University Press, 2001) pushes the post-colonial thesis that the nineteenth-century encounter shaped both Britain and India; in doing so, it follows some fascinating byways on the cultural map of both countries.

Two contentious and much cited books have to be mentioned here. Scholars have been falling over themselves in recent years to decry or disprove Edward Said's *Orientalism* (Harmondsworth: Penguin, 2003); it is indeed poorly researched, and it frequently overstates its case, but it remains provocative and fascinating. The same is true – in even greater degree – of Michel Foucault's seminal introductory volume to his *History of Sexuality*, published as *The Will to Know*, translated by Robert Hurley (Harmondsworth: Penguin, 1998); this book's ignorance of the facts of sexual history – especially outside Europe – is only matched by its confidence in making general statements about it.

Chapters 6 and 7: The Twentieth Century

The 1963 *Kamasutra*, with W.G. Archer's preface and K.M. Panikkar's introduction, is frequently republished; a recent edition is *The Kama Sutra of Vatsyayana* (New York: Berkley Trade, 2004). S.C. Upadhyaya's translation has recently appeared as *Kama Sutra: the Hindu Art of Love* (London: Watkins, 2004), complete with his explanatory notes. Sadly, it is hard to get hold of Mulk Raj Anand and Lance Dane's *The Love Teachings of Kama Sutra* (London: Spring, 1980).

Alain Daniélou's *The Complete Kama Sutra*, translated by Ken Hurry (Rochester, Vermont: Inner Traditions International, 1994) continues to remain in print, as does one of his more curious works, *The Phallus: Sacred Symbol of the Male Creative Power*, translated by Jon Graham (Rochester, Vermont: Inner Traditions International, 1995). Daniélou's oddly egotistical autobiography is entitled *The Way to the Labyrinth: Memories of East and West*, translated by Marie-Claire Cournand (New York: New Directions, 1987). The only biography of Daniélou is a French-language double-hander that also covers his cardinal brother: Emmanuelle Boysson's *Le Cardinal et l'Hindouiste. Le Mystère des frères Daniélou* (Paris: Albin Michel, 1999).

Arthur E. Salmon's workmanlike biography, *Alex Comfort* (Boston: Twayne, 1978) and Comfort's own *Sexual Behaviour in Society* (London: Duckworth, 1950) are out of print. *The Joy of Sex*, of course, continues to sell handsomely; it was recently republished for its thirtieth anniversary with accompanying photographs (London: Mitchell Beazley, 2004). Books living in the twilight world of popular 'Kama Sutras', however, seem to live pretty disposable existences. Anne Hooper's *K.I.S.S. Guide to the Kama Sutra* (London: Dorling Kindersley, 2001) is one of the few worth recommending – either as a sex guide or as an introduction to the *Kamasutra*. The two 'pop-up' *Kamasutras* are Jonathan Biggs and Bob Robinson's *The Pop-up Kama Sutra* (New York: Bonanza, 1984); and Keith Finch and Andy Crowson's *The Kama Sutra of Vatsyayana in Pop-up* (London: Collins & Brown, 2003).

Intimate Relations: Exploring Indian Sexuality (Chicago: University of Chicago Press, 1989) is a collection of typically thoughtful essays from the psychologist, novelist and *Kamasutra* expert Sudhir Kakar. Two solid academic books on homosexuality in India are *Same-Sex Love in India: Readings from Literature and History*, edited by Saleem Kidwai and Ruth Vanita (Basingstoke: Macmillan, 2000), and *Queering India: Same-sex Love and Eroticism in Indian Culture and Society*, edited by Ruth Vanita (New York and London: Routledge, 2002). The former includes Vanita's excellent essay on the early reception of the *Kamasutra* in India, 'The *Kamasutra* in the Twentieth Century', and her study of homosexuality in the *Kamasutra*, 'Vatsyayana's *Kamasutra*'. *Queering India* has an intriguing essay by Michael J. Sweet on 'Eunuchs, Lesbians and Other Mythical Beasts: Queering and Dequeering the *Kama Sutra*'.

Two useful academic essays focus on the career of the *Kamasutra* in modern India and 1960s America, respectively: Jyoti Puri, 'Concerning Kamasutras: Challenging Narratives of History and Sexuality', in *Signs: Journal of Women in Culture and Society*, 27/3 (2002); Valerie Peterson, 'Text As Cultural Antagonist: The *Kama Sutra* of Vatsyayana', in the *Journal of Communication Inquiry* 26/2 (April 2002).

William Mazzarella's lively and intelligent essay, 'Citizens have Sex, Consumers Make Love: Marketing KamaSutra Condoms in Bombay', can be found in Brian Moeran (ed.), *Asian Media Productions* (London: Curzon Press; Honolulu: University of Hawaii Press, 2001).

Sudhir Kakar's *The Ascetic of Desire: A Novel of the Kama Sutra* (New York: Overlook Press, 2000) is an insightful conjuring of Vatsyayana's world, but *Ecstasy* (New York: Overlook Press, 2002), his disturbing pseudo-biography of a guru not entirely dissimilar to Sri Ramakrishna, is perhaps more successful as a novel. Avatar Prabhu's *The Revised Kamasutra: A Novel* (Fairfield, Iowa: Sunstar Publishing, 1998) is both clever and funny. Lee Siegel's *Love in a Dead Language: A Romance* (Chicago: University of Chicago Press, 1999) is brilliant, playful and outrageous; if you read only one book mentioned in this essay – apart from the *Kamasutra* itself, of course – make it this one.

Acknowledgements

I would like to thank the many librarians, archivists and biblio-philes around the world who have helped me in my search for obscure editions of the *Kamasutra* and material relating to Arbuthnot, Burton and Indraji. My thanks go to: Keith Arbuthnot; William Arbuthnot; Nicholas Bacuez at the Harry Ransom Center, The University of Texas at Austin; Susan Bellany at the National Library of Scotland; Jacques Cloarec; Amy Deuink at Penn State Schuylkill; Sylvain Dumont at Alain Danielou.org; Gillian Evison, Doris Nicholson and all the staff at the Indian Institute, Bodleian Library, Oxford; Ivana Frlan at the University of Birmingham; John Goldfinch, Michael O'Keefe and the staff at the British Library's Oriental and India Office Collection; Diane Hudson at the Fitzwilliam; Caroline Hay at Christies; Betsy Kohut at the Smithsonian; Alice McEwan at the Royal Asiatic Society, London; Mark de Novellis at Orleans House; Steve Pepple at Buddenbrooks; Loren Rothschild; David E. Schoonoverat at the University of Iowa; Kiran Sethi at Raymond India; Arlene Shaner at the New York Academy of Medicine; Punita Singh and Mark Tewfik at Maggs Bros Rare Books.

Many Sanskritists and other writers and scholars have been extremely generous with their expertise. I would like to thank: Tony Brown; Simon Dawson; Vidya Dehejia; Laura Desmond; Virchand Dharamsey; Rachel Dwyer; Phillip Ernest; Ben Grant;

Lesley Hall; Justine Hardy; Anne Hooper; Hanco Jürgens; Sudhir Kakar; Dane Kennedy; Christopher Minkowski; Klaus Mylius; Isabel Onians; Cinzia Pieruccini; Michael Rabe; Ludo Rocher; Rosane Rocher; David Smith; Linda Sonntag; Matthew Sweet; Somdev Vasudeva; Marika Vicziany; Peter Wyzlic; and Kenneth Zysk. Especial thanks must go to Wendy Doniger; Mary Lovell; Lee Siegel; and Chlodwig H. Werba. Their advice and inspiration have been invaluable. All errors remain, of course, my own. ·

For their help and friendship, I would like to thank Jerry Goodman; Anne-Celine Jaeger; Ita Mac Carthy; Jan Piggott; Caroline Schafer; John Scholar; Andrew Vereker; and Theodore Zeldin. My particular thanks go to my television agent, Sophie Laurimore at William Morris; my Nepali 'Jifea' friends, who first introduced me to the *Kamasutra*; and Jonathan Buckley, who has always encouraged me.

Finally, I'd like to thank my editors, Louisa Joyner and Sarah Norman, and everyone else at Atlantic — especially Toby Mundy, for trusting me with this book. And, for their incredible support and for reading so intelligently, I would like to thank Robin, Gwen and Moray McConnachie; Richard Scholar; and, above all, Alice Hunt.

Index